TRANSLINGUAL AND TRANSNATIONAL GRADUATE EDUCATION IN RHETORIC AND COMPOSITION

T0344991

TRANSLINGUAL AND TRANSNATIONAL GRADUATE EDUCATION IN RHETORIC AND COMPOSITION

EDITED BY
NANCY BOU AYASH
AND CARRIE BYARS KILFOIL

UTAH STATE UNIVERSITY PRESS
Logan

© 2023 by University Press of Colorado

Published by Utah State University Press
An imprint of University Press of Colorado
1624 Market Street, Suite 226
PMB 39883
Denver, Colorado 80202-1559

The University Press of Colorado is a proud member of
the Association of University Presses.

The University Press of Colorado is a cooperative publishing enterprise supported,
in part, by Adams State University, Colorado State University, Fort Lewis College,
Metropolitan State University of Denver, University of Alaska Fairbanks, University
of Colorado, University of Denver, University of Northern Colorado, University of
Wyoming, Utah State University, and Western Colorado University.

∞ This paper meets the requirements of the ANSI/NISO Z39.48-1992
(Permanence of Paper).

ISBN: 978-1-64642-405-4 (hardcover)
ISBN: 978-1-64642-325-5 (paperback)
ISBN: 978-1-64642-326-2 (ebook)
https://doi.org/10.7330/9781646423262

Cataloging-in-Publication data for this title is available online at the Library of Congress.

Cover illustration © calvindexter/iStock

CONTENTS

TRANSLINGUAL AND TRANSNATIONAL GRADUATE EDUCATION IN RHETORIC AND COMPOSITION

INTRODUCTION
Translingual and Transnational Graduate Education in Rhetoric and Composition

Nancy Bou Ayash and Carrie Byars Kilfoil

Translingual and transnational scholarship have marked a conceptual, epistemological, and ideological milestone in composition studies. By challenging dominant monolingualist approaches to teaching and research, this scholarship has worked to dismantle a disciplinary parochialism that restricts composition's focus to one language (English) and one nation (United States), imagined in static, homogenized, commodified, and mutually dependent terms. Translingual composition theory surfaces the linguistic heterogeneity of all written communication, even that which appears to take place in one language (as conventionally defined), and promotes writers' adeptness working across languages, dialects, genres, and discourses to make meaning in global-local contexts. Transnational composition theory highlights and encourages uptake from these contexts by promoting a view of writing and reading as dynamic material social practices that move across nation-state borders and the current and historical consolidations of capital and resources these borders mark. Further, transnational composition inquiry develops cross-border connections and sustained exchanges of ideas and resources, which introduce alternative ways of understandings and responding to—in teaching, research, and administration—these socially constructed literacy practices as constantly entangled in complex webs of ideologies and power structures.

Translingualism and transnationalism are related concepts often conflated in composition's discourse. This conflation reflects a more general conflation of language and nation advanced by a monolinguist ideology. Monolingualism, Suresh Canagarajah (2013) explains, is based on an "equivalence of language, community, and place," such that each language is "stamped with the essence of the particular community it is associated with" and "the language [is] capable of naturally expressing only the values and thoughts belonging to that community"

https://doi.org/10.7330/9781646423262.c000

(20). Community itself is imagined as homogeneous and bounded by geographical spaces "colonized for one language or another" (21). As Yasemin Yildiz (2012) argues, this one-to-one equation of language, community, and territory leads to the popular (and incorrect) assumption that "individuals and social formations . . . possess one 'true' language, their 'mother tongue,' and through this possession [are] organically linked to an exclusive, clearly demarcated ethnicity, culture, and nation" (2). These links are inflected by and work to reinforce global hierarchies of symbolic power attached to "official" and "unofficial" languages and their associated regions, cultures, and communities.

Notions of a language's social prestige in various contexts work to advance racist and colonialist ideologies and the institutional projects through which these ideologies are exercised and reinforced. We join our contributors in recognizing the need to attend to and contest hegemonic ways of thinking about and engaging with standardized national languages, language varieties, identities, and nation-states that might result from past and/or current training and professional acculturation at both the undergraduate and graduate level. We believe it is necessary to confront the dominant monolingualist and nationalist orientation of our field, as it is reproduced through the professionalization that takes place in graduate studies, in order to establish composition as a disciplinary space for linguistically and socially just epistemologies and social practices.

Translingual theory unsettles a monolingualist understanding of languages as discrete, static entities indexing belonging to equally static and hierarchically organized national-cultural collectives. In their 2011 opinion piece, "Language Difference in Writing: Toward a Translingual Approach," Bruce Horner, Min-Zahn Lu, Jacqueline Jones Royster, and John Trimbur introduce the concept of "translingualism" to refer to a "disposition of openness and inquiry toward language and language differences" that resists the monolingualist reification of language, nation, and sociocultural identity (311). From this perspective, translingualism foregrounds the fluid, changeable, and performative character of language, always part of the fashioning and refashioning of identity but never in any pregiven, bounded, and predictable manner. In the context of writing and writing teaching, a translingual orientation recognizes heterogeneity in all linguistic practices, even those we are conditioned to perceive as taking place in one language and culture (Lu and Horner 2013), and values writers' creative capacities to work across languages, dialects, genres, and registers to meet communicative exigencies. As Steven Alvarez (2016) argues, emphasis on translingual repertoires and practices can help dismantle hegemonic language hierarchies and the policing of language standards upon which they rely. In this way, translingualism can inform composition pedagogies that "frame, conceptualize, interpret, and highlight the plurality of local histories and social struggles" (24) in minoritized communities and "create transformative educational experiences that give students theoretical tools for foregrounding social justice" (20).

This sense of translingualism, which our collection adopts, is closely linked to transnationalism insofar as transnational approaches to writing research and education often require engagements in deliberate and visible cross-language work and/or involve analysis of literacy practices easily identifiable as translingual in historically complicated geopolitical networks of dominance and resistance. As Christiane Donahue (2009) argues, transnational writing scholars must "develop rigorous practices and a grounded vocabulary for collaborative literacy research across national contexts" (235) through utilizing the full range of linguistic resources in their repertoires, including knowledge of the speech and writing patterns of other national languages. Moreover, as Rebecca Lorimer Leonard, Kate Vieira, and Morris Young (2015) note, while transnational inquiry in writing "should not be conflated with nor limited to the study of multilingualism," "including language in analysis can reveal how writers make sense of their own practices or how they position themselves across multiple cultural, linguistic, and political contexts" (x). Analyzing the ways writers work across languages in various global-local contexts is one way to apply a transnational focus to composition, since Lorimer Leonard, Vieira, and Young define the "transnational" as "an optic or analytic that traces how individuals build social fields across real or perceived boundaries" in the context of global change (vi). Though issues of language and language plurality run through transnational composition, its focus is not restricted to them. While translingual composition scholarship has been enhanced by transnational composition research (see the "Selected Bibliography" in Horner et al.'s opinion piece [2011], which cites scholars from across the globe), translingualism is not the sole application of transnational research or the domain of transnational composition more generally.

In keeping with disciplinary trends, translingual and transnational composition scholarship to date has mainly focused on undergraduate writing pedagogy and practices in the United States (US) and abroad (Bou Ayash 2019; Canagarajah 2013; Horner and Tetreault 2017; Martins 2015). Some scholars have acknowledged that the effective implementation of translingual and transnational approaches will require changes to the teacher-scholar training that takes place in rhetoric and composition graduate programs (Canagarajah 2016; Horner, NeCamp, and Donahue 2011; Tardy 2017; You 2016); however, these and similar engagements with the specific implications of this changing terminological and ideological landscape for graduate students' academic life and work remain dependent on the strong leadership and commitment of individual proactive faculty and their forward-looking course designs and pedagogies and have not yet widely altered existing disciplinary structures and discourses. Given connections among graduate education, disciplinary identity, and (re)production, large-scale, collaborative investigations of the ramifications of emerging translingual and transnational paradigms for the field's graduate programs are necessary if these theories are to shape composition's identity and professional practices in the long term.

Since their emergence in the late 1970s, graduate programs in rhetoric and composition have contributed to the professionalization of the field, mapping its parameters via coursework, reading lists, exams, and other requirements in distinct, sometimes idiosyncratic programmatic ways (Lauer 1984; Phelps 1995). While these curricular structures offer shape to the discipline, it is through graduate students and faculty navigating them that composition as a field of study is reproduced. As David Shumway and Craig Dionne (2002) argue, graduate students become "disciplined" through the completion of coursework and requirements to "internalize the values, norms, and standards the discipline upholds" (3). After graduation, these internalized assumptions structure their academic labor (teaching, administration, and scholarship) in what amounts to a self-policing of disciplinary boundaries (Shumway and Dionne 2002), at least in the traditional sense of the term. As far as composition is concerned, Bruce Horner (2016) forwards a model of academic disciplinary labor and knowledge as practice that crosses and remakes boundaries, borders, and traditions and that is "more true to the experience of those working in composition" (204). Counteracting the discipline's nationalist history and containment by English-only monolingualism, this collection contributes to such ongoing social material practice in its reimagining and rewriting of rhetoric and composition graduate studies.

To understand the role graduate programs play in the disciplinary uptake of translingual and translingual theories in the field, there is a pressing need for more scholarly attention to (1) the design of graduate courses and curricula that aspire to implement translingual and transnational theories of composition; (2) graduate students', faculty's, and administrators' feelings of frustration, (in)security, or (dis)empowerment in the wake of these theories and their implied professional labor; and (3) what is at stake for graduate programs and their members working toward (and ultimately reworking) the tenets of translingualism and transnationalism in learning, teaching, scholarship, and/or the administration of existing programmatic arrangements.

With a primary focus on graduate studies and professionalization in rhetoric and composition, this collection explores the ways translingual and transnational perspectives can and should shape the labor and experiences of graduate students entering the field and staffing most first-year writing courses. It includes a range of theoretical, empirical, and narrative-based perspectives with examples and analyses from actual graduate-level programs, course designs, and campus initiatives. To maintain coherence amid this rich variety of voices, we encouraged contributors to frame their chapters around the following central questions:

- In what ways do contemporary graduate-level rhetoric and composition coursework, program design, and/or professional-development and mentorship opportunities align with and/or diverge from the tenets of translingual and transnational composition scholarship?
- How are, can, and should graduate students be professionalized to work across (language, social, cultural, and national) differences at various points in their programs ranging from coursework, to teaching, to the production/circulation of scholarship?
- How do graduate faculty and their students negotiate disciplinary traditions of graduate-level education and professionalization with emerging composition theories and pedagogical practices that call for rethinking dominant conceptualizations of language and nation and the material labor involved in researching and teaching them?
- How must twenty-first-century graduate professionalization and education be reworked in light of new understandings of and approaches to language and nation, as well as increasing global mobility and connectivity?
- How do we cultivate different types of scholarly and pedagogical expertise to counter the residual effects of past monolingualist, monocultural training and professionalization practices?
- If we accept that all teaching and mentorship is local and situated practice, how do we connect local institutional/programmatic/ departmental expectations with broader disciplinary conversations on the normalcy of and necessity for translingual and transnational competence and labor?
- What can graduate students themselves do en route to take control, either individually or collectively, of their own translingual and transnational positioning and preparation?

The chapters in this collection do not provide definitive answers to these complex questions, nor are they intended to, but they do illustrate how graduate students, fellow faculty, and administrators alike continually negotiate constraints and possibilities for change and critical innovation. We invite our readers to consider these questions along with us and the ways they have been addressed and interpreted in each chapter as the field continues to reimagine the full scope and structure of its graduate education along translingual and transnational lines. In what follows, we summarize the individual chapters and put them in communication with one another in relation to these central questions. Several currents run through the upcoming chapters, including the importance (and frequent lack) of graduate student agency in program design and assessment, models for assessing the challenges and successes of graduate programs attempting to engage in translingual and transnational work, and viable pathways for destabilizing the racist and colonialist monolingual ethos implicitly built into rhetoric and composition graduate programs and the institutions in which they are situated.

The University of Louisville graduate program in rhetoric and composition, and its current and former members, figures prominently in several chapters. This program, and the biennial Thomas R. Watson Conference it hosts, has long been a locus of translingual and transnational work in the field and was instrumental in the development of the landmark 2011 *College English* opinion statement on translingualism and its key tenets and implications (Horner et al. 2011) and in the creation of the Transnational Composition Standing Group, which has met annually and sponsored a panel at the annual meeting of the Conference on College Composition and Communication (CCCC) since 2015. As such, its faculty and former graduate students are well positioned to participate in the discussion this collection works to engage, and the program itself is a useful site for analysis of the ways translingual and transnational theories influence graduate education as material social practices situated in spatiotemporal contexts. That said, other institutional locations are also represented in this collection—such as the University of Texas at El Paso, the University of Washington, Penn State University, the University of Arizona, and Barry University, illustrating that translingual and transnational concerns are not exclusive to one graduate program but emerge in locally situated ways as graduate students and faculty negotiate the material conditions of writing teaching and research, currently and historically.

Based on perspectives from specific graduate-level programs and courses, this collection presents potential pathways for developing translingual and transnational orientations in such primary sites of disciplinary socialization. Insights from various chapters suggest rhetoric and composition graduate programs and curricula are caught up in what Yildiz (2012) describes as the "postmonolingual condition" of twenty-first-century Western social and academic life, a complex "field of tension" (5) in which a dominant nationalist-monolingualist ideology continues to assert and sustain itself just as emergent translingual, transnational representations of and practices with language and literacy are increasingly gaining ground. Though such programs and curricula are inflected by the flow of diverse discourses, knowledge constructions, Englishes, languages, and language varieties as a result of transnational patterns of migration and border crossings, these flows remain largely conditioned by the privileging of English-only, US–centric ways of languaging, reading, writing, and knowing. In response to deeply entrenched national and language-ideological allegiances in graduate-level work, the chapters that follow represent small-scale, localized efforts to confront disciplinary blinders imposed by nationalistic views of the world and perspectives on languages as closed systems with clearly demarcated boundaries impervious to foreign influence. Such efforts are not meant to be read as ultimate solutions for all problems pertaining to the current state of graduate education but rather as invitations for further exploration, experimentation, and collaboration among graduate faculty, advisors, administrators, and students. In other words, these invitations bring the rigorous ideological work of translingualism and transnationalism within the scope of various stakeholders' power, available program and/or campus resources, and funding opportunities (for compensation, hiring, professional development, new course development and design, pedagogical innovation, policy reform, etc.).

Taken together, these chapters identify rhetoric and composition graduate programs as potential sites of transformation to expose and intervene in the dominant ideologies of monolingualism and nationalism that continue to shape compositionists' belief systems and professional practices as teachers, scholars, and administrators in linguistically and culturally heterogeneous institutions. Such transformation in graduate education, however, can only begin by moving beyond the kind of *ideologiekritik* of nationalist monolingual ideologies that characterizes the field's contemporary translingual and transnational writing scholarship toward a deeper attention to and examination of their real, damaging effects of linguistic racism and the erasure of difference—intellectual as well as linguistic, racial, and ethnic (Bou Ayash 2019, 165; Gilyard 2016, 287). In fact, pointing toward "models for radical, translingual engagement" in the field, Keith Gilyard (2016) advocates for dedicating time and energy to documenting the negotiation efforts and "stories of struggle . . . and . . . triumph" (288) of students,[1] especially so-called ethnic minorities, in order to get "a fuller portrait" of their complex life and work amid the productive tensions of working closely and collaboratively with faculty and each other across racial, ethnic, linguistic, and other differences.

Taking up Gilyard's calls, part 1, "Invisible and Dislocated: Graduate Student Insights in Translingual and Transnational Contexts," is comprised of graduate student accounts of their experiences negotiating tensions among the monolingual assumptions of US higher education generally, rhetoric and composition graduate education specifically, and the porous national and linguistic borders that define their lives. At every turn in their graduate studies, students are positioned on the front lines of these ideological tensions largely not of their own making and are most burdened with the task of confronting them. Therefore, we open the collection with fresh graduate student perspectives on how the advent of translingual and transnational theories and pedagogies in the field has affected their lived experiences and daily labor in order to set the scene for the chapters that follow in part 2, which offer practical applications of translingual and transnational writing theories and pedagogies to graduate education.

Representing the voices of students socially designated as mainstream and language minoritized, as users of English as a first and additional language, these critical reflections document a significant lack of graduate student agency and autonomy, a lack monolingualism has structured into graduate curricula and programs. We echo our contributors' conviction that graduate students at various stages of their academic careers are to be seen as agentive language users and active collaborators on program development and revision (Lerma et al., chapter 1; Zaleski and You, chapter 6). Graduate faculty can and should play a significant role in designing student-fronted pedagogies and courses that value their students' language expertise and cross-border experiences and closely attend to their narratives of meso-level negotiations across spaces, times, knowledges, national languages, language practices, cultures, and (racialized, classed, gendered, sexed, abled) identities.

The chapters by Corina Lerma, Moisés García-Rentería, Patricia Flores, Kate Mangelsdorf, and Lucía Durá, and Joseph Franklin, Emily Yuko Cousins, and Alex Way attest to the fact that new and continuing rhetoric and composition graduate students too have responsibilities in taking more control of their academic and professional careers. They can do so through recognizing the constant interplay between socially dominant ideologies of linguistic nationalism, on one hand,

and counterhegemonic ideologies, on another hand, and how their complex negotiations of these inform their subject positionings in relation to texts, contexts, readers/writers, and conventions. Consequently, graduate students can ultimately participate in the construction and reconstruction of their sociocultural and political realities and futures.

In their contribution, "Doing Translingualism through Panoramic Ethos: Three Transnational Graduate Students' Pathways across Multiliteracies and Implications for Program Practices," Lerma, García-Rentería, Flores, Mangelsdorf, and Durá use the concept of "panoramic ethos" to highlight and extend translingual theories of language and subjectivity, as well as their implications for graduate teaching and learning. University of Texas at El Paso graduate students' testimonios of lived experiences on the US-Mexico border illustrate their facility as sophisticated translingual practitioners working across racial and ethnic lines, negotiating national, sociocultural, and linguistic borders in material and theoretical educational contexts. By contrast, programmatic literature tends to deny student agency, especially around "language," casting their expertise as "invisible, ignored, or exoticized." To address the disconnect between graduate program expectations and students' linguistic practices, histories, and subjectivities, a panoramic ethos extends translingual theory's assertion that difference is normative and further highlights the "deficits" in student, teacher, and programmatic understanding that normative difference in the classroom implies. The authors suggest possibilities for program designs that engage all stakeholders'—students', teachers', and administrators'—multiple subjectivities and languages, focusing not on the unidirectional pursuit of preestablished objectives and standards but rather on renegotiating understandings of and motivations for rhetoric and composition learning in diverse, situated contexts.

Franklin, Cousins, and Way join Lerma, García-Rentería, Flores, Mangelsdorf, and Durá in making visible the often-overlooked challenges graduate students face as they confront the complex ideological entanglements, contradictions, and ruptures that characterize their education and training. In "(En)countering Monolingualism: A Transnational Sensemaking of Graduate Education," Franklin, Cousins, and Way offer further evidence of graduate-program practices that deny student agency, and add that such practices reproduce "sedentarist, monolingualist" assumptions advancing fast-capitalist agendas in higher education across the globe. They begin with narratives of their experiences as international English-language teachers and US rhetoric and composition graduate students, recounting in painful detail the commodification of their language practices, labor, and professional subjectivities in the context of the neoliberal values driving "English" higher education in the United States and abroad. The authors then reflect on their experiences with translingual and transnational scholarship as graduate students, observing that these theories provided a way to locate themselves as liminal subjects working across national and professional borders, as well as ideological frameworks to resist alienating, unsustainable subjectivities and labor practices.

By virtue of their experiences, Franklin, Cousins, and Way argue that translingual and transnational approaches to rhetoric and composition graduate education can and should accent the valuable experiential knowledge students bring to their programs, disrupt programmatic assumptions about language and identity tied to uncritical perceptions of the demands of "the market," and summon shifts in ideology and practice to enhance collaboration and community. Their narratives and sensemaking highlight the ways monolingual ideology lays the groundwork for the commodification of language, language users (including teachers and students), and languaging, imagined in terms of decontextualized language "skills" exchanged on academic and professional markets. Translingual ideology—in so much as it offers an alternative to monolingualism—can offer new conceptualizations of disciplinary members and work that resist this commodification, and, by extension, the broader fast-capitalist, monological structures increasingly imposed on composition teaching and learning. Making these changes can position programs to more fruitfully address the changing conditions of teaching, learning, and even the "market" in twenty-first-century contexts of internationalizing higher education.

Our student-centered section concludes with Carrie Kilfoil's "The Postmonolingual Condition and the Rhetoric and Composition PhD: Norming Language Difference in a Doctoral Program." In her empirically driven chapter, Kilfoil presents data from a 2013 survey of University of Louisville graduate students' perceptions of language diversity to illuminate how disciplinary language ideology is being restructured to account for growing awareness of linguistic heterogeneity in writing and writing teaching. Offering a postmonolingual reading of her data, Kilfoil attunes to the presence of multilingual perceptions and practices among graduate students amid the continued forcefulness of the monolingual paradigm. Specifically, she notes how respondents consistently indicate their awareness of and appreciation for language differences in their writing program, as well as desires to engage multiple languages and English dialects in composition teaching and research. However, she argues the continued dominance of monolingualist ideology is evidenced by the ways respondents tended to imagine these engagements as taking place through curricular add-ons and extracurricular activities that pose practical barriers to their timely progression through the program. Drawing from student comments and recommendations, Kilfoil suggests ways this program, and others like it, can leverage students' positive perceptions of and attitudes toward multilingualism to "norm" language differences in its mainstream rhetoric and composition graduate curriculum, thus lessening the material barriers graduate students perceive to engaging language issues in their professional development.

Shifting from student-centered to departmental, programmatic, and institutional perspectives and the necessary work of revamping curricula, structures, and practices in graduate education, part 2, "(Trans)Disciplinarity and Knowledge Building in Graduate Curricula and Mentorship," opens with the theoretically oriented essay "Transforming Graduate Education in Rhetoric and Composition: Toward a Transnational and Translingual Revaluation" by Bruce Horner.

With its central argument that graduate-level rhetoric and composition programs and courses must rethink and revalue what they are already doing so it may be done "differently," Horner's chapter helps bridge the student experiences and perspectives shared in the previous section and the practices and initiatives outlined in this section. Since the graduate student narratives and accounts offered in part 1 articulate how monolingualist, nationalist ideologies negatively impact graduate student experiences and learning processes, it is tempting to read translingualism and transnationalism, as depicted in this section, as stable bodies of knowledge and practices that offer shiny new "solutions" to these "problems." That said, such understandings obscure how translingualism and transnationalism operate as ways of seeing that expose the linguistically and culturally fluid, heterogeneous character of rhetoric and composition, currently and historically, to enable and foreclose particular opportunities for meaning making in its graduate programs. In his chapter, Horner emphasizes the need to acknowledge the ordinariness and normativity of translingual and transnational relations in that "matters of language and nationality" are and have always been part and parcel of rhetoric and composition graduate education. The seeming uniqueness and newness of translingual and transnational relations, as Horner notes, "attests *not* to their actual novelty, but, rather, the new awareness of their presence," hence of their force and significance (emphasis added).

Tracing the trajectory of the graduate seminars he taught at his home institution, the University of Louisville, and offering a reflective analysis of the place and role of translinguality and transnationality in his course designs and syllabi, Horner stresses the growing tensions of reconciling the desire for pedagogical innovation and creativity, on one hand, and a crucial realization, on another hand, that there is nothing "new" or "special" about the translingual and transnational in composition. In response to such felt tensions, he voices skepticism toward the design of individual graduate-level courses with the explicit goal of transmitting and securing "a stable body" of specialized knowledge on the translingual and/or transnational character of various aspects of composition work. Alternatively, Horner calls for a more integrated approach to curricular changes and revisions, demanding of both graduate faculty and their students a qualitative, not additive, "revaluation and transformation" of the full set of threshold concepts that have come to shape ways of seeing and doing language and nationality in graduate programs and courses. In his own words, this approach requires endorsing and cultivating "a different understanding of language, language relations, users, contexts of use, and the relations among these, and a different understanding of the transnational location and movement of work in and on composition." After all, as Horner (2016) points out in earlier work with Min-Zhan Lu, it is the "labor of revision that is always what we, in concert with our students, take up, and take responsibility for (whether or not we acknowledge that responsibility) in our thinking, teaching/learning, writing" and re-envisioning of programmatic structures and designs (216).

Echoing Horner's call for integrative curricular revisions aimed at normalizing translingual, transnational practices and identities endemic to rhetoric and composition graduate programs, the rest of the chapters that comprise part 2 offer insights on how to more effectively shape the experiences and practices of graduate students through carefully structured curriculum design, mentorship, and teacher/tutor training. We encourage readers to approach the pedagogical and curricular transformations some of these chapters describe not as contradictory to Horner's suggestions but rather as interconnected and a further indication of the difficult work ahead of us in unveiling the intrinsically translingual and transnational character of graduate rhetoric and composition work that has been *un*noticed and *un*examined in theory, policy, and practice for so long under a monolingual nationalist paradigm. In fact, because a monolingual, nationalist mindset is both pervasive and pervasively naturalized, it is often difficult for our graduate students and many of our colleagues to see the ordinariness of translinguality and transnationality in their literate work and life without the aid of sensitizing pedagogical praxis and curricular interventions like the ones Bou Ayash, Michelle

Zaleski and Xiaoye You, and Madelyn Pawlowski and Christine M. Tardy, have designed. Put differently, the translingual and transnational connections this collection strives to promote in rhetoric and composition graduate education are in reality both *not new and new* and, therefore, necessitate closer, louder, and more open engagements among graduate students, mentors, researchers, teachers, and/or administrators.

Detailing concrete ways to work from graduate students' needs and concerns regarding foreign-language learning, Bou Ayash, in her chapter "Translation and Translingual Competence in Graduate Training," presents critical translation as a valuable pedagogical resource for actively promoting their translingual competence and sensibilities. With an eye toward how translation might reorient translingual inquiry and how translingualism might reorient translation practice, Bou Ayash describes a locally sensitive pedagogic initiative at the University of Washington, a large public research university in the Pacific Northwest US region, that prepares graduate students for agentively pursuing cross-language relations in their writing, research, and teaching practices. Reflecting on the affordances and challenges of teaching a graduate seminar on the theoretical and practical approaches to translation from a transdisciplinary perspective, she emphasizes how through centralizing translation in its full complexity, such pedagogical spaces can become key institutional sites for promising discussions among graduate students, faculty, and program administrators surrounding the often-ignored, undisturbed PhD language requirement. As Bou Ayash demonstrates, a strong focus on the complex politics and problematics of translation brings graduate students (even those traditionally labeled as *monolingual speakers* for whom English is a first and dominant language) face to face with the reality of difference in today's translingual and transnational literate world. In this sense, Bou Ayash argues rhetoric and composition graduate curricula must provide opportunities for their students to fully integrate translation practice into their scholarly and pedagogical pursuits.

The chapters by Zaleski and You, and Pawlowski and Tardy, emphasize that the complexities of language and rhetoric in today's local-global contact zones merit strong representation in rhetoric and composition graduate programs. In their chapter entitled "Comparative Rhetoric and the Translingual Future of Mentorship," Zaleski and You share insights on the transformative relationships to "texts, rhetorical traditions [and practices], and authority" emerging out of You's teaching of a comparative rhetoric graduate seminar, on one hand, and, on another hand, Zaleski's active participation and coursework in that seminar. Disrupting the strict binaries of novice versus expert that define traditional teacher-student/mentor-mentee relationships, Zaleski and You specifically describe forging a translingual-oriented mentoring relationship marked by curiosity, deliberative inquiry, informed risk taking, experimentation, self-reflexivity, and productive dialogue across difference. The "cosmopolitan dispositions" and relations such translingual mentorship affords contribute to leveling the playing field in graduate training in that these demand from graduate faculty not only the willingness to accept the agentive role students play as fellow writers and rewriters of disciplinary knowledge, but also the humility to let go of their positioning as the sole authority figures with the final word on research- and teaching-related matters. In conclusion, Zaleski and You call for cultivating translingual and transnational sensibilities through incorporating comparative rhetorical studies into graduate rhetoric and composition curricula.

In "The Role of Graduate Education in Building Writing Teachers' Knowledge of Language," Pawlowski and Tardy also call for changes to rhetoric and composition graduate curricula that decenter graduate-faculty expertise, thereby making space for language-related coursework and concepts that trouble traditional disciplinary boundaries. Pawlowski and Tardy trace the decline of language-related research and scholarship in rhetoric and composition and its graduate programs, noting recent concerns that, as a consequence, many disciplinary professionals lack the formal language-related knowledge to engage in translingual teaching and scholarship responsibly. They then report on a study of graduate student teachers in a US writing program that suggests students need what Pawlowski (2019, 55) has elsewhere termed enhanced "pedagogical language knowledge" (PLK): a knowledge of language and its pedagogical relevance in the writing classroom. Through survey data and interviews with individual graduate students, Pawlowski and Tardy illustrate tensions between students' critical language awareness, often informed by multilingual experiences outside their graduate work, and low levels of confidence applying pedagogical practices that reflect that awareness. Pawlowski and Tardy conclude that graduate students' metalinguistic insecurity, lack of confidence designing and facilitating lessons for L2 students, and tendency to consider language instruction solely in terms of grammar correction indicate programs must apply an interdisciplinary approach to graduate students' development of PLK. They encourage programs to both allow for and require outside coursework, in, for instance, applied linguistics and modern languages, and for rhetoric and composition faculty to apply greater attention to "bridging concepts like genre, transfer, and code" in core coursework to better prepare graduate students for the mobile, multilingual realities of contemporary composition teaching.

The final chapter, "A Translingual Approach to Tutoring International Graduate Students" by Aimee Jones, presents how the translingual and transnational directions this collection is forwarding can materialize in writing center work. Uniquely situated outside but alongside graduate programs, writing centers as "third spaces" (Reiff et al. 2015, 15) contribute to the language and literacy socialization of graduate students and help build opportunities for them to skillfully network various aspects of their academic and professional lives. More specifically, Jones reports on a case study of international multilingual graduate students' motivations and expectations for using the writing center at a large R1 public university in Florida. Interviews and tutoring-session transcripts illustrate how the widely accepted binary model of writing center tutoring, which breaks down client needs into higher-order concerns (HOCs) and lower-order concerns (LOCs), risks eclipsing the specific language needs of these students. As a corrective, Jones advocates for a translingual approach to tutor training that eschews the implicit monolingualism of the binary model, instead highlighting the productive labor of writing center clients as language users working across languages. This model for writing center tutor training, according to Jones, would disrupt the HOC and LOC binary and work to replace nondirective, Socratic styles of tutor-client interaction with dialogue and negotiation. In addition, a translingual approach to tutor training would professionalize writing center tutors to see multilingual student writers' motivations and expectations as dynamic and shifting in relationship to their developing semiotic repertoires and academic identities.

The collection concludes with a collection of short response essays that critically engage with the perspectives, arguments, and recommendations already presented in parts 1 and 2. The individual responses by Amy J. Wan, Anselma Widha Prihandita, Joe Wilson, and Brice Nordquist comprising part 3 highlight the important yet complex work still to be done if we are to pursue translingual and transnational relations in graduate rhetoric and composition studies. In her response, "Shifting the Paradigm of Translingual and Transnational Graduate Education," Wan reflects on the "messy" and "deliberate" nature of the contributors' work to centralize translingual and transnational orientations in rhetoric and composition graduate education. For Wan, the contributors' efforts illustrate that applying such orientations is about much more than simply promoting the "acceptance of people who speak languages other than English or who come to the US to study from other countries" in individual graduate courses. Indeed, she cautions against seeing the movement this collection seeks to document and advance only in terms of increasing representation of diverse languages, discourses, and people in graduate pedagogy, lest the "the optics of diversity" become a cover for maintaining oppressive institutional structures in which we and our field are deeply enmeshed. In this sense, Wan urges readers to see the chapters in this collection as examples of concerted efforts to go against the grain of dominant institutional ideologies, illustrative of the hard work involved in changing a racist, monolingualist system of higher education from the bottom up through various points of intervention: pedagogical, programmatic, and institutional. Wan emphasizes the important role of institutionally secure tenure-line faculty who can and should bravely and actively engage in this process as she highlights connections between monolingualist sensibilities and "white supremacist dispositions and structures" to clarify what is at stake in making these changes and why we must fight for them.

In "Translingualism and Transnationalism as Decolonial Recovery," Prihandita demonstrates a similar commitment toward social justice within the academy more broadly and graduate education in particular. Informed by her own struggles negotiating difference in academic writing as a female international graduate student of color, she argues that the field's translingual and transnational approaches to writing must be researched and taught as a form of what she terms "decolonial recovery" for them to reach their full counterhegemonic potential in graduate-level academic work and life. Such acts of "*recovery from coloniality*" place a strong focus on recognizing, reclaiming, and capitalizing on the diverse meanings, knowledges, language resources, rhetorical traditions, and literacy practices graduate students inevitably bring with them into their writing and learning but that get lost, silenced, and erased under traditional colonized models of graduate training. The difficult task of dismantling such colonial logics in rhetoric and composition graduate education, according to Prihandita, begins by enacting sustained structural critique, developing cosmopolitan dispositions of openness and accommodation, and, most important, constantly questioning how naturalized beliefs and practices continue to maintain—albeit inadvertently—linguistic, racial, and epistemic privilege and institutional power.

Wilson, in "Distributing the Labor of Translation in the Context of Graduate Education in Writing Studies," takes up the question of labor—and the translingual and transnational orientations it is associated with—and how "we conceive of and locate" its concrete manifestation in active translations across genres, named languages, and language practices in diverse writing situations. Considering the interplay between rhetorical genre studies, on one hand, and, on the other hand, translingual and transnational scholarship in the field, Wilson prompts us to think more critically about the many genres we purposefully select for our graduate seminars, program policies, curricula, and assessment tools and the ways these genres can further support, leverage, and reward our graduate students' labor of "translating their rhetorical, linguistic, and disciplinary knowledges" while developing deeper translingual and transnational sensibilities.

In his response, "Translingual and Transnational Graduate Education for the Local Public Good," Brice Nordquist reflects upon the goals of this collection in the context of various environmental, sociopolitical, and public health crises that have further contributed to inequality and injustice on a local and global level. He specifically notes that rhetoric and composition's "productions and applications of knowledge . . . are struck in fixed tracks of professional preparation and performance" that seem ill equipped to address the current moment. Following Lerma et al.'s recommendations, he confirms that translingual and transnational attention to the "language practices and mobilities that constitute our classrooms and programs" can offer graduate faculty and their students opportunities to reframe disciplinary knowledge building to be more socially attuned and responsible. In this sense, Nordquist suggests, "attention to local language practice and coconstructions of localities, along with a commitment to the boundary-crossing work of democratic education, can broaden our understandings of graduate and postgraduate success and thus open up more possibilities for conceiving of and enacting graduate education as a public good."

Rhetoric and composition graduate programs and classrooms are useful sites for facilitating intellectual curiosity and risk taking and subsequent ideological clarity about the operation and profound impacts of monolingual nationalism on writing and writers. Just as important, they are also sites of some of the most creative thinking and innovation about what to do differently and how. Therefore, translingual and transnational change in rhetoric and composition must start with graduate education as a critical gap in disciplinary research. As Stephen North (2000) observes of English studies generally, composition "appears to have very little historical sense, shared or otherwise, of its efforts at doctoral education" and, moreover, "no significant tradition of dealing with doctoral education as education" (2). In fact, identifying a paradox in rhetoric and composition graduate studies, Sidney Dobrin (2005) notes how it works to enculturate students into the field, yet its practices often run counter to, and even tacitly argue against, disciplinary theories and research. Along the same lines, Louise Wetherbee Phelps (1995) argues, "The maturation of Ph.D. programs in composition and rhetoric creates a rhetorical exigency to study and theorize doctoral practices of education as deeply and seriously as we have undergraduate teaching" (117).

As we point out at the beginning of our introduction, composition-ists have spent considerable time and energy discussing undergraduate writing teaching and learning and not as much time understanding the complexity of graduate students' sociocultural positioning, linguistic and cultural practices, and lived experiences as scholars and teachers. Moreover, little attention has been applied to thinking about how our current practices and standards might be inadvertently perpetuating and strengthening, rather than challenging, the marginalization of these positionings, practices, and experiences. To do so, we must begin to see graduate education as education: a set of (meta)pedagogical and epistemic practices that are rich, multilayered, and locally oriented insofar as they involve the socialization of prospective writing teachers and scholars. These practices map out the conditions of possibility in the field and in so doing inculcate the conceptions of language and nation that shape the ways its members see themselves as professionals and conduct disciplinary work.

As Barbara Gleason (2006) reminds us, complex decision-making about the design of graduate curricula must take into consideration the "value a knowledge base may have for improving the opportuni-ties and lives of individuals, families, and entire communities" (267). Collectively, our contributors suggest ways translingual and transna-tional writing theories and pedagogies can improve the "opportuni-ties and lives" of stakeholders in rhetoric and composition graduate education during a time of unprecedented challenge. As the COVID-19 pandemic amplifies fast-capitalist influences on institutions, humanities-based disciplines like rhetoric and composition (and the new faculty they produce) are increasingly called upon to prove their relevance and worth in internationalizing institutions beset by declining enrollments and ensuing budget cuts. Like the virus, the market and its pressures highlight the illusory quality of national borders, across which neolib-eral ideologies and their commodified visions of language, students, faculty, and disciplines (and the reified job-ready "skills"—linguistic and otherwise—they represent) pass as institutions struggle for financial sol-vency, or growth beyond it. As the graduate student contributions in this collection suggest (Lerma et al., chapter 1; Franklin, Cousins, and Way, chapter 2), translingualism and transnationalism provide a knowledge base for future faculty to locate themselves within the dynamic ideological landscape of global higher education and resist the damaging subjectivities and labor practices fast-capitalist, monolingualist interpretations of "English" teachers and teaching impose on them, their students, and the wider disciplinary community they are working to join.

At this crucial stage in graduate students' professional development, it is incumbent on graduate faculty, program directors, and institutions to integrate translingual and transnational sensibilities into curricular planning and pedagogy, as our contributors have demonstrated, in order to ensure graduate students find strong support, modeling, and training for the counterhegemonic teaching and research needed at this critical moment in the field. That said, we are mindful that, for many graduate faculty, administrators, and students, making revisions to graduate programs already underresourced and overextended in terms of their goals and responsibilities is an intimidating prospect. This collection aims to provide inspiration and models for making these curricular and pedagogical changes while illustrating the importance of productive collaboration and transdisciplinarity to make them feasible and sustainable in a dominantly "individualistic," insular "graduate school culture that prevails in the humanities" and beyond (Cassuto 2015, 2).

A small first step in that direction would be to draw graduate students and their faculty into the kind of collaborative relationships several of our contributors have taken up in the very act of composing their own chapters, namely Lerma et al., Zaleski and You, and Pawlowski and Tardy. By deliberately engaging with the language resources and experiences students and faculty bring into programs, finding ways to reimagine core courses along transdisciplinary lines, and forming partnerships with allied departments and programs in global studies, applied linguistics, translation studies, foreign and second-language studies, and modern languages, graduate programs can integrate translingual and transnational orientations in epistemologically and materially attainable, sustainable ways. As Bruce Horner, Samantha NeCamp, and Christiane Donahue (2011) note, a translingual orientation to language difference and heterogeneity "shifts our focus away from individuals, located on a fixed scale of competence toward 'mastery' of a reified 'target' language, and toward groups of people working in collaboration to use all available linguistic resources; and it shifts our focus away from disciplinary boundaries separating specific traditions of scholarship on writing and its teaching, and toward putting these diverse traditions in dialogue with one another to the benefit of all those working 'in' them" (288).

By working together, dialogically, to deconstruct research silos and create alternative linguistic practices and institutional structures inspired by innovative modes of professionalization, graduate faculty and students can do more than just weather the unprecedented shock of shuttered campuses, faculty layoffs, and historically low tenure-track hiring in the humanities. We can remake rhetoric and composition graduate programs to foster the disciplinary dispositions needed for future faculty to meaningfully address challenges posed by this particular moment of geopolitical crisis and what lies beyond it.

The pandemic has laid bare and amplified the material, existential consequences of stark and persistent inequities among races, ethnicities, cultures, nations, genders, sexualities, and differently abled bodies. At this juncture, expanding access to (and definitions of what counts as) research-based knowledge, the symbolic capital it carries, the material capital for which it can be exchanged, and the sociomaterial resources of academic institutions is critically important for marginalized and underserved individuals across the globe. Antiracist and decolonial projects in composition studies have worked to destabilize widely accepted (and traditionally institutionally transmitted and reinforced) hegemonic assumptions about writing and its teaching to claim space for minoritized people and rhetorics in academic institutions. These projects are bound up in issues of language, nation, and sociocultural identity and share many practical and epistemological concerns with scholarship in translingual and transnational studies, including matters of linguistic justice, epistemological exclusion, and faculty inclusion and representation. As Wan suggests in her response to this collection, scholars of translingualism, transnationalism, decolonialism, and antiracism in composition are potential "accomplices and allies" in a collective struggle to shift dominant disciplinary paradigms regarding "what it means to build knowledge within the institution of higher education" and who is invited to participate in this knowledge building.

Though beyond the scope of this collection, several chapters suggest connections between translingual and transnational theories and antiracist, decolonial work aimed at opening up and redefining academic literacies, rhetorics, and writing program teaching and administration along inclusive and equitable lines. We see these connections as a point of departure for future research in composition studies and urge further consideration of how translingual and transnational scholarship and sensibilities, as conducted and inculcated in rhetoric and composition graduate education, can further support antiracist and decolonial initiatives in the field. Such research would highlight the power of rhetoric and composition graduate programs to improve the lives and labor of the many people our field touches, thereby revaluing our graduate studies as matters of social responsibility in linguistically and socioculturally diverse institutions and the communities in which they are situated.

NOTE

1. Gilyard here addresses college students, but his views hold equally true on the graduate level.

REFERENCES

Alvarez, Steven. 2016. "Literacy." In *Decolonizing Rhetoric and Composition Studies: New Latinx Keywords for Theory and Pedagogy*, edited by Iris Ruiz and Raúl Sánchez, 17–30. New York: Palgrave Macmillan.

Bou Ayash, Nancy. 2019. *Toward Translingual Realities in Composition: (Re)Working Local Language Representations and Practices.* Logan: Utah State University Press.

Canagarajah, Suresh. 2013. *Translingual Practice: Global Englishes and Cosmopolitan Relations.* London: Routledge.

Canagarajah, Suresh. 2016. "Translingual Writing and Teacher Development in Composition." *College English* 78 (3): 264–72.

Cassuto, Leonardo. 2015. *The Graduate School Mess: What Caused It and How We Can Fix It.* Cambridge, MA: Harvard University Press.

Dobrin, Sidney I. 2005 "Introduction: Finding Space for the Composition Practicum." In *Don't Call It That: The Composition Practicum*, edited by Sidney I. Dobrin, 1–37. Urbana, IL: NCTE.

Donahue, Christiane. 2009. " 'Internationalization' and Composition Studies: Reorienting the Discourse." *College Composition and Communication* 61 (2): 212–43.

Gilyard, Keith. 2016. "The Rhetoric of Translingualism." *College English* 78 (3): 284–89.

Gleason, Barbara. 2006. "Reasoning the Need: Graduate Education and Basic Writing." *Journal of Basic Writing* 25 (2): 49–75.

Horner, Bruce. 2016. *Rewriting Composition: Terms of Exchange.* Carbondale: Southern Illinois University Press.

Horner, Bruce, Min-Zhan Lu, Jacqueline Jones Royster, and John Trimbur. 2011. "Language Difference: Toward a Translingual Approach." *College English* 73 (3): 299–317.

Horner, Bruce, Samantha NeCamp, and Christiane Donahue. 2011. "Toward a Multilingual Composition Scholarship: From English Only to a Translingual Norm." *College Composition and Communication* 63 (2): 269–300.

Horner, Bruce, and Laura Tetreault, eds. 2017. *Crossing Divides: Exploring Translingual Writing Pedagogies and Programs.* Logan: Utah State University Press.

Lauer, Janice. 1984. "Composition Studies: Dappled Discipline." *Rhetoric Review* 3 (1): 20–29.

Lorimer Leonard, Rebecca, Kate Vieira, and Morris Young. 2015. "Special Editors' Introduction." *Literacy in Composition Studies* 3 (3): vi–xii.

Lu, Min-Zhan, and Bruce Horner. 2013. "Translingual Literacy, Language Difference, and Matters of Agency." *College English* 75 (6): 586–611.

Martins, David. 2015. *Transnational Writing Program Administration.* Logan: Utah State University Press.

North, Stephen. 2000. *Refiguring the Ph.D. In English Studies: Writing, Doctoral Education, and the Fusion-Based Curriculum.* Urbana, IL: NCTE.

Pawlowski, Madelyn T. 2019. "Locating and Supporting the Developing Pedagogical Language Knowledge of College Writing Instructors." PhD dissertation, University of Arizona, Tucson.

Phelps, Louise Wetherbee. 1995. "Reproducing Composition and Rhetoric: The Intellectual Challenge of Doctoral Education." *Composition Studies* 23 (2): 115–32.

Reiff, Mary Jo, Anis S. Bawarshi, Michelle Ballif, and Christian R. Weisser. 2015. *Ecologies of Writing Programs: Program Profiles in Context.* Anderson, SC: Parlor.

Shumway, David, and Craig Dionne, ed. 2002. *Disciplining English: Alternative Histories, Critical Perspectives.* Albany: SUNY Press.

Tardy, Christine. 2017. "Crossing, or Creating, Divides? A Plea for Transdisciplinary Scholarship." In *Crossing Divides,* edited by Bruce Horner and Laura Tetreault, 181–89. Logan: Utah State University Press.

Yildiz, Yasemin. 2012. *Beyond the Mother Tongue: The Postmonolingual Condition.* New York: Fordham University Press.

You, Xiaoye. 2016. *Cosmopolitan English and Transliteracy.* Carbondale: Southern Illinois University Press.

PART I

Invisible and Dislocated

Graduate Student Insights in Translingual and Transnational Contexts

1

DOING TRANSLINGUALISM THROUGH PANORAMIC ETHOS

Three Transnational Graduate Students' Pathways across Multiliteracies and Implications for Program Practices

Corina Lerma, Moisés García-Rentería,
Patricia Flores, Kate Mangelsdorf, and Lucía Durá

Over the last decade, translingual ideology has been conceptualized as one that "treats language as a social, embodied act that is not only diverse and hybrid but also in a constant state of flux, mobility, and fluctuation" (Bou Ayash 2019, 35). In this view, all language users, all language practices, are translingual. Even individuals who think of themselves as monolingual engage in translingual practices. Translingual practices, as Suresh Canagarajah (2018) has noted, are expansive and situated, leading to "a spatial orientation that embeds communication in space and time, considering all resources as working together as an assemblage in shaping meaning" (31). In this chapter we take up a spatial orientation to translingualism and apply it to graduate education and program design through the concept of a *panoramic ethos*. In a panorama, we see a wide view of an area or space in all directions. The multiperspectival view provided by a panoramic ethos creates an inventive space where all stakeholders are seen as meaning-making agents with the capability to negotiate and change subjectivities, identities, and languages. Panoramic ethos is an antiracist framework that can inform teaching philosophies and curriculum design within graduate programs from inception through evaluation by humanizing cross-linguistic realities in the contested spaces of geographic, sociocultural, linguistic, and institutional-professional borders. To view ourselves and los otros with real openness, as a panorama invokes, implies the important recognition that *all of us* are also constantly negotiating not only what we see and perceive but also what we don't see and perceive. A panoramic ethos not only necessitates a

https://doi.org/10.7330/9781646423262.c001

critical lens but also offers an actionable perspective-taking framework to ver con los otros. Perspective taking happens through empathetic listening to understand the Other and also by adopting a panoramic view of deficiencies. In this regard, we advocate for a Freirian teacher-student, student-teacher exchange but one that, in addition, centers a specific notion of deficiencies. Centering deficiencies, we argue, allows us to view them as common and not simply belonging to an Other. We propose that adopting this framework enables programs to make visible colonizing writing standards and oppressive language ideologies and practices and to attempt to transform each person's ethos based on what we learn from a panoramic view.

Our perspective on deficiencies is similar to that proposed by Patricia Roberts-Miller (2019), in which every person, including the teacher—and in the context of programs, the policy and decision makers and curriculum designers—walks into the learning space deficient based on what they see as well as what they don't see. Deficiencies are the results of narrow, limited perspectives, which we all possess. A common view of students whose language practices do not match an imaginary Standard English is to see them as deficient and unable to succeed in their graduate programs. These so-called language deficiencies can only be fixed when students learn to use the imaginary English academic standard, a standard closely associated with white America. In contrast, we are perceiving deficiencies in a broader, perceptual sense, related to language but not *just* related to language. We see these deficiencies in perspective as potential sites ripe for invention, resistance, and change in a panoramic space. In particular, students whose language practices are seen as inferior to an imaginary and powerful standard have a chance of escaping victimization narratives and can transform themselves into meaning-making members of different communities.

To illustrate the value and need for doing translingualism through the lens of panoramic ethos for graduate-program development, we first provide the testimonios of current graduate students that highlight their educational histories and language practices. Then, we point out the mismatch between these testimonios and common practices in traditional rhetoric and composition graduate programs with asymmetrical power relations, and finally we suggest how graduate programs might change through the lens of a panoramic ethos that favors intentional perspective taking, understanding, and negotiation.

PATY FLORES HUTSON, *CONTIGO EN LA CRUZADA*: BRIDGING THE LANGUAGE AND SPATIAL DIVIDE

Fifteen years ago, I enrolled at the University of Texas at El Paso (UTEP) as a second-language (L2) student. I was born and raised on the Mexico-US border. I do not consider myself from one country or the other, as I am a member of both cultures. Mi mamá, like countless others, crossed the border to give birth to her children in the hopes they would one day live in the United States permanently for a chance at a better life. Growing up on the border allowed me to cultivate a bicultural identity that has helped me navigate two worlds. This bicultural identity is directly tied to the way I use language. My mother enrolled me at a very young age in English classes hoping I would be proficient enough to attend school in El Paso, Texas. She constantly reminded my brothers and me that "allá hay más oportunidades que aquí." I remember disliking and skipping my English classes often, as I felt my identity as a young Mexican girl was being stolen. I despised the English language, and as a result I had difficulty learning it.

In her canonical text *Borderlands/La Frontera*, Gloria Anzaldúa (1987) describes the border as "*una herida abierta* [an open wound] where the Third World grates against the first and bleeds" (3). In this essay, she refers to the physical border between Mexico and the United States as a site of a continuous power struggle, where multiple worlds live both harmoniously and in conflict. As a transnational member of the Ciudad Juárez–El Paso region, I feel that wound personally. To me, that wound was first opened after being forced to learn the English language, and I have attempted to treat the wound by bringing my Mexican and US cultures into harmony.

Due to its proximity to the Mexico-US border, UTEP is uniquely suited to serve students living with the "open wound." Approximately six hundred students make a daily commute from Ciudad Juarez to UTEP and are classified as border commuter (BC) students. Most of these students cross the Mexico-US bridge every single day, with crossing times usually in excess of two hours. Every morning, BC students wait in line hoping to not be interrogated, mistreated, or even humiliated by a US Customs official. Throughout my undergraduate degree at UTEP, I was a BC student and had to cross the Mexico-US bridge every single morning in order to get to class. I usually left my house around 5 a.m. in order to make it on time to my 9 a.m. class. I remember specifically one instance of being interrogated by a border customs officer for over four hours because I was carrying my brother's chemistry book in my backpack. I was asked such questions as, "Are you planning on making a bomb?" and "Are you planning on making drugs?" When I tried to respond in Spanish, the border customs officers demanded I speak in English. That day, I didn't make it to my first class, and upon arrival to my second class, I had already lived a traumatic experience that would remain with me for a very long time. Crossing the bridge every morning to get to class can make BC students feel vulnerable. Through these experiences, my identity was shaped into that of an insecure college student who understood my ability to speak English would grant me not only better opportunities in my future but more humane treatment. Without it, I often felt helpless navigating every aspect of my life, from commuting to school to being present in the classroom.

Upon arrival to UTEP, I tested out of the ESOL (English for speakers of other languages) courses and was placed directly into first-year composition (FYC) classes. Although I felt hesitant about my course placement, at that point I wasn't even aware challenging that decision was an option. More important, as an undergraduate student, I felt that having confidence in my scores from the TOEFL examination, in combination with the administration's advice to skip the ESOL courses, was the right decision for my academic success.

Throughout the first semester as an undergraduate student, I had to overcome many challenges, which were compounded by the language barrier I faced inside the classroom. However, I was fortunate enough to be placed in a first-year composition class with a sympathetic instructor. As I walked inside the classroom, I noticed the instructor speaking Spanish with another student, which immediately made me feel welcome as a transnational student. Every day throughout the semester, the instructor greeted me with a "bueños diás!" She also gave me feedback in Spanish, which gave me a sense of freedom and confidence, as I could better express myself and receive more meaningful feedback. This small gesture helped me work on healing my personal "open wound."

My experience as a transnational student at UTEP has allowed me to understand Anzaldúa's theory, which holds that epistemology begins with the awareness of personal truths. To Anzaldúa, one cannot be the most effective learner without an awareness of self-identity, which is directly linked to one's preferred language. Further, Anzaldúa's work has impressed upon me that accepting my own language, and the ways I choose to use it, inside and outside the classroom, are the most important aspects for remaining truthful to my individuality.

JUAN MOISÉS GARCÍA RENTERÍA, STRATEGIC CONTEMPLATION OF ACADEMIC THIRD SPACES (*OJOS PARA VER CON LOS OTROS*): TRANSLINGUALISM AND THE COPRESENCE OF THE *RETÓRICA POVERA*

I came to the Mexico-US border because I wanted to live there and pursue a doctoral degree, to become a doctorando. I was born in the central western coast of México to an urban de-Indianized Mestizo household that provided me with material and spiritual support and sustenance over my life in academia, my mother especially, who had always loved school but could not pursue anything beyond primaria lest she became una volada. She always thanked God I inherited her will to continue through higher education. I had now come in her place. As a first-generation transnational student, I read much about the situation of my community and went there on the holidays; the border's materiality came to stand for an epistemological regime embedded in academia, a unified nation I sought admission into but which constantly tore apart the relation between the imaginaries that made me up and the ones that count as true knowledge.

Make no mistake, academia is a site of contest over epistemological territories. Oftentimes, those battles make use of strategies of legitimization in which socially situated intellectual specialties are canonized as universal, neutral symbolic systems. The codification of literacies as standard norms serves to support and sustain social hierarchies by replicating the commonsensical notion that only certain intellectual specialties, which reflect the values of specific discourse communities, can work towards the creation of new knowledge. Therefore, writing instruction in academia often becomes a disciplining of public and private subjectivities into the tastes and values of socially situated communities. The educational system of the liberal arts, an institution born to police the symbolic economy of a white male elite, brought into being the tradition of belletristic composition still embedded in English studies these days (Crowley 1998).

In México, the institutions in charge of disciplining academic subjectivities follow a parallel path to that of English belletristic composition. The project of instruction into Castilian literacy, which started alongside the Conquista alfabetización, was tied from the beginning to a nationalist project that explicitly sought to assimilate "el indio" and "las masas" to Hispanic culture (Torres Montero 2001). Once México became an independent country, and as we progressed into modernity, intellectual professionalization continued to be explicitly motivated by this rhetorical strategy, taking its cues from cultural critics like Matthew Arnold

(1993), the English poet who was also determined to erase the "narrow, harsh, unintelligent, and unattractive spirit and culture" of the working classes (22). Spanish undergraduate programs in México served to institutionalize a means of cultural mobilization, a process that implied a migration from "functional illiteracy" into the Western canon. This is perhaps why, much like Michel Foucault (2005), who noted that only an ethical constitution of subjectivity could disrupt "political power" (252), my cuñada, as I set out to move to the border to become a doctorando, literally nudged me and said, "No te vayas a hacer crema."

The embodied aspect of this academic training meant unlearning my own vernacular literacies in order to become—arguably, always arguably—proficient in the dominant, belletristic variation. Writing instruction was supposed to dispel every trace of ignorance and raise the moral stature of my ordinary self by providing me with a brand of critical thinking, a rationalist frame of acceptance, that disparaged affective and faith literacies through the constant and "pervasive mood of irony and world-weariness" typical of critique (Anker and Felski 2017, 3). Because I am someone who grew up in a community that values spirituality, care, humility, and humor, this version of composition instruction made me feel uprooted from the people I originally set out to honor. I became the archetype of the colonized intellectual that Frantz Fanon (2004) imagines as "a sentinel on duty guarding the Greco-Roman pedestal" (211); I learned to recognize the mark of "indigence and innate depravity" (7) in the intellectual specialties of the very people who, ironically, sponsored my education through their care and knowledge.

Recognizing this feeling of uprootedness as a liminal space we venture into as colonized intellectuals constituted for me the disciplinary shuddering Jesús Martín-Barbero (2017) calls an "escalofrío epistemológico." The *escalofrío epistemológico* is a moment of self-reflexivity in which a scholar questions the ethics behind the stance that scrutinizes subaltern intellectual specialties as deficient. It is a moment of postcritical epiphany that problematizes the "diagnostic quality of critique" (Anker and Felski 2017, 67) and dares to wonder "a quién y para qué [sirven] mis acuciosos análisis semióticos, mis *lecturas ideológicas*" (Martín-Barbero 2017, 19). Adopting the vantage point of my intellectual specialties, I recognized my *escalofrío epistemológico* as a mystical experience of sorts, a "scrupulous attention to what makes itself known in . . . moments of numinous experience" (Ulanov 2011, 54). This openness to the awe-inspiring dimension of a secret pulse is, if you will, the Christian kairos, "a change in the pulse and tempo of experience . . . where the notion of end, the notion of definitive occurrence and rupture in the passage of the ordinary customs and habits, is highlighted" (Latour 2017). This mystical openness to "transpersonal input" (Barnard 1997, 64) was crucial for me to give pertinence to new possibilities of reconfiguring my academic self, allowing me to legitimize in it the literacies of my community.

For Martín-Barbero (2017), the experience of the *escalofrío epistemológico* entails the displacement of research methodologies to a practice of ver con los otros. Ver con los otros is a disposition to listen intently to the sensibilities and imaginaries of the "culturas pobres" (16). For me, it became a tool for debordering and rebordering the epistemological territory of academia, my own means of enacting what Jacqueline Jones Royster and Gesa E. Kirsch (2011) call "critical imagination" and "strategic contemplation" in order to honor my disembedded imaginaries and negotiate agency. The space this methodology opens is where the reconfiguration of composition as a translanguaging occurrence takes place, disrupting monolingual ideologies by "making connections and seeing possibility," "insight, inspiration, and passion" (19, 22). By ver con los otros I have realized I came to academia because my mother gave me the eyes to find hope in los estudios, ojos para ver in nonnormative intellectual specialties, the voices of the socially oppressed filtering through the cracks and crumbling mortar of the Mexico-US border wall.

CORINA LERMA, *NI DE AQUÍ, NI DE ALLÁ*: NEGOTIATING SUBJECTIVITIES THROUGH TRANSLINGUALISM AND MEMORY AS SPACES FOR INVENTION

There is a phrase used in Spanish to describe people like me, ni de aquí, ni de allá, or "not from here, not from there." I was born and schooled in El Paso, Texas, United States of America, and I grew up thinking the piece of land where one is born dictates one's citizenship; therefore, for all intents and purposes, I defined myself as an American. However, I became bilingual at a very young age. My behaviors and identity centered on the idea that I was an American—even a typical American. Despite my American status, I was placed in bilingual classes at school where my pronunciation of English words became a constant internal battle and source of anxiety.

By the time I was in second grade, I had already internalized the hierarchy established in my public-education experience and developed a student subject position, one who avoided talking unless absolutely necessary. The culturally normative social practices in the classroom developed one of my earlier subject positions, a successful student. I performed this subject position, through discourse and social practices, and therefore reproduced the same ideological subject position (Althusser 1971). The restrictive and repressive classroom made me adopt a subjectivity in which emotional responses had no place and had to be eliminated if I wanted to become a successful student (hooks 1994). I continued with this mentality of being emotionless and doing exactly as teachers wanted as I advanced in school.

Halfway through the school year, Mrs. Kuntz, my second-grade teacher, informed the class she would begin scheduling visits to our homes. I obediently gave the form to my mom, and performing a routine we had established silently, I translated for her what it was saying to Spanish. On the day of the visit, Mrs. Kuntz discussed my progress, and I became somewhat distracted with *Clifford*, which was playing on the television in the background with no volume. Mrs. Kuntz noticed and asked, "What kind of shows or cartoons does Corina watch?" My mom proudly replied, "She loves cartoons like *Clifford*, *Barney* and *Zaboomafoo*." Mrs. Kuntz smiled and said, "That's great! Make sure she continues to only watch English television shows and cartoons and speaks English at home." Her admonition to my mother made me feel like my parents' language was somehow detrimental to my education.

Her hegemonic discourse, made more insidious by her innocuous presentation, convinced me it was in my best interest to stop speaking Spanish. Although her approach was not intimidating or forceful, she had used her authority and power as an instructor to persuade me my language was inferior and to influence me to feel shame for speaking in my first language (Phillips 2006). I began to wonder if I would ever be able to hide the fact that I spoke Spanish, and I worried about how much I needed to continue working on removing all trace of an accent. Unbeknownst to me, I was not simply removing an accent, I was also making attempts to hide half my identity as a Mexican American.

Even though Spanish served as a bond in my family and home life through a common identity, heritage, and history, this experience told me speaking Spanish was a sign of inferiority. Language, in this case, was not used as a means to adapt but as a weapon of conquest and domination (Balderrama and Rodriguez 2006). Henry Giroux (1988) says, "Students have memories, families, religions, feelings, languages and cultures that give them a distinctive voice. We can critically engage that experience and we can move beyond it. But we can't deny it" (99). Mrs. Kuntz's perhaps well-intentioned advice denied me access to that voice because as I moved on in my education, I developed a positionality in which I resented my family's attachment to their language and feared they would somehow hold me back. Gloria Anzaldúa (1987) captures this pain when she says in *Borderlands/La Frontera,* "So if you want to really hurt me, talk badly about my language" (59).

As I advanced to middle and high school, I continued to write, speak, and perform Standard English and even avoided any instance of Spanglish at home or school, leading me to develop a fragmented sense of identity. My ability to repress "all longing to speak in tongues other than Standard English without seeing this repression as political was an indication of the way we act unconsciously, in complicity with a culture of domination" (hooks 1994, 173). Mexican American children of immigrants often experience linguistic violence and a legacy in which English becomes a marker of education and success and Spanish a language of inferiority and Otherness.

This experience, however, only marked the beginning of several experiences that placed in conflict the ideologies of my different subject positions, causing me cognitive dissonance. For instance, this dissonance occurred again in sophomore year of high school when I was asked to answer the following question: "In a well-supported essay argue if Pancho Villa was a hero or anti-hero to the Mexican Revolution of 1910." Although I had no knowledge of that historical time from a Mexican perspective, I felt I had somehow betrayed a part of me. It was the first time I felt a strong sense of resistance to teachers, books, and my education. This epiphany or space of discomfort shined a light on my previous feelings of personal dissonance and confusion about my identity (Denzin 2014).

Throughout my life, up to that moment, I had unconsciously worked on mechanisms to live a completely compartmentalized life in terms of my home and school. It was in that moment that I was forced to confront the imbrication of what had been separate subject positions and enculturations. This contradiction captured my ambiguous subjectivity as a daughter to Mexican parents and my subjectivity as an American pursuing an education in the United States. At that moment, I had to choose a language attached to subjectivity and performance. I chose to adopt and perpetuate the ideas and beliefs I had learned as an American student, but, in reality, I had no other option. Michel Foucault's (1977) notions of power describe how the people who determine our choices have tremendous power because they legitimize the viable responses. He writes, "The perpetual penality that traverses all points and supervises every instant in the disciplinary institutions compares, differentiates, hierarchizes, homogenizes, excludes. In short, it *normalizes*" (183). The unilateral representation of history was normalized, leading me to only have one option, to legitimize the US perspective on this chapter of history.

These ideas led me, for the first time in my whole academic career, to bridge my fragmented senses of identity and explore all these moments that had haunted me as spaces for invention and resistance. Kendall Phillips (2002, 2006) describes the rhetorical maneuver as one that shows the subject's potential to draw from the resources of memory, agency, artistry, and invention. All these past experiences of friction. as I encountered power in the form of authority, or overlapping and conflicting subject positions, were moments of possibility and potential agency. Most of those times, I silenced that sense of tension as I encountered power, but as I move forward and recognize similar feelings, I will not stand idly by. The process of undergoing this experience of reflection has created a space or an inventional pause in which I am able to analyze how these experiences of dissension, contradiction, and cognitive dissonance are points of possibility. I understand I am the granddaughter of a Mexican American and repatriate of the 1930s who married a Mexican national and who worked in the United States under the bracero program during the 1940s. I am American born and raised in El Paso, Texas, and daughter to Mexican parents. I understand that all these aspects of myself define some of the subject positions and subjectivities I use on a daily basis to negotiate the world around me but are also means of self-empowerment.

ADOPTING PANORAMIC ETHOS AS A TRANSLINGUAL PRAXIS

By foregrounding the testimonios of three transnational/translingual students at a university on the Mexico-US border, we seek to open up possibilities for rethinking traditional notions of graduate education and program design. UTEP is more than 80 percent Hispanic, which leads to a unified perception of our student body's identity. Testimonios are a form of "storying" used to represent the "small voice of history" (Guha 1996), but they are also the mobilization of symbols to articulate identities and ideologies. More important, testimonios transcend any methodology, as they are a form of political action. Testimonios then do not have to necessarily yield something but have inherent value in meaning-making practices. The testimonios presented here are of three graduate students who would normally be described monolithically as Latinx, Hispanic, or transnational. Yet, in consort, these testimonios show there is a clear disconnect between student subjectivities and standard, product-oriented educational structures. Common program requirements such as language exams, comprehensive exams, and required core classes, intended to help students be successful in their academic discipline, can end up producing a single consistent subjectivity that defines academic experience. Standard, one-size-fits-all program structures and requirements seem particularly out of sync with the rapidly changing academic (and post-COVID-19) job market.

To illustrate the disconnect between graduate program expectations and students' subjectivities, we would like to give as an example the "Expertise Grid for Rhetoric, Composition, and the Teaching of English" at the University of Arizona, as given on the website of the Doctoral Consortium in Rhetoric and Composition (n.d.). This grid describes the characteristics of students as they move through the program and develop as teachers and scholars. The expertise grid starts with several characteristics students should exhibit before entering the program: "Students should be intrigued about how language—broadly speaking—works as an expressive, communicative, and/or persuasive tool; [they should have an] expressed interest in learning how to use and better understand language; [they will have] no understanding of methods and theories yet."

We certainly do agree that being intrigued about how language works, or wanting to learn more about language, is a good thing. But as these testimonios show, students' language journeys and understandings extend far beyond "interest and intrigue." Like Paty, Moisés, and Corina, many students entering a doctoral program are already sophisticated translingual practitioners who have maneuvered throughout their lives within oppressive, colonizing, and frequently traumatizing linguistic and rhetorical spaces. They know how language works and how it connects to power, resistance, and invention. Yet their expertise is often invisible, ignored, exoticized, or subsumed under the visible, vetted, and normalized academic fluency of an instructor or program. Further, students' language use and practices are not specific or inherent to marginalized students or multilingual writers; to think so is to risk the commodification of difference, which as Roberts-Miller (2019) notes, gives rise to "the racist hierarchies of a culture or society; and racist hierarchies are hierarchies that are socially constructed categories that claim to be essential and inherent in groups." Panoramic ethos stands to counter these prevalent ideologies and practices in traditional graduate rhetoric and composition curricula.

Panoramic ethos espouses several theories of translingual ethos: (1) the notion that difference is the norm (Horner and Alvarez 2019); (2) critical reflection of negotiation in code-meshing performances (MacDonald and DeGenaro 2017); and (3) language as plurilingual, an intersubjective social practice with a grammar that is emergent, hybrid, and multimodal

(Canagarajah and Liyanage 2012). However, panoramic ethos also insists on the understanding and redefinition of *deficient* students and teachers in a classroom. While the concept of deficit holds strong historical implications, as we mention earlier, there is a difference between saying everyone—including the teacher—enters a classroom with differences and everyone enters a class with deficits, in the panoramic sense. A focus on deficits suggests the need for teachers' development in the design of the program and implies an unfinished process in which teachers and students seek interventions of their reality and in which the student helps the teacher understand. In other words, a program design informed by a panoramic ethos understands *all* stakeholders, not just students, have multiple subjectivities, languages, and identities and does not privilege the creation of a single or standard subjectivity through recursive pedagogical practices. In this sense, a panoramic ethos is not about intrigue and achievement of previously established milestones, which give the illusion of something to grasp or obtain. It is about reframing our motivations for learning with and by each other.

A concrete example of an enactment of panoramic ethos we can draw from in shaping our own translingual programs and pedagogies is the "intenciones pedagógicas" articulated by the Mexican certificate "Escuela y Comunidad" of the Instituto de Investigaciones para el Desarrollo de la Educación of the Universidad Iberoamericana, an initiative directed at training community-based elementary and middle-school instructors. The purpose of the certificate was to open up a space in which the "*miradas*" of researchers, program directors, and both mestizes and Indigenous instructors could "establecer un diálogo" (García Uriza 2016, 70) that addressed the linguistic discrimination and cultural relevance of the basic education programs in their communities. As a way to encourage critical reflexivity of the instructor's role in oppressive and exclusionary power relations, stakeholders decided to articulate pedagogical intentions that explicitly encouraged the "interacción entre las lenguas" (289). These articulations resulted in a combination of individual and shared program objectives that disrupted the view of "the student as end product" (Moore 2015, 56), in which the teacher's job is to "help students understand," and suggested instead that teachers should aim at experiencing "la lengua y el lenguaje que permite la comunicación y la interrelación en el territorio vivo" (García Uriza 2016, 298), language and the way of expression that facilitates communication and interrelation in the living territory. We believe this example acknowledges the partial quality of our perspectives and has implications for programmatic materials such as syllabi, curricula, and program design.

Like the University of Arizona, many graduate programs, including ours at UTEP, have created documents that communicate program expectations of students. Often in response to the dictates of accreditation agencies or university systems, these documents describe programmatic goals and learning objectives. At UTEP, for instance, students are required to take courses in rhetorical history, composition studies, and research methods that have been developed by faculty over a number of years. Though we do occasionally ask students for input into these courses, and a few students have cotaught these courses with us, the focus is on the faculty *helping students understand* what faculty and directors think they need to understand, in essence positioning ourselves not as teacher-students and the students not as student-teachers, when in reality, we each have something to learn from the other, not the Other. We wonder, though, what might have happened if, as with the Instituto de Investigaciones para el Desarrollo de la Educación, we had started with "establecer un diálogo" from the beginning that involved all stakeholders, students, faculty, and program directors seeking to understand each other through a panoramic ethos. What if this diálogo happened every semester or every year? What courses would be created, and recreated? How might typical academic performances in the form of exams, conference presentations, and articles be transformed? How would this approach be different from a mere consultation with students? Where would the sophisticated and complex language practices of students, including transnational students, be foregrounded and centered?

More specifically, we imagine inventive spaces—physical and virtual—in graduate programs in which all program participants—students, faculty, advisors, coordinators, administrative staff—contribute testimonios, or other culturally relevant and appropriate accounts, of their own language journeys in whatever length, modality, and language they choose. These various perspectives from all program stakeholders would (1) foreground the multiple subjectivities, identities, and languages that create and maintain a graduate program, and they would (2) serve to populate the program's panorama of deficiencies and expertise, which would impact recruitment, curriculum, and programmatic practices and events. For instance, a testimonio or storytelling event could replace or supplement the typical meet-and-greet that starts the academic year in so many programs and could reoccur periodically. While one strategy won't be enough to work against the pull of racialized language standards that come from tests (i.e., the GRE or TOEFL) and English-only classrooms, conferences, and journals, adopting a panoramic ethos across program practices can have a positive impact on practices that are no longer relevant. For example, traditional language-proficiency exams, in which students are supposed to show proficiency in a non-English language through translating a literary passage, derive from the assumption that all students are native English speakers and occludes the rhetoricity of language translation. Like this one, many other programmatic and professionalization practices are narrow in accounting for program/teacher expertise and student deficits. To work against these pressures, a panoramic ethos must permeate all aspects of a program so all participants are understood to have multiple perspectives and meaning-making ways that open up possibilities for negotiation and change. Beyond offering a specific critical imperative, a panoramic ethos is an intentional way to seek to understand: to see through others' eyes.

CONCLUDING THOUGHTS: *VIENDO CON LOS OTROS*

The testimonios in this chapter highlight the importance of advocating for different learning practices in graduate programs and classrooms in rhetoric and composition. Adopting a panoramic ethos would allow an openness for individuals from different communities and backgrounds to interact more mindfully and expansively. With openness, understanding, and negotiation, these "nontraditional" approaches can strive to break the barriers many transnational students currently face, as well as create a more inclusive setting where different languages are not only welcomed or encouraged but built into the fabric of a classroom or curriculum. The experiences of transnational students are not unique and transcend the Mexico-US border region and minority-serving institutions like UTEP. Over half a million international students are currently enrolled at US college institutions, with the majority hailing from countries where English is not the primary language (Matsuda 2014). Further, as noted in the introduction, even monolinguals from the United States enact translingual practices.

Panoramic ethos can be viewed as an identity-building process that is far from static or finite and does not intend to be a fixed or suitable solution for all graduate-program design situations. A panoramic ethos expands the complex negotiations of language use and identities from what is often perceived as a single category, that is, the transnational student, to everyone in the classroom. By approaching academic spaces as being in need of multiple perspectives, we seek to equalize in order to open up to diversity, a plurality in which every member contributes to their own intelligibility of the world, rather than having to adopt a commodified identity to gain access to a symbolic economy. A panoramic ethos approaches teaching and learning as an intersubjective ongoing dialogue in which the result is a widening of the horizon for both student and teacher.

Mapping the territory of academia through panoramic ethos means abandoning the will to replicate a fixed academic identity on the student, and through viendo con los otros, opening up a space for a student identity shared and added to by everybody in the classroom. Graduate-program design can be an event that emerges from conjoined meaning-making practices against monolithic iterations of academia, from the transformative potential of transnational graduate students' community wealth: our testimonios *ground* the theories of academia, rather than theories grounding our experience.

REFERENCES

Althusser, Louis. 1971. "Ideology and Ideological State Apparatuses." In *Lenin and Philosophy and Other Essays*, 127–86. London: New Left Books.

Anker, Elizabeth S., and Rita Felski. 2017. *Critique and Postcritique*. Durham, NC: Duke University Press.

Anzaldúa, Gloria. 1987. *Borderlands/La Frontera: The New Mestiza*. San Francisco: Aunt Lute Books.

Arnold, Matthew. 1993. "Democracy." *Arnold: Culture and Anarchy and Other Writings*, edited by Stefan Collini, 1–25. Cambridge: Cambridge University Press.

Ayash, Nancy Bou. 2019. *Toward Translingual Realities in Composition: (Re)Working Local Language Representations and Practices*. Logan: Utah State University Press.

Balderrama, Francisco E., and Raymond Rodriguez. 2006. *Decade of Betrayal: Mexican Repatriation in the 1930s*. Albuquerque: University of New Mexico Press.

Barnard, William G. 1997. *Exploring Unseen Worlds: William James and the Philosophy of Mysticism*. New York: SUNY Press.

Canagarajah, Suresh. 2018. "Translingual Practice as Spatial Repertoires: Expanding the Paradigm beyond Structuralist Orientations." *Applied Linguistics* 39 (1): 31–54.

Canagarajah, Suresh, and Indika Liyanage. 2012. "Lessons from Pre-colonial Multilingualism." In *The Routledge Handbook of Multilingualism*, edited by Marilyn Martin-Jones, Adrian Blackledge, and Angela Creese, 49–65. London: Routledge.

Crowley, Sharon. 1998. "The Bourgeois Subject and the Demise of Rhetorical Education." In *Composition in the University: Historical and Polemical Essays*, edited by Sharon Crowley, 30–45. Pittsburgh: University of Pittsburgh Press.

Denzin, Norman K. 2014. *Interpretive Autoethnography*. Thousand Oaks, California: Sage.

Doctoral Consortium for Rhetoric and Composition. n.d. "Expertise Grid for Rhetoric, Composition, and the Teaching of English." https://ccccdoctoralconsortium.org/materials/.

Fanon, Frantz. 2004. *The Wretched of the Earth*. Translated by Richard Philcox. New York: Grove.

Foucault, Michel. 1977. *Discipline and Punish: The Birth of the Prison*. New York: Vintage Books.

Foucault, Michel. 2005. *The Hermeneutics of the Subject: Lectures at the Collège de France, 1981–1982*, edited by Frédéric Gros. New York: Palgrave Macmillan.

García Uriza, and Brenda Idahena. 2016. *Escuela y communidad: Caminos de aprendizaje desde la fuerza del corazón*. Ciudad de México: Universidad Iberoamericana.

Giroux, Henry A. 1988. "The Hope of Radical Education: A Conversation with Henry Giroux." *The Journal of Education* 170 (2): 91–101. http://www.jstor.org/stable/42742123.

Guha, Ranajit. 1996. "The Small Voice of History." *Subaltern Studies* 9: 1–12.

hooks, bell. 1994. Teaching to Transgress: Education as the Practice of Freedom. New York: Routledge.

Horner, Bruce, and Sara P. Alvarez. 2019. "Defining Translinguality." *Literacy in Composition Studies* 7 (2): 1–30.

Latour, Bruno. 2017. Interview with Lynda Walsh. "Forum: Bruno Latour on Rhetoric." *Rhetoric Society Quarterly* 47 (5): 403–62.

MacDonald, Michael T., and William DeGenaro. 2017. "Negotiating a Transcultural Ethos from the Ground Up in a Basic Writing Program." *Journal of Basic Writing* 36 (1): 25–55.

Martín-Barbero, Jesus. 2017. "Entre el mirar y el ver: Los inesperados efectos de un escalofrío visual." In *Ver con los otros: Comunicación intercultural*, edited by Jesús Martín-Barbero and Sarah Corona Berkin, 15–43. Ciudad de México: Fondo de Cultura Económica.

Matsuda, Paul Kei. 2014. "The Lure of Translingual Writing." *PMLA: Publications of the Modern Language Association of America* 129 (3): 478–83.

Moore, Alex. 2015. *Understanding the School Curriculum: Theory, Politics and Principles*. London: Routledge.

Phillips, Kendall R. 2002. "Spaces of Invention: Dissension, Freedom, and Thought in Foucault." *Philosophy & Rhetoric* 35 (4): 328–44.

Phillips, Kendall R. 2006. "Rhetorical Maneuvers: Subjectivity, Power, and Resistance." *Philosophy & Rhetoric* 39 (4): 310–32.

Roberts-Miller, Patricia. 2019. "The Deficit Model of Education and Unintentional Racism." Patricia Roberts-Miller. http://www.patriciarobertsmiller.com/2019/12/11/the-deficit-model-of-education-and-unintentional-racism/.

Royster, Jaqueline Jones, and Gesa Kirsch. 2011. *Feminist Rhetorical Practices: New Horizons for Rhetoric, Composition, and Literacy Studies*. Carbondale: Southern Illinois University Press.

Torres Montero, Gabriela. 2001. "La educación profesional en la posrevolución: El caso de la Universidad de San Luis Potosí (1920–1923)." In *La educación superior en el proceso histórico de México*, vol. 2, edited by David Piñera Ramírez, 379–97. Mexicali: Universidad Autónoma de Baja California.

Ulanov, Ann Belford. 2011. "Encountering Jung Being Encountered." *Jung Journal: Culture & Psyche* 5 (3): 54–62.

2

(EN)COUNTERING MONOLINGUALISM
A Transnational Sensemaking of Graduate Education

Joseph Franklin, Emily Yuko Cousins, and Alex Way

When we applied to graduate school, we were all working outside the United States: Alex was teaching English for Academic Purposes (EAP) at a university in Japan, Joe was directing a writing center in the United Kingdom, and Emily was teaching first-year writing at a liberal arts college in Bangladesh. We shared a common hope that graduate school, specifically in rhetoric and composition, would train us for future work as internationally mobile compositionists and writing program administrators. As difficult as it was to uproot our lives and move to the United States to be full-time students again, we were also seeking a sort of break, an escape from exhausting and often disorienting working conditions, to have a chance to reflect meaningfully on our experiences in these various global locales before moving on to the next chapter of our careers. The three of us were drawn to our university because of its association with translingualism and transnational composition studies via faculty, prior graduates, conferences, seminars, symposia, and publications.

Engaging with translingual and transnational theory as graduate students gave us a critical lens to bring into focus the monolingualizing forces we had encountered in our international workplaces and provided a sense of relief when it felt like our experiences did not seem legible to others in the field, or even to ourselves. Approaches in transnational inquiry, which challenge an assumed binary of frictionless global flows clashing with stable, authentic local interests (Zenger 2018), resonated with the messiness of our international work and positionalities. Monolingualism upholds essentialist links between language, nation, and identity, each imagined as stable and singular (Yildiz 2012). As a counter to monolingual language ideology, translingualism offers a reconceptualization of languages as emerging from and constantly transformed by practices of language users, whose identities are similarly

https://doi.org/10.7330/9781646423262.c002

in flux. In the context of US college composition, translingual pedagogies challenge the enforcement of "standard" English and the treatment of "nonstandard" varieties of English as deficient or deviant (Horner et al. 2011). As graduate students, we recognized an expansiveness in the decolonial potential of translingual pedagogies that help us confront and counter forms of language-based discrimination, within and beyond US-based higher education. Translingual composition theory offered us terms with which to describe an orientation toward language difference we had begun cultivating while working with students of diverse backgrounds and helped us engage in the difficult mental labor necessary to unlearn monolingual assumptions we carried.

When we turned the translingual lens toward examining rhetoric and composition graduate education itself, however, we were increasingly compelled by how monolingual, fast-capitalist conditions that inhibited our sensemaking had followed us from our different contexts abroad into our graduate training. Monolingualism conceptualizes languages as a fixed code or set of rules, which can be standardized and then parceled off for purchase (e.g. Intermediate Japanese, English for Business Communication, and Conversational Portuguese). In this way, the monolingual language ideology lays the groundwork for the commodification of English, which is then distributed as an immutable entity regardless of context (Pennycook 2008, 34). For many in the current global fast-capitalist knowledge economy, learning English is "virtually a must" to keep up with the competitive global marketplace and involves investing in textbooks, standardized tests, courses, and private tutoring (Prendergast 2008, 1). The high financial burdens of these investments perpetuate unequal access around the globe. In parallel, in US college composition, the commodity to be delivered is Standard Written English (SWE): instructors are paid to transmit SWE to student-consumers who, in turn, expect to be given SWE as a tool for their future success (Horner 2016, 113).

In this chapter, we offer narratives to serve as illustrations of how it felt to navigate the uncanny resemblances to fast-capitalist monolingualism within and outside rhetoric and composition. As graduate students, we had the freedom to think through our work with the help of translingual and transnational composition theory, but we also saw how monolingualist and fast-capitalist values were uncritically reproduced in the materials we read and through the practices of those around us, including ourselves, our peers, and faculty. These practices reminded us of the compromising positions we experienced abroad in that they unnecessarily inhibited and constrained our sensemaking through marginalizing our ideas and denying paths for meaningful resistance or change. First, we struggled to draw from and build on our cross-cultural, cross-language experiences within the monolingualist, US-centric terms of discussion that characterized much of our graduate work. Second, we recognized exhausting conditions arising from labor demands of graduate work constructed in response to imagined careers and fast-capitalist market pressures treated as fixed. We believe translingual and transnational composition theory is not just another competency, pedagogical application, or specialization but should serve as a critical foundation for current and future reimaginings of rhetoric and composition graduate programs that resist monolingual influences that hold us *all* back in different ways.

ALEX

Graduating with my BA in the midst of the Great Recession (and disappearing job prospects), I began searching for employment abroad. After a brief stint teaching in South Korea, which ended when my employer went bankrupt, I jumped ship to Japan and became a native English teacher (NET) at an *eikaiwa*, or English conversation school.

The *eikaiwa* industry resembled the fast-food industry at times. For instance, my *eikaiwa* franchise coordinated all its operations so students on vacation could travel to any of the other franchise locations throughout Japan and resume their studies on the same textbook unit. Such convenience came at a price. The newly developed in-house textbooks and teaching methods were pedagogically questionable, and the work culture in my *eikaiwa* was brutal—my twenty-two-year-old coworker died from a combination of "power harassment" and *karoushi*, or death from overwork leading to suicide. While my time spent abroad was special—I loved learning new languages, and Japan is where I met my wife—I never wanted to teach in such hypercapitalistic and exploitative conditions again. I also never wanted to lose another colleague to overwork. I thought perhaps graduate school would allow me better working conditions and grant me the freedom to design and teach classes myself rather than being led by a corporate curriculum.

I started a rhet/comp program at a university in the Pacific Northwest that offered a TESL (teaching English as a second language) certificate, but the timing for the required graduate seminar did not fit my MA trajectory. So, feeling I needed to go outside rhet/comp to earn the proper credentials, I became acquainted with a linguistics professor, took her applied linguistics course, and wrote an English for academic purposes (EAP) pedagogical rationale for my final project. Upon graduation, the professor offered me the opportunity to teach a composition course for international students, and I accepted in hopes it would position me to teach EAP back in Japan. However, I felt like an imposter in another discipline—despite my many years of teaching ESL, I had never received any official credentials.

Through a personal connection, I found a part-time position teaching EAP in Japan after getting my MA. My worries about lacking credentials were unfounded, for better or worse. Similar to US universities, personal connections and cheap labor were valuable. I was, essentially, an adjunct in working conditions similar to those in US universities (e.g., in order to make ends meet, I had to combine this job with two other part-time jobs). At my university, I wanted to try out a translingual approach, which I had explored in my master's program. This approach would have likely involved error negotiation, students interweaving multiple languages in their work, and translation; but the EAP curriculum to me seemed like an immovable brick wall. In a course devoted to writing paragraphs, I found myself counting individual words on exam papers to ensure students wrote within word limits and nit-picking topic sentences for slight (yet grammatically correct) deviations that would result in severe grade reductions, as per the shared EAP rubric. Nevertheless, I had déjà vu of being trapped in a rigid curriculum, but this time it was through the university, not an *eikaiwa*.

Now that I am teaching in a US university context as a PhD student, I realize that the monolingualist structure of US composition, which assumes and contains a linguistically homogeneous student body of Standard English users (Matsuda 2006), yet again makes it difficult to draw upon my cross-cultural and multilingual background in the classroom. Furthermore, while translingualism has encouraged rhet/comp teachers to see students' multilingual backgrounds as resources, teachers' multicultural and multilingual resources remain overlooked as assets. I want to experiment with translingual pedagogies, and I have, for instance, experimented with small-scale translation assignments. But I cannot help feeling pressured to just stick with the SWE script. I also worry students will view my translingual approach as irrelevant, or even contrary, to learning academic writing. Moving forward, I remain unsure how to negotiate my translingual orientation to teaching under monolingual expectations.

EMILY

As a high-school student attending a US international school in Tokyo, I was extremely anxious about studying Japanese. I was ashamed of my lack of language skills, which I felt were a direct contradiction of my identity as half Japanese. The dread I felt before and during every class was visceral: it sat heavily in my stomach and made my heart race. Worst of all was the fear of being called on to read from the textbook aloud in front of everyone and mispronouncing an unfamiliar kanji. I felt discouraged and alienated by a language I would have loved to enjoy learning. Looking back, I understand how my language anxiety was rooted in monolingual language ideology that treats language fluency as a prerequisite to legitimate citizenship. Taking a seminar on translingualism in graduate school led me to this realization and helped me critically examine and confront this self-doubt. I was drawn to translingual articulations of labels and categories as mere constructions placed on top of a reality of constant in-betweenness, and this shift in thinking helped me more effectively sort through language and identity-based anxieties.

Before attending graduate school, I had been working at an English-medium liberal arts women's university in Bangladesh, teaching first-year writing and managing a staff of peer tutors at the writing center. Students came from over a dozen countries across the region, and many were the first women in their hometowns ever to attend university; all were learning English as a second, third, or fourth language. It was a fascinating backdrop of many translingually informed pedagogies and interactions, with students and faculty working across linguistic and cultural differences on a daily basis. At the same time, I struggled to make sense of my position and complicity within an institution that was held afloat by Western corporate donations and whose funding was contingent on telling stories of underprivileged young women being empowered through a US-style education. The writing center was tasked with composing these profiles for the grants office, following templates that reinforced autonomous literacy narratives. When I asked why we couldn't ask students to write their own narratives, in their own voices, I was told it would take far too long to edit them all. In our close interactions with students, we in the writing center were positioned to see how this grand narrative obscured the much messier, more complex situations our students faced and the material consequences that came along with an institutional ignorance of students' lived realities. Monolingual pressures were felt in various ways: while some faculty seemed to embrace a translingual disposition toward language difference, others scrutinized student writing for grammatical errors. Students scraped together their savings for months to register for the IELTS or TOEFL exam, with scholarships and conditional acceptances hinging on their scores. My increasingly exhausting work conditions made it difficult for me to make sense of the complexity of my surroundings in any meaning-ful way, and I hoped graduate school would provide the chance to do so.

When I began my studies, however, I got the sense that discussions would often structure and segment the world in ways that didn't reso-nate with my experiences, and the conversations I wanted to have were not necessarily happening. It was difficult to unpack the unspoken assumptions and histories packed within common terms and concepts while also trying to think of new things to say. When I did try to share my perspectives from non-US contexts in class, I could not help but question the value of my contributions against the pragmatic US-based takeaways everyone appeared to seek. I also found myself adjusting anec-dotes in anticipation of assumptions or biases I felt needed to be cor-rected. In describing my work in Bangladesh, for example, after giving a basic institutional overview, I would pause and ask myself, Do I now list examples of academic genres students were working on (literacy narra-tives, IRB proposals for senior thesis research) to make this unfamiliar setting more relatable? Do I mention many students would go on to pursue graduate studies in the United States or the United Kingdom? I felt the need to assert the academic capabilities of my students, as if to counter an assumption that a university in a non-Western, developing country could not possibly house a thriving writing program.

The traditional disciplinary frames with which we were being trained to produce knowledge as graduate students seemed to constrain our efforts to think through diverse subjectivities or research from different cultural, national, and institutional contexts. This constraint meant that when I attempted to draw from my linguistic, cross-cultural background as translingual approaches encourage, these moments felt peripheral, just beyond the scope of meaningful uptake and engagement. Much of my sensemaking ended up happening, unexpectedly, in informal, in-between spaces: emails with professors, discussions during office hours, and informal chats with peers.

JOE

My first job abroad was teaching English in South Korea at a *hagwon* (private, after-school academy). For my entire contract I never had two days off in a row; we taught sometimes eight classes per day; we had unpaid, uncomfortable social and professional requirements; and we (foreign teachers) were always reminded of our value as appealing accents and exotic (white) faces. Pedagogically, I felt particularly upset that all my students' writing was sent to the Philippines to be assessed at a lower cost by anonymous strangers. We were told to reprimand any student if they ever used Korean in class, but constantly telling my students "no Korean!" grew increasingly uncomfortable, personally and pedagogically. I grew more and more aware of compromises and feeling simultaneously revered, exhausted, and insulted, like the time foreign teachers were required to sing and dance for parents but not allowed to speak with them at all. The constant work to parse whether my frustrations were from business practices, cultural norms, individual personalities, or whatever else meant I was mentally and physically exhausted by constantly trying to make sense of things. That exhaustion came to underwrite all my experiences in a negative light and propelled me to leave and attend graduate school as a way to move forward in my understanding and to get better jobs.

Later, as a composition grad student/teacher, I cherished the freedom to craft my own course and focus on writing. But with a heightened awareness of insider/outsider dynamics, I noticed something. All the care and attention given in the scholarship to help students seemed to really mean *undergraduate* students. Reasonable workload consideration, in-class writing, collaboration, assigning multimodal/multilingual texts—somehow these were not part of *our* curriculum as grad students. It felt surreal to hear about these values from the same instructors in a teaching practicum who would later ignore them during a seminar.

After my MA, I took a job starting up a writing center in a Russell Group university in England. I felt empowered and invigorated to build something, but at the same time it was a struggle, as the composition approaches I tried to deliver met a series of ideological, disciplinary, and pedagogical brick walls. I brought these experiences to my PhD program in the hopes of making sense of them. In a seminar on translingualism, I was overjoyed to be articulating and understanding so many prior confusions about why things didn't work out how I'd hoped. Talking through experiences at the ideological level offered a lot of value along with differing identities and discourses. But I also felt a power shift in moving from my role in the United Kingdom to the role of a graduate student in the United States, a perceptible change from being in a position to make change (however difficult) to being *told* how things worked with no interest in adapting.

At a departmental forum for graduate students and faculty, I raised concerns about workload. The norm voiced by my peers was of struggling to meet demands, sometimes by going to therapy, going on medication, or neglecting family. Each grad student attempted to cap their work somewhere between sixty and eighty hours per week but often failed. We grappled with finding some way to accept feeling like a failure for not doing more. Faculty shared their own experiences as graduate students under sometimes even worse conditions and collectively sympathized while pointing out things really only get worse. They pushed back against easing workloads because graduate school was a place to "prepare" for the intense realities coming next. There was no space for resistance; this was just the market.

Early on, I was grateful for my program's focus on professional preparation, but after studying and reflecting on translingualism, I began to feel more critical about the terms by which I was being "prepared." One supposedly benign check-in meeting with members of the department quickly became a sort of interrogation and assessment of my accomplishments based on some confusing set of standards. I was repeatedly asked to brand myself: Are you a WPA person or a translingual person? I was told not to bother with collaborative publications because they mean nothing on the market. Yet, the one course I took framed explicitly for publishing my work was *outside* the composition department. The people in the meeting who were telling me how important it was to publish weren't making space in classes in our own program for me to "prepare" for it. During advising, the recently removed foreign-language requirement was treated like a reprieve. My oral-exam questions and feedback were mostly focused on what I'd be required to say on the job market, not so much to do with ideas. Because these expectations were framed as responses to "the market," when I tried to ask questions or resist them, I was treated as unprepared. It felt I was hearing "no Korean!" if I tried to speak back to these standards, but instead of being told to speak English, I was expected to speak the language of the market. Being compromised in this way, the same way as working in a *hagwon*, felt very disempowering—which was not how I envisioned a PhD program.

DISCUSSION

As we engaged in conversations comparing our experiences of teaching writing in different parts of the world, we found many of the challenges we had faced internationally, and had hoped to leave behind, were just as present in graduate school. Translingual and transnational lenses helped us recognize the role of monolingual, fast-capitalist forces in diverse contexts abroad and in hindering our growth as graduate students. In this chapter, we leverage our experiences of dissonance and exhaustion to offer translingual critique of rhetoric and composition graduate curriculums in hopes of moving toward more socially just environments for graduate student professionalization and knowledge making.

In our international work, we all witnessed firsthand the commodification of English and English teaching, including the extreme standardization of lesson content, curricular mandates that scrutinized student work for error, and the prevalence of standardized testing. This commodity approach to language is rooted in a monolingual language ideology that treats languages as "ready-made, self-evident, discrete object[s]" (Lu 2004, 25). Despite the *actual* heterogeneity of English as practiced by language users worldwide, the English-language industry exports English as a set of skills detached from its contexts of use, draining it of the rich meanings and practices emerging from its actual global intermingling with diverse languages and language users. The homogenization of English in the global English-language-teaching industry overlooks all the ways "English always needs to be seen in the context of other languages" (Pennycook 2008, 34). This monolingual approach is particularly evident in the "no Korean" policy Joe recounts. As Joe and Alex observe, the commodification of English went hand in hand with commodification of language teachers themselves, who may face degrading and exploitative working conditions.

As graduate students, we saw how rhetoric and composition programs can also act as conduits to fast-capitalist, neoliberal values with an uncritical emphasis on career preparedness via the acquisition of commodified, specific competencies for a very particular job market. Forms of learning or professionalization outside built-in curricular structures, such as foreign-language learning or writing for publication, are not only unsupported but are rendered almost impossible because of demands of coursework and dissertating (Kilfoil 2018). In the English-language-teaching industry, our job was to deliver "authentic, native-like" English, while in graduate school we are expected to deliver Standard Written English (SWE) to student-consumers. Even though translingual theory inspired us to draw from students' diverse linguistic and cultural backgrounds in the classroom and to draw from our own language repertoires, these messages felt fragile against the exigencies of market demands. As Alex notes, our efforts to apply translingual pedagogies were complicated by the programmatic expectation that instructors should deliver SWE to students. Just trying to keep up with the rapid pace of the semester, we were unable to figure out how translingual approaches could be justified to our supervisors and students in a way that was meaningful and satisfying to us. We were wary of the usual critiques, as Min-Zhan Lu and Bruce Horner (2009) note, that critical pedagogies "ignore the pragmatic needs and interests of the very students they claim to serve" (113). As a result, we experienced dissonance between the values of translingual theory we wanted to embrace as writing instructors and the monolingual, fast-capitalist values being implicitly reinforced in our day-to-day surroundings.

We also observed monolingual parallels between the native-speaker ideal in the English-language-teaching industry and the assumed native-speaker status among writing instructors in rhetoric and composition. According to the monolingual paradigm, native speakers have exclusive access to the most authentic forms of their mother tongue (Yildiz 2012). Stemming from this, the English-language-teaching industry has long preferred native speakers with British or American accents, referred to in ELT scholarship as "native-speakerism" (Holliday 2006). Alex and Joe witnessed these discriminatory hiring practices in Korea and Japan: their privileged and sought-after status as white, male, native speakers with Western American accents meant their English-teaching abilities went unquestioned. The native/nonnative speaker binary within the ELT industry has been heavily critiqued, yet discrimination persists based on an assumed correlation between whiteness and native speaker status (Jenkins 2017). In parallel, in rhetoric and composition, the dominance of SWE as the language and content of instruction marginalizes and diminishes the credibility of speakers of nonstandard varieties of English. As Wendy Hesford, Edgar Singleton, and Ivonne Garcia (2009) note, "Other than the international instructor's attempt to adapt and adopt the university's culture, there is no value in what the multilingual instructor brings to the writing classroom as an individual who is not a native speaker of English or a U.S. citizen" (116). We became more and more aware of how "good" academic writing seems to reward and reify a particular white discourse.

Regardless of linguistic identity, as graduate students with experiences outside the United States, we struggled to draw from and build on our backgrounds. There seemed to be a discrepancy between the field's apparent interest in global perspectives, as seen in publications and conferences, and the lack of structures to support and encourage global perspectives in graduate-program settings. As Emily's narrative indicates, this discrepancy was partly because of market pressures implicitly telling us to devalue certain experiences as irrelevant (what is "here" is immediately practical and therefore valuable, while "over there" is distant and anecdotal). The parochialism embedded in terms of discussion also limited our capacity to engage in meaningful sharing. Even when graduate students are offered spaces to share their perspectives, taking advantage of such moments can be a struggle if the terms by which they are expected to share render their experiences illegible. Another obstacle is the general expectation to be able to communicate expertly in SWE. As Horner (2016) describes, SWE "has legitimacy as the currency of the academic realm," and those who can use it "thus are authorized to communicate thought, and deemed able to think" (119). Such expectations may act as a barrier, especially for speakers of "nonstandard" varieties of English.

Meanwhile, we observed the influence of fast-capitalist, neoliberal values on our work conditions, which we had sought to escape when applying to graduate school but which continued to get in the way of our sensemaking as graduate students. Our unsustainable work conditions were intertwined with monolingualist assumptions that assert the primacy of a particular form of English (SWE), which graduate students must seek to master through their coursework while simultaneously managing other work in teaching or administrative roles. The unsustainable workload is routinely rationalized as preparation for a singular job market in which future exhaustion is inevitable. We saw a certain level of hyperproductivity being normalized in ways that had direct consequences on well-being, with graduate students often accepting their exhaustion as an issue of self-management and as a normal part of the graduate school experience. The workload, the sink-or-swim mentality, was particularly discouraging in the absence of critical discussions about market pressures and monolingual assumptions about the primacy of certain literacies and competencies. We can deeply relate to the frustrations described by Kaylin in her narrative about her time as an MA student, during which she felt increasingly "disheartened, dissatisfied, and dispassionate" (Fredrick et al. 2020, 155). The disregard for graduate students' day-to-day struggles also places a disproportionate burden on anyone whose life circumstances or backgrounds place them outside the mainstream graduate student identity prototype.

IMPLICATIONS

We believe rhetoric and composition graduate programs should take care not to limit translingual and transnational theory to pedagogical applications for approaching language difference in the writing classroom but instead should weave this theory throughout coursework, orientations, and mentoring. A special week during GTA training, or a one-time guest lecture or workshop, is not enough. Furthermore, translingual pedagogies should be used to inform teaching in graduate-level courses, not just first-year writing. Translingualism is a disposition-in-progress, and cultivating a translingual disposition on the programmatic level should be a collective effort. Ellen Cushman (2016) suggests that a translingual, decolonial reimagining for composition should not merely change the content of what is taught but "revise the paradigmatic tenets of thought structuring everyday practices" (236). We should draw from translingual and transnational theory to replace and expand traditional terms and frames with which graduate students communicate and produce knowledge, and this change requires more than add-ons to the curriculum.

Just as translingual pedagogies encourage us to draw from undergraduate students' backgrounds, graduate programs need to assume graduate students possess valuable experiential knowledge that can be mobilized toward improving programs and the field more broadly. Sedentarist, monolingualist conceptions of student identity perpetuate essentialist approaches, treating graduate students primarily as disciplinary outsiders who need to be assimilated into the field; to counter these conceptions, we need translingual critiques to highlight graduate students' ongoing work negotiating their shifting subjectivities and their agency in shaping programs. Allowing programs to be shaped by knowledge graduate students bring with them would mean normalizing questions such as: What can composition learn from someone who has previously worked at an English-conversation school in China? Taught at a two-year college? Raised a child bilingually? What can composition learn from graduate students who are learners of languages other than English? When the terms of discourse in the field perpetuate assumptions that these experiences are not relevant because they do not contribute to our professionalization as US-based compositionists, the field's scope of knowledge production is restricted.

We also call for a critical interrogation of the term *preparation* as it is used to justify unsustainable work demands while treating future career trajectories as known and fixed. Programs should take care not to act as conduits for market pressures without also making equivalent space to critique and resist them. Meetings in which graduate students raise concerns about how their workloads are having damaging effects on physical, mental, and emotional well-being, as Joe recounts in his narrative, should be taken seriously and as an opportunity for the program to critically address market pressures. It is not enough to ask; advisors, mentors, and supervisors should actually listen to what graduate students are saying about how exhausted, confused, or frustrated they feel, and those concerns should be taken up seriously enough to lead to meaningful change in workloads, schedules, curricula, and hiring. A first step is to be cautious of the messages we continue to reproduce: that the workload is to prepare students for future unforgiving demands, that students should lower their expectations about the quality of their work, or that no one really does all the readings. Catherine Chaput (2002) urges graduate programs to "carefully examine our departmental, professional, and university rhetorical practices for their complicity in proliferating the effects of a global political economy and then to invent new constructions of graduate student education that more adequately resist such economic abuses" (179). Each time we all uncritically treat the market as solid or inevitable, even to ourselves, we miss an opportunity to deconstruct it and end up positioning graduate students as separate from and against faculty, instead of aiming our critique at the structures pressing on us all in different ways. We should ask ourselves, How do we all understand and reinforce notions like productivity or preparation? On what terms are certain kinds of work and knowledge being sidelined and devalued?

CONCLUSION

In reflecting on our experiences, we saw the influence of monolingualism and fast capitalism in our rhetoric and composition programs, including narrow market expectations molding our curricular options, the normalization of superproductivity and exhaustion, the inertia of disciplinary tradition demarcating what we talked about and how. Translingualism is often taken up as a pedagogical approach for negotiating language difference in the classroom, but here we have focused on how translingual and transnational composition theory can enable more productive discussions about how monolingualist pressures constrain graduate student professionalization and knowledge making in the field more broadly. These frameworks help us look inward to recognize our complicity in reinforcing monolingualist values and practices that commodify certain competencies and uncritically emphasize marketability. We suggest that this shared complicity results in a cumulative loss in the field's capacity to grow and learn from the diverse experiences graduate students bring with them. A transnational perspective prompts us to recognize how issues that may have appeared distant and foreign—the seemingly strange and extreme practices of commodified English teaching in Asia, for example—may actually hold more relevance to our "local" US-based work experiences than we might expect.

A translingual orientation prompts us to critically examine our own exhausting efforts to attain certain competencies or titles, and to what ends. Collectively, we should resist seeing important stories of disorientation or exhaustion as signs of individual failure and try to see them as red flags pointing us to limitations of existing structures within which we all find ourselves—structures we might then look at together and ask, Why is it the way it is, and does it need to be this way? When programs teach undergraduates one way and graduate students another, when we uncritically treat certain texts, languages, and identities as more valid, when we answer only with "this is what the market demands" or "that's just how it's done," when we normalize struggle as preparation and ignore liminal realities, we are giving power to sedentarist, monolingualist thinking when more mobile orientations are what we need. To question structures through translingual and transnational approaches, to seek nuance and adaptation, creates a level of attention and care that makes room for progress. The work begins with revising and reflecting on the terms by which graduate student experiences and concerns can be taken up as valid and urgent.

REFERENCES

Chaput, Catherine. 2002. "The Rhetoric of Globalization, Graduate Student Labor, and Practices of Resistance." In *Professing Rhetoric: Selected Papers from the 2000 Rhetoric Society of America Conference*, edited by Frederick J. Antczak, Cinda Coggins, and Geoffrey D. Klinger, 187–94. Mahwah, NJ: Lawrence Erlbaum.

Cushman, Ellen. 2016. "Translingual and Decolonial Approaches to Meaning Making." *College English* 78 (3): 234–42.

Fredrick, Terri, Kaylin Stravalli, Scott May, and Jami Brookman-Smith. 2020. "The Space Between: MA Students Enculturate to Graduate Reading and Writing." In *Graduate Writing Across the Disciplines: Identifying, Teaching, Supporting*, edited by Marilee Brooks-Gillies, Elena G. Garcia, Soo Hyon Kim, Katie Manthey, and Trixie G. Smith, 143–65. Fort Collins, CO: WAC Clearinghouse. Across the Disciplines Books.

Hesford, Wendy, Edgar Singleton, and Ivonne M. Garcia. 2009. "Laboring to Globalize a First-Year Writing Program." In *The Writing Program Interrupted: Making Space for Critical Discourse*, edited by Donna Strickland and Jeanne Gunner, 113–25. Portsmouth, NH: Boynton/Cook.

Holliday, Adrian. 2006. "Native-Speakerism." *ELT Journal* 60 (4): 385–87.

Horner, Bruce. 2016. *Rewriting Composition: Terms of Exchange*. Carbondale: Southern Illinois University Press.

Horner, Bruce, Min-Zhan Lu, Jacqueline Jones Royster, and John Trimbur. 2011. "Language Difference: Toward a Translingual Approach." *College English* 73 (3): 299–317.

Jenkins, Sulaiman. 2017. "The Elephant in the Room: Discriminatory Hiring Practices in ELT." *ELT Journal* 71 (3): 373–76.

Kilfoil, Carrie. 2018. "The Postmonolingual Condition and Rhetoric and Composition Ph.D.: Norming Language Difference in a Doctoral Program." *Composition Forum* 40. http://compositionforum.com/issue/40/postmonolingual.php.

Lu, Min-Zhan. 2004. "An Essay on the Work of Composition: Composing English against the Order of Fast Capitalism." *College Composition and Communication* 56 (1): 16–50.

Lu, Min-Zhan, and Bruce Horner. 2009. "Composing in a Global-Local Context: Careers, Mobility, and Skills." *College English* 72 (2): 113–33.

Matsuda, Paul Kei. 2006. "The Myth of Linguistic Homogeneity in U.S. College Composition." *College English* 68 (6): 637–51.

Pennycook, Alastair. 2008. "English as a Language Always in Translation." *European Journal of English Studies* 12 (1): 33–47.

Prendergast, Catherine. 2008. *Buying into English: Language and Investment in the New Capitalist World*. Pittsburgh: University of Pittsburgh Press.

Yildiz, Yasmine. 2012. *Beyond the Mother Tongue: The Postmonolingual Condition*. New York: Fordham University Press.

Zenger, Amy. 2018. "Writing Program Administration, Mobility, and Locality at the American University of Beirut, 1970 to Present." In *Western Higher Education in Global Contexts*, edited by Mohanalakshmi Rajakumar, 59–80. Lanham, MD: Lexington Books.

3

THE POSTMONOLINGUAL CONDITION AND THE RHETORIC AND COMPOSITION PHD
Norming Language Difference in a Doctoral Program

Carrie Byars Kilfoil

In "Reproducing Composition and Rhetoric: The Intellectual Challenge of Doctoral Education," Louise Wetherbee Phelps (1995) argues every doctoral program "expresses and acts out vividly in concrete features a theory of the discipline: in its curricular content, requirements, qualifying exams and reading lists" (118). Rhetoric and composition PhD programs reflect and reinforce matters of disciplinary "epistemology, ethics, and politics" (17), including conceptions of language and language relations that structure disciplinary labor. Subsequently, these programs can be useful sites to examine dominant and emergent disciplinary language ideologies, the practices that follow from these ideologies, and the dispositions toward language that shape compositionists' professional practices as teachers, scholars, and administrators in linguistically heterogeneous institutions.

This chapter presents data from a 2013 survey of students enrolled in a long-standing rhetoric and composition PhD program at the University of Louisville (U of L), a midsized public institution in the American South. In my analysis, I suggest the survey data reflect the "postmonolingual condition" of the program, insofar as Yasemin Yildiz (2012) defines postmonolingualism as "a field of tension in which the monolingual paradigm continues to assert itself and multilingual practices persist or reemerge" (5). The persistence and reemergence of multilingual practices is indicated by responses demonstrating doctoral students' awareness of and appreciation for language differences in their writing program, as well as desires to engage multiple languages and English dialects in composition teaching and research. However, the continued dominance of monolingualist ideology is evident in the ways many

https://doi.org/10.7330/9781646423262.c003

participants tended to imagine these engagements as taking place through curricular add-ons and extracurricular activities that place practical barriers to their timely progression through the program. Drawing from student recommendations, I suggest ways this program, and others like it, could leverage students' positive perceptions of and attitudes toward multilingualism to "norm" language differences in its mainstream rhetoric and composition graduate curriculum, thereby making issues of language diversity central and necessary components of composition graduate training.

BACKGROUND

In *Beyond the Mother Tongue: The Postmonolingual Condition,* Yildiz (2012) argues the growing visibility of multilingualism in Western art, culture, and public discourse must be understood in terms of the postmonolingual condition of twenty-first-century Western social life. For Yildiz, the prefix *post* has both historical and critical dimensions. On the one hand, it references the time since the emergence of monolingualism in the late eighteenth century as a dominant Western paradigm of language and sociocultural identity. On the other hand, *post*monolingual references growing resistance to monolingualism as "increased migration and mobility, the advance of communication technologies, and the spread of media have . . . contributed to the sense that multiple languages coexist and interact in new constellations" in global-local contexts (3). Although Yildiz maintains a fully articulated ideological alternative to monolingualism does not yet exist, she notes that writers in a variety of fields are beginning to "suggest the possible contours of such a multilingual paradigm and contribute variously to just such a restructuring" (5).

In composition studies, the restructuring of disciplinary ideology to account for multilingualism is apparent in what Brian Ray (2015) describes as the "norming of language difference" in professional discourse (89). Ray cites and reviews Suresh Canagarajah's (2013b) *Translingual Practice: Global Englishes and Cosmopolitan Relations,* Vershawn Young, Rusty Barrett, Y'Shanda Young-Rivera, and Kim Brian Lovejoy's (2013) *Other People's English: Code-Meshing, Code-Switching, and African American Literacy,* Scott Wible's (2013) *Shaping Language Policy in the U.S.: The Role of Composition Studies,* and Canagarajah's (2013a) edited collection *Literacy as Translingual Practice: Between Communities and Classrooms* to illustrate "linguistic diversity's inevitable yet tumultuous move to the center of [composition] teaching and research" (89). Paul Kei Matsuda

(2013) also notes the "unprecedented attention" (128) language issues have received in recent composition monographs, journal articles, edited collections, awards, and featured sessions at the annual meetings of the Conference on College Composition and Communication (CCCC). Matsuda observes that "the issue of language differences [in composition] . . . has joined the ranks of new intellectual undertakings worthy of attention from all U.S. college composition scholars" (131). However, as mentioned in the introduction to this collection, the vast majority of disciplinary scholarship on language diversity has focused on undergraduate students enrolled in FYC or developmental/basic writing courses administered by university writing programs, which is in keeping with general trends in composition research. Empirical studies like the one described in this chapter can help shed light on the ways rhetoric and composition graduate students experience and account for curricular structures (their own and their undergraduate students') and labor in the context of competing and shifting language ideologies in the field they are working to enter.

SURVEY

This survey was designed to investigate rhetoric and composition doctoral students' backgrounds and perceptions of language diversity in the context of their professional development as composition teacher-scholars. For the purposes of this survey, language diversity was defined as the simultaneous presence of multiple, shifting language codes (including both national languages and English dialects) in composition teaching and research. The web-based survey consisted of twenty-four questions. Participants completed background questions regarding their stage in the program, the courses they taught, and the languages and English dialects they use for communication. They were then were asked to rate their agreement with statements about their teaching and scholarly practices on a six-point Likert scale (1=Strongly disagree, 6=Strongly agree) and clarify their responses through a series of open-ended prompts.

Survey questions solicited information about doctoral students' awareness of language differences in undergraduate composition classes and their professional preparation to teach students with minoritized language backgrounds, including but not limited to undergraduate students identified as ESL in US universities. Additionally, the survey worked to gather information about doctoral students' perceptions of language differences in writing research, both as a focus of composition scholarship and as a condition of international writing research that takes place in a variety of languages. It also attempted to gauge participants' desires and professional preparation to conduct composition research on language diversity using English and other languages. Finally, the survey attempted to identify participants' perceptions of their language practices in the program to determine the degree to which they were using multiple languages and English dialects in their teaching and scholarship.

The invitation to participate in the study was emailed to all thirty-nine enrolled rhetoric and composition doctoral students at U of L. It elicited seventeen responses. The relatively low response rate (43.6%) impeded the generalizability of the data and the conclusions that could be drawn from it. However, I suggest the survey data are valuable for several reasons. First, the quantitative Likert-scale data revealed trends in doctoral students' professional-development experiences related to language and language relations within their program. Second, the comments participants made to gloss their Likert-scale answers provided further insight into these trends, as well as recommendations for how their program could increase support for graduate students navigating composition teaching and research in the context of multiple languages. Finally, I believe the survey instrument, data, and analysis (see appendix 3.A) can provide a model for other programs seeking input from their graduate students to access the strength of curricula and inform local decisions about graduate training to support language diversity.

PARTICIPANTS

The first three survey questions solicited background information about the participants. Responses to question 1 indicated three of the seventeen respondents were completing coursework, six were completing exams, one was completing their dissertation prospectus, and seven were writing their dissertations. Responses to question 2 indicated all participants were fully funded graduate students who had either taught or were currently teaching as graduate teaching assistants (GTAs). Respondents reported teaching courses in the first-year composition sequence (English 101: Introduction to College Writing [39%; n=17] and English 102: Intermediate College Composition [27%; n=12], English 105: Honors College Writing [5%; n=2], as well as English 303: Science and Technical Writing [5%; n=2], English 306: Business Writing [16%; n=7], and ENG 309: Inquiries in Writing [n=1]). Three students also reported teaching literature courses, including Women and Literature, Writing about Literature, and American Literature II.

Responses to question 3 (What national languages and/or dialects of English do you use currently or have you used in the past and where and when have you developed your knowledge of these languages? Please discuss all languages you feel you have some familiarity with, even if not "fluent.") indicated all students who responded to the survey considered themselves to be, at least on some level, multilingual. All respondents reported using or having used other national languages in either personal or academic contexts or both, although most described their knowledge of languages other than English as limited to basic conversation and reading skills. Four participants reported speaking and writing multiple languages as a product of their experiences in the United States as foreign nationals or abroad as exchange students from the United States. The majority described their language knowledge beyond English as developed through high-school and college coursework. Three participants described themselves as "multidialectals" who used conventions associated with nonmainstream dialects like African American Vernacular English (AAVE) and Southern American English in addition to the Standard American English conventions they used as teachers and scholars. Although these responses suggest participants' knowledge and use of other languages was primarily limited to contexts outside the PhD program, they also counter the monolingualist assumption that rhetoric and composition doctoral students, like the undergraduate students they are being trained to teach (Matsuda 2006), are US-educated, English-only monolinguals with little to no experience communicating in other languages (Hesford, Singleton, and García 2009).

DATA ANALYSIS AND DISCUSSION

Questions 4–8 referred to participants' work as GTAs and ongoing development as teachers through coursework, workshops, and other programmatic resources and requirements. Responses showed that most participants (76.47%, n=13) noticed undergraduate students whose language practices reflected a variety of national languages and English dialects in their classes (see table 3.1). Moreover, the majority (88.23%, n=15) thought language diversity was increasing in US higher education as compared to thirty years ago when their graduate program was first developed and implemented (see table 3.2).

Most respondents (82.35%, n=14) also indicated they felt responsible for addressing the specific language needs of students with language backgrounds different from mainstream English monolinguals, including students commonly identified as multilingual, multidialectal,

Table 3.1. Graduate students' responses to the statement, "I notice students whose language practices reflect a variety of national languages and dialects of English in the classes that I teach." (*N*=17)

Response	N	%
Strongly agree	5	29.41
Agree	4	23.53
Somewhat agree	4	23.53
Somewhat disagree	2	11.76
Disagree	1	5.88
Strongly disagree	1	5.88

Table 3.2. Graduate students' completions of the statement, "Compared to 30 years ago, language diversity in US higher education is:" (*N*=17)

Response	N	%
Increasing	15	88.24
Largely the same	2	11.76
Decreasing	0	0

basic writers, or ESL writers (see table 3.3). However, fewer participants (76.47%, n=13) felt confident in their ability to teach students with noticeably diverse language backgrounds. Of those who agreed they felt confident, only three strongly agreed, while eight only somewhat agreed (see table 3.4).

Participants' feelings of insecurity teaching undergraduates with diverse language backgrounds reflect their responses to questions about their professional preparation to teach composition in linguistically diverse institutions. Most students (82.45%, n=14) said they felt underresourced in this area. These responses aligned with the results of several studies in which writing teachers report a lack of professional preparation to teach multilingual students (Braine 1996; Ferris et al. 2012; Matsuda, Saenkhum, and Accardi 2006; Williams 1995). However, in this case, a number of participants made a distinction between their theoretical introduction to language differences in composition teaching through coursework and their practical training in these matters. The vast majority (94.12%, n=16) agreed they felt "knowledgeable about scholarship devoted to language diversity in writing teaching," although only three strongly agreed with this statement. One participant wrote, "I feel like I've read a lot about this issue, but have received little concrete training in how to teach to it," while another wrote, "I have had a few courses which promote the theoretical value of respecting and engaging with students from different language backgrounds, but I really haven't seen any resources or support which expound upon the practical side of that issue."

Several participants commented on how the program could provide them with more practical training to respond to language differences in the composition classroom. One student recommended an optional TESOL certification, one recommended a "separate course for those interested in special attention to this subject," four participants suggested incorporating language teacher training into the English 602 teaching practicum course, and seven others recommended optional pedagogy workshops. Most recommendations involved adding on to the current curriculum, which some participants acknowledged would be practically problematic. New certifications, courses, and workshops would require additional resources to create and maintain them and would compete with core courses and requirements for the time and attention of students and faculty alike. As one student wrote, "I'm not sure how these activities could scale. . . . It seems like most resources—workshops, websites, handouts, whatever—would be necessarily simplistic."

Curricular add-ons also risk reinforcing what Matsuda (2006) identifies as a monolingualist "policy of linguistic containment" in US institutions, through which linguistically diverse students and communicative practices (at least, as traditionally recognized) are "quarantined from the rest of higher education" in special classes and programs (641). Under this policy of containment, language differ-

Table 3.3. Graduate students' responses to the statement, "In my teaching, I feel responsible for addressing the specific language needs of students with language backgrounds different from mainstream English monolinguals, including students commonly identified as multilingual, multidialectal, basic writers or ESL writers." (N=16)*

Response	N	%
Strongly agree	4	25
Agree	7	43.75
Somewhat agree	3	18.75
Somewhat disagree	1	6.25
Disagree	0	0
Strongly disagree	1	6.25

* Due to a technical problem with the survey instrument, only sixteen answers were recorded to this question.

Table 3.4. Graduate students' responses to the statement, "I feel confident in my ability to teach students with diverse language backgrounds, including students commonly identified as multilingual, multidialectal, basic writers or ESL writers." (N=17)

Response	N	%
Strongly agree	3	17.65
Agree	2	11.76
Somewhat agree	8	47.06
Somewhat disagree	2	11.76
Disagree	2	11.76
Strongly disagree	0	0

ences are approached "as a defining problem for and characteristic of the socially 'different,' seen as both linguistically and socially embodying something other than 'the norm' and hence requiring a 'different' approach—likely in a different location, curriculum, or program segregated from 'normal' writers" (Lu and Horner 2013, 583). However, the suggestion that language training be incorporated into the existing teaching practicum course, the only required course for all students in the program,[1] works against the often-prevailing sense that language issues are separate and marginal matters to be taken up through additional, non-credit-bearing workshops and programs. As Sidney Dobrin (2005) argues, the teaching practicum course is "the largest, most effective purveyor of cultural capital in composition studies," a space in which teachers are not only "trained . . . but one in which they are enculturated into cultural ideologies of composition" (21).

In terms of their own language practices as teachers, most participants disagreed with statements that they used language conventions associated with other national languages (82.35%; n=14) or nonstandard varieties of English (64.70%; n=11) in their classes. However, those participants who acknowledged using multiple languages and English dialects in their teaching described these practices as productive. One wrote that discussing English dialects and language change helped them teach academic writing in the context of the globalization of academic research and the linguistic heterogeneity of modern academic discourse. Another wrote that their unintentional use of Texas and South Texas dialects sometimes "opens up discussions of different words for different object, phrases, and actions." Three others wrote that they used discussion of the plurality of languages and dialects to teach students about the contextual nature of "correctness" in writing. One of these participants wrote,

> Because I have some experience with southern and midwestern dialects, I've sometimes brought scans and transcripts of actual Civil War letters, and used them to illustrate points about grammar and "correctness" (in conjunction with some scholarly texts, like Joseph Williams' "Phenomenology of Error"). I find that students enjoy "negotiating" with these texts, and I can usually get them to change their ideas about error and correctness when I teach these.

Several participants suggested undergraduate composition students can find pleasure in discussing nonmainstream linguistic forms and practices perhaps seen as transgressive in an "English" writing class and that this pleasure can be pedagogically productive.

However, as one participant acknowledged, GTAs take risks when they use language conventions associated with non-Standard English dialects in the classroom. They wrote,

> I speak in a Southern dialect sometimes in the classroom and that is just because it occurs when I am speaking so I do not plan it. I think more students feel comfortable talking to me because they recognize the authority is different in that way. However, I have had students in class make fun of how I say certain words because of my Southern accent/dialect. That is actually uncomfortable to be honest, and I could have used it as a teaching

moment about different dialects, but because I am a graduate teaching assistant and did not feel so much authority, I did not say anything.

This comment suggests that while the use of diverse language resources can help instructors develop solidarity with their students, GTAs using nonmainstream dialects risk undermining their institutional authority, which, as Wendy Hesford, Edgar Singleton, and Ivonne M. García (2009) argue, is built in relationship to their ability to represent and transmit linguistic forms and practices associated with mainstream academic culture and, by extension, Standard American English.

As Hesford, Singleton, and García (2009) observe, graduate programs often tacitly discourage multilingual teaching assistants from using their full range of linguistic resources in their teaching. Handbooks and workshops for international GTAs work to assimilate them to mainstream academic forms and practices, and in so doing, cast linguistic and cultural differences as barriers to graduate student teachers' institutional legitimacy and effective teaching of mainstream students. Hesford, Singleton, and García limit their critique of the monolingualist assumption that GTAs should teach exclusively in (Standard American) English to international graduate students and institutional authorities (e.g., the graduate school, the English department, the writing program) who enforce these expectations. However, the above participant's response suggests this critique can be extended to domestic GTAs who identify as multidialectal and undergraduate students who, ironically, can work to enforce a Standard American English–only norm, even if these students (as at U of L) are often the victims of such enforcement. Given the institutional monolingualist bias that frames their liminal role as both students and instructors, it is perhaps unsurprising that most participants reported not using their full range of language resources in their teaching.

As with the questions about their teaching, participants' responses to questions about their scholarship revealed ambivalence about the place of linguistic forms and practices divergent from a perceived Standard American English–only norm in their professional development. While most participants felt responsible for addressing students' language differences in their classes, fewer participants were interested in making language diversity in writing teaching a focus of their research (see table 3.5). This lack of interest might seem surprising given the recent prominence of research about language issues in composition and the fact that most participants felt knowledgeable about scholarship devoted to language diversity in writing teaching (see table 3.6). Moreover, while only two students strongly agreed they felt confident conducting

Table 3.5. Graduate students' responses to the statement, "I am interested in conducting research on and writing about language diversity in writing teaching." (N=17)

Response	N	%
Strongly agree	2	11.76
Agree	3	17.65
Somewhat agree	4	23.53
Somewhat disagree	3	17.65
Disagree	5	29.41
Strongly disagree	0	0

Table 3.6. Graduate students' responses to the statement, "I feel knowledgeable about scholarship devoted to language diversity in writing teaching, including but not necessarily limited to work on students commonly identified as multilingual, multidialectal, basic writers, or ESL writers." (N=17)

Response	N	%
Strongly agree	3	17.65
Agree	6	35.29
Somewhat agree	7	41.18
Disagree	0	0
Somewhat disagree	1	0
Strongly disagree	0	0

Table 3.7. Graduate students' responses to the statement, "I feel confident in my ability to conduct research on language diversity in writing teaching." (N=17)

Response	N	%
Strongly agree	2	11.76
Agree	5	29.41
Somewhat agree	2	11.76
Somewhat disagree	3	17.65
Disagree	5	29.41
Strongly disagree	0	0

this type of research, slightly more students indicated they felt confident in their ability to perform this research than indicated they were interested (see table 3.7).

Discrepancies in participants' interest in, awareness of, and confidence pursuing scholarship on language diversity could be accounted for in various ways. Language-related knowledge has been historically devalued in rhetoric and composition graduate education (MacDonald 2007; Tardy 2017), due in part to "the field's disciplinary origins and relations that link it more strongly to the humanities and areas like cultural studies than to the social sciences and fields like applied linguistics" (Tardy 2017, 186). While participants in this study may have become conversant in recent scholarship associated with translingual literacies and approaches through coursework and other doctoral requirements, they may not have developed the background in theoretical and applied linguistics necessary to conduct language-related composition research. Moreover, as the MLA Ad Hoc Committee on Foreign Languages (Modern Language n.d.) has described, language study in the humanities is often associated with instrumentalist practices, introductory courses, and contingent faculty positions. Participants may have been wary of linking themselves with low-status language-teaching practices and, by consequence, failing to position themselves to compete as new scholars for secure academic appointments, high-impact publications, grants, awards, and so forth, all of which are associated with established traditions of high-status disciplinary research and theory (Horner and Lu 2010).

The sense that language differences were not matters of scholarly inquiry for most participants was further reflected in the linguistic practices they reported as researchers. Only two students (11.76%) agreed they used language resources in their scholarship beyond those typically identified with Standard American English (see table 3.8). Other responses reinforced the sense that most participants read and wrote exclusively English-medium scholarship and did not pursue research and publishing in non-English-medium contexts. Most did not feel knowledgeable about non-English-medium scholarship on writing and writing instruction (see table 3.9), and most indicated they did not feel confident in their ability to read scholarship in other languages (see table 3.10).

These responses suggest that a lack of strong multilingual knowledge and confidence led participants to adopt a linguistically parochial perspective about writing and writing instruction in their preprofessional scholarly development. As a number of scholars have argued, this perspective is endemic to the field of rhetoric and composition, notwithstanding the fact that scholarship in writing and its teaching takes place worldwide in a variety of languages (Donahue 2009; Foster and Russell 2002; Horner, NeCamp, and Donahue 2011; Muchiri et al. 1995), and, as Tony Silva, Ilon Leki, and Joan Carson (1997) state, "Examination of the large area of studies of writing in languages other than English . . . would repay consideration by adding needed depth to theories of rhetoric and writing" (402).

As with teaching, relatively low levels of knowledge of and confidence in using other languages for research purposes can be linked to participants' assessment of their professional preparation in these areas. Five students wrote they felt the graduate program did not provide any resources or support for graduate students to read and write scholarship in languages other than English. Several others wrote the foreign-language requirement was the sole gesture toward this goal but questioned its usefulness. At the time of the survey, the program required students to demonstrate competence in two approved foreign languages (i.e., French, German, Spanish, Italian, Latin, Greek, or Russian) or proficiency in one through graduate modern-language coursework, which would not otherwise count toward their degrees, or a translation exam. However, one student wrote that the "culture around the requirement is that it is a 'hurdle' to get past and not an enriching and useful activity." Another wrote that restrictions

Table 3.8. Graduate students' responses to the statement, "I use languages beyond 'Standard English' in my scholarship, including but not necessarily limited to conventions associated with other national languages and dialects of English." (*N*=17)

Response	N	%
Strongly agree	1	5.88
Agree	1	5.88
Somewhat agree	2	11.76
Somewhat disagree	3	17.65
Disagree	6	35.29
Strongly disagree	4	23.53

Table 3.9. Graduate students' responses to the statement, "I feel knowledgeable about non-English medium-scholarship on writing and writing instruction." (*N*=17)

Response	N	%
Strongly agree	1	5.88
Agree	1	5.88
Somewhat agree	2	11.76
Somewhat disagree	3	17.65
Disagree	6	35.29
Strongly disagree	4	23.53

Table 3.10. Graduate students' responses to the statement, "I feel confident in my ability to read non-English-medium scholarship for the purposes of my research." (*N*=17)

Response	N	%
Strongly agree	1	5.88
Agree	2	11.76
Somewhat agree	4	23.53
Somewhat disagree	2	11.76
Disagree	4	23.53
Strongly disagree	4	23.53

around the language requirement limited its usefulness, stating, "The language requirements are a bit strict in what is or is not counted as a viable language option. For example, I'm interested in scholarship coming out of Scandinavia, but neither Norwegian or Swedish are 'approved' languages."[2] Finally, one student linked the ineffectiveness of the language requirement to the ways the language exams, which required students to translate short passages from another language into English to certify their proficiency, failed to reflect disciplinary views on learning and assessment. They wrote, "The language exam/requirements were just not useful. I think they should be removed and replaced with courses we could take or directed study where we could study languages and it's not based on proficiency, especially since many scholars in rhetoric and composition complicate what proficiency means. Therefore, it seems rather ironic that this program makes us become 'proficient' in a language when we critique 'proficiency.'" This irony reinforces the sense that language requirements are outside the mainstream rhetoric and composition graduate curriculum and the skills and resources they are intended to impart are inessential to the real work of composition professionals (Horner et al. 2011; Kilfoil 2015; Tardy 2017).

Several participants offered suggestions for making the language requirement more useful and palatable to students. Six called for more opportunities for graduate students to take modern-language courses outside the department, with one suggesting students be advised to take these courses after completing their departmental coursework toward the degree. Another suggested foreign-language coursework might count as graduate credit toward the degree.[3] However, some participants raised questions about the feasibility of learning other languages in light of the material conditions of graduate student labor in the program. As one wrote, "I'm not sure how the time needed to learn any of these languages would be grafted onto our current model of PhD studies. I used Christmas money to buy some books to self-teach myself Latin, but because of the demands of writing a diss, I have not cracked those books." Another wrote, "If I really wanted to take other language classes, I expect I would be allowed to do so—but it would be on my own time, and I have precious little free time for extracurricular activities."[4]

Five participants wrote they would benefit as scholars from developing additional language resources. One was "interested in scholarship coming out of Scandinavia" but indicated they didn't have the language knowledge necessary to access this scholarship, while another wrote, "For my dissertation, it would help me to be able to read French, and for my own research interests in classical rhetoric, it would be great to have reading knowledge of Latin and Greek." Another wrote about the need to teach rhetoric and composition graduate students to use other languages for scholarly purposes in response to the global dominance of English: "English may be the dominant language in the world, but there is a variety of untapped scholarship/voices that, because they are not translated into English, are silenced. If we are able to read German or French or Spanish, I think graduate students could utilize a very rich source of information on language use and writing that is ignored due to our monolingual society and value of scholarship that is English only. Teach us the skills, technologies, and literacies of translation, and we could start untapping [sic] those sources sooner than later." And finally, one other wrote, "Additional resources (classes in foreign languages, etc.) might be helpful for those of us planning to read foreign scholarship and/or translate, but I think a lot of us have research interests that don't necessitate those goals."

While this last comment casts graduate research involving reading and/or translating foreign scholarship as outside the norm, all the students surveyed agreed the acquisition of language knowledge beyond Standard English is useful for graduate students entering the field of

Table 3.11. Graduate students' responses to the statement, "I believe that the acquisition of language knowledge beyond 'Standard English' is useful for graduate students entering the field of rhetoric and composition." (N=17)

Response	N	%
Strongly agree	7	41.18
Agree	6	35.29
Somewhat agree	4	25.53
Somewhat disagree	0	0
Disagree	0	0
Strongly disagree	0	0

rhetoric and composition (see table 3.11). The answers elicited by this question, along with other survey responses, suggest that while institutionalized monolingualism had worked to shape graduate students' professional-development experiences in the program, many were adopting dispositions toward language that recognized multilingualism as a condition of composition teaching and research in global-local contexts. Moreover, many responses indicated participants saw language differences as a resource for, rather than impediment to, meaning making in composition scholarly and pedagogical discourses (Horner et al. 2011).

CONCLUSION

Yildiz argues the pressures of the monolingual paradigm "have not just obscured multilingual practices across history; they have also led to active processes of monolingualization," and education "has been one of the primary means of such a social engineering of monolingual populations" (2–3). Various studies of composition's history suggest the field's development can be read as part of the norming of monolingualism in US colleges and universities, insofar as composition has ensured that US writing instruction takes place in "English-only" (Horner and Trimbur 2002), aligned its programs and pedagogies with English-native-speaker discourse (Trimbur 2008), and maintained a "myth of linguistic homogeneity" in writing programs that informs their frequent neglect of second-language writers (Matsuda 2006). In historical context, the contemporary move to embrace language difference as "a new norm" (Ray 2015) in college writing instruction suggests a paradigmatic shift in disciplinary work that will require compositionists to develop new knowledge and capabilities in order to be meaningful.

Matsuda (2013) argues that composition's history, which "can be characterized as a struggle to dissociate itself from language issues," has created the conditions for "a huge void in the knowledge of language issues" in the field (130). Consequently, many modern compositionists aware of and interested in language differences in writing and writing programs lack the knowledge base to explore this new "linguistic frontier" (130) in teaching and research. Christine Tardy (2017) agrees that compositionists often lack the metaknowledge about language to address linguistic diversity in pedagogically informed and effective ways. Tardy argues for integrating insights from second-language acquisition and bilingualism into rhetoric and composition graduate education to better equip future teachers with the knowledge to "understand, support, and facilitate the multi(or trans)lingual development of their students, to make pedagogical choices that are broadly informed and context sensitive, and ultimately, to adopt dispositions that value and build upon the linguistic resources of their students" (187).

I believe graduate programs like U of L's can adjust their curricula to leverage their students' awareness of and positive perceptions of multilingualism in public, classroom, and disciplinary discourses to support their development of informed professional dispositions toward language. To do so, surveys like the one I discuss here can be useful, since listening to graduate students about how they perceive their professional abilities, interests, and practices related to language and languages relations can help administrators and faculty imagine how to make these changes. In this case, the program might consider developing specialized courses, workshops, and materials that address language issues in composition. The program might also consider ways to support students taking courses in allied fields, like applied linguistics. However, the program should be mindful of graduate students' limited time and resources and also consider ways to integrate transdisciplinary research in language and multilingual professional practices into its mainstream rhetoric and composition graduate curriculum.

For instance, including research from applied linguistics in core courses, like the composition-teaching practicum, and the exams that follow from these courses, might lessen the material burden of pursuing knowledge "outside" rhetoric and composition proper. Additionally, revamping the language requirement to make graduate students' development of new language resources a central component of their learning, through inviting and supporting scholarship in multiple languages in seminars, comprehensive exams, and dissertations, might better position students to teach and conduct research across languages. Of course, any adjustments to curricula are often challenging and involve time and resources many programs struggle to provide. However, if language differences are to become the new norm in composition's professional practices, as well as discourse, adjustments are needed to ensure future faculty develop the desire, confidence, and tools to address matters of language and language diversity in writing programs in thoughtful and effective ways.

APPENDIX 3.A
SURVEY QUESTIONNAIRE AND TABULATED
LIKERT-SCALE RESPONSES

Rhetoric and composition PhD students' perceptions of language diversity

For the purpose of this survey, "language diversity" refers to the simultaneous presence of multiple, shifting language codes (including both national languages and dialects) in US higher education.

1. At what stage are you currently in your PhD program?

    Drop-down menu: coursework, exams, prospectus, dissertation

2. What courses have you taught or are you currently teaching?

    Drop-down menu: ENG 101, ENG 102, ENG 105, ENG 303, ENG 306, ENG 309, other (space for text), not teaching/on fellowship

3. What national languages and/or dialects of English do you currently use or have you used in the past and where and when have you developed your knowledge of these languages? Please discuss all languages you feel you have some familiarity with, even if not "fluent."

4. I notice students whose language practices reflect a variety of national languages and dialects of English in the classes I teach.

Strongly agree	5
Agree	4
Somewhat agree	4
Somewhat disagree	2
Disagree	1
Strongly disagree	1
TOTAL	17

5. Compared to 30 years ago, language diversity in US higher education is:

Increasing	15
Largely the same	2
Decreasing	0
TOTAL	17

6. In my teaching, I feel responsible for addressing the specific language needs of students with language backgrounds different from the mainstream English monolinguals, including students commonly identified as multilingual, multidialectal, basic writers, or ESL writers.

Strongly agree	4
Agree	7
Somewhat agree	3
Somewhat disagree	1
Disagree	0
Strongly disagree	1
TOTAL	16

7. I feel confident in my ability to teach students with diverse language backgrounds, including students commonly identified as multilingual, multidialectal, basic writers, or ESL writers.

Strongly agree	3
Agree	2
Somewhat agree	8
Somewhat disagree	2
Disagree	2
Strongly disagree	0
TOTAL	17

8. What resources and support (coursework, requirements, trainings/workshops, etc.) does your PhD program provide to prepare you to teach students with a wide range of different language backgrounds? Would additional resources be helpful? If so, please specify. [space for text]

9. I feel knowledgeable about scholarship devoted to language diversity in writing teaching, including but not necessarily limited to work on students commonly identified as multilingual, multidialectal, basic writers, or ESL writers.

Strongly agree	3
Agree	6
Somewhat agree	7
Somewhat disagree	1
Disagree	0
Strongly disagree	0
TOTAL	17

10. I am interested in conducting research on and writing about language diversity in writing teaching.

Strongly agree	2
Agree	3
Somewhat agree	4
Somewhat disagree	3
Disagree	5
Strongly disagree	0
TOTAL	17

11. I feel confident in my ability to conduct research and write about language diversity in writing teaching.

Strongly agree	2
Agree	5
Somewhat agree	2
Somewhat disagree	3
Disagree	5
Strongly disagree	0
TOTAL	17

12. I feel knowledgeable about non-English-medium scholarship on writing and writing instruction.

Strongly agree	1
Agree	1
Somewhat agree	2
Somewhat disagree	3
Disagree	6
Strongly disagree	4
TOTAL	17

13. I feel confident in my ability to read scholarship written in languages other than English for the purposes of my research.

Strongly agree	1
Agree	2
Somewhat agree	4
Somewhat disagree	2
Disagree	4
Strongly disagree	4
TOTAL	17

14. I feel confident in my ability to write scholarship in languages other than English for contribution to a non-English-medium conference or journal.

Strongly agree	1
Agree	1
Somewhat agree	0
Somewhat disagree	1
Disagree	2
Strongly disagree	12
TOTAL	17

15. What resources and support (coursework, requirements, trainings/workshops, etc.) does your program provide to prepare you to read and write scholarship in languages other than English? Would additional resources and support be helpful? If so, please specify. [space for text]

16. In my teaching, I use language conventions associated with other national languages.

Strongly agree	0
Agree	1
Somewhat agree	2
Somewhat disagree	5
Disagree	8
Strongly disagree	1
TOTAL	17

17. In my teaching, I use not only Standard English dialect but also other dialectal forms of English.

Strongly agree	3
Agree	2
Somewhat agree	1
Somewhat disagree	6
Disagree	4
Strongly disagree	1
TOTAL	17

18. If you agreed with the previous statements, please describe the languages and dialects of English you use: when, why, and how you use them and what teaching opportunities they enable. [space for text]

19. I use languages beyond Standard English in my SCHOLARSHIP, including but not necessarily limited to conventions associated with other national languages and dialects of English.

Strongly agree	1
Agree	0
Somewhat agree	0
Somewhat disagree	5
Disagree	8
Strongly disagree	3
TOTAL	17

20. If you agreed with the previous statement, please describe these languages: when, why, and how you use them and what lines of scholarly inquiry they enable. [space for text]

21. I believe the acquisition of language knowledge beyond Standard English is useful for graduate students entering the field of rhetoric and composition.

Strongly agree	7
Agree	6
Somewhat agree	4
Somewhat disagree	0
Disagree	0
Strongly disagree	0
TOTAL	17

22. If you agreed with the previous statement, please describe what type(s) of language knowledge you feel is most useful and why. [space for text]

23. What resources and support does your program provide to help you develop language knowledge beyond Standard English? Would additional resources and support be helpful? If so, specify. [space for text]

24. If you have any other experiences with or opinions about language diversity in the context of your role as a graduate student, please feel free to add them here. [space for text]

NOTES

1. English 602 Research in Composition is also required of all students. However, students have the option to substitute other research-methods courses in the department. No substitutions are offered for English 602.

2. This student's comment does not acknowledge that according to the Graduate Program Guidelines (University of Louisville 2013), students could petition the

graduate committee to approve other languages for them to use to complete the requirement. However, the comment reflects the perceived barrier listing particular approved languages in program policies places on students' development of additional language knowledge.

3.   While, according to the rules at the time, one graduate foreign-language course could count toward the degree, this student seemed to be referring to undergraduate language coursework. Undergraduate language courses focus on developing students' language knowledge, rather than on their knowledge of the literature and culture of that language. The latter is the focus of modern-language graduate courses at U of L (and many other institutions), which assume the student already has substantial language knowledge.

4.   Though graduate programs have traditionally assumed graduate students would have a background in another language by virtue of undergraduate coursework, this presumption is increasingly problematic. Under the pressure of state and federal budget cuts, many universities have scaled back their modern-language programs and classes. For instance, at the University at Albany, State University of New York, in 2010, administrators responded to sweeping budget cuts by eliminating undergraduate majors in a number of languages. In 2011, George Washington University's Columbian College of Arts and Sciences eliminated undergraduate language requirements as a budget-saving measure. As reporter Lisa Foderaro observes in a December 3, 2010, article in the *New York Times*, "Small, interactive" foreign-language courses are expensive to run and can seem unnecessary in a world increasingly dominated by English. The paradox, however, is that universities are eliminating these courses at the same time they "embrace an international mission." SUNY Albany's motto is, after all, "the world within reach."

REFERENCES

Braine, George. 1996. "ESL Students in First-Year Writing Courses: ESL Versus Mainstream Classes." *Journal of Second Language Writing* 5 (2): 91–107.

Canagarajah, Suresh, ed. 2013a. *Literacy as Translingual Practice: Between Communities and Classrooms.* London: Routledge.

Canagarajah, Suresh. 2013b. *Translingual Practice: Global Englishes and Cosmopolitan Relations.* London: Routledge.

Dobrin, Sydney, ed. 2005. *Don't Call It That: The Composition Practicum.* Urbana, IL: NCTE.

Donahue, Christiane. 2009. "'Internationalization' and Composition Studies: Reorienting the Discourse." *College Composition and Communication* 61 (2): 12–43.

Ferris, Dana, Jeffrey Brown, Hsiang (Sean) Liu, Maria Eugenia, and Arnaudo Stine. 2012. "Responding to L2 Students in College Writing Classes: Teacher Perspectives." *TESOL Quarterly* 45 (2): 207–34.

Foster, David, and David R. Russell, eds. 2002. *Writing and Learning in Cross-National Perspective: Transitions from Secondary to Higher Education.* Urbana, IL: NCTE.

Hesford, Wendy, Eddie Singleton, and Ivonne García. 2009. "Laboring to Globalize a First-Year Writing Program." In *The Writing Program Interrupted: Making Space for Critical Discourse*, edited by Jeanne Gunner and Donna Strickland, 113–25. Portsmouth: Boynton/Cook.

Horner, Bruce, and Min-Zhan Lu. 2010. "Working Rhetoric and Composition." *College English* 72 (5): 470–94.

Horner, Bruce, Min-Zhan Lu, Jacqueline Jones Royster, and John Trimbur. 2011. "Opinion: Language Difference in Writing: Toward a Translingual Approach." *College English* 73 (3): 303–21.

Horner, Bruce, Samantha NeCamp, and Christiane Donahue. 2011. "Toward a Multilingual Composition Scholarship: From English Only to a Translingual Norm." *College Composition and Communication* 63 (2): 269–300.

Horner, Bruce, and John Trimbur. 2002. "English Only and U.S. College Composition." *College Composition and Communication* 53 (4): 594–630.

Kilfoil, Carrie Byars. 2015. "Beyond the 'Foreign' Language Requirement: From a Monolingual to a Translingual Ideology in Rhetoric and Composition Graduate Education." *Rhetoric Review* 34 (4): 426–44.

Lu, Min-Zhan, and Bruce Horner. 2013. "Translingual Literacy, Language Difference, and Matters of Agency." *College English* 75 (6): 582–607.

MacDonald, Susan Peck. 2007. "The Erasure of Language." *College Composition and Communication* 58 (4): 585–625.

Matsuda, Paul Kei. 2006. "The Myth of Linguistic Homogeneity in U.S. College Composition." *College English* 68 (6): 637–51.

Matsuda, Paul Kei. 2013. "It's the Wild West Out There: A New Linguistic Frontier in U.S. College Composition." In *Literacy as Translingual Practice*, edited by A. Suresh Canagarajah, 128–38. London/New York: Routledge.

Matsuda, Paul Kei, Tanita Saenkum, and Steven Accardi. 2013. "Writing Teachers' Perceptions of the Presence and Needs of Second Language Writers: An Institutional Case Study." *Second Language Writing* 22 (1): 68–86.

Modern Language Association. n.d. *Foreign Languages and Higher Education: New Structures for a Changing World.* Report of the MLA Ad Hoc Committee on Foreign Languages. https://www.mla.org/Resources/Guidelines-and-Data/Reports-and-Professional-Guidelines/Teaching-Enrollments-and-Programs/Foreign-Languages-and-Higher-Education-New-Structures-for-a-Changed-World.

Muchiri, Mary N., Nshindi G. Mulamba, Greg Myers, and Deoscorous B. Ndoloi. 1995. "Importing Composition: Teaching and Researching Academic Writing Beyond North America." *College Composition and Communication* 46 (2): 175–98.

Phelps, Louise Wetherbee. 1995. "Reproducing Composition and Rhetoric: The Intellectual Challenge of Doctoral Education." *Composition Studies* 23 (2): 115–32.

Ray, Brian. "'It's Beautiful': Language Difference as the New Norm in College Writing Instruction." 2015. *College Composition and Communication* 67 (1): 87–103.

Silva, Tony, Ilona Leki, and Joan Carson. 1997. "Broadening the Perspective of Mainstream Composition Studies: Some Thoughts from the Disciplinary Margins." *Written Communication* 14 (3): 398–428.

Tardy, Christine M. "Crossing, or Creating, Divides? A Plea for Transdisciplinary Scholarship." 2017. In *Exploring Translingual Writing Pedagogies and Programs*, edited by Bruce Horner and Laura Tetreault, 181–89. Logan: Utah State University Press.

Trimbur, John. 2008. "The Dartmouth Conference and the Geohistory of the Native Speaker." *College English* 71 (2): 142–69.

University of Louisville. 2013. Graduate Program Guidelines. University of Louisville Graduate Program, Louisville, KY.

Wible, Scott. 2013. *Shaping Language Policy in the U.S.: The Role of Composition Studies.* Carbondale: Southern Illinois University Press.

Williams, Jessica. 1995. "ESL Composition Program Administration in the United States." *Journal of Second Language Writing* 4 (2): 157–79.

Yildiz, Yasemin. 2012. *Beyond the Mother Tongue: The Postmonolingual Condition.* New York: Fordham University Press.

Young, Vershawn, Rusty Barrett, Y'Shanda Young-Rivera, and Kim Brian Lovejoy. 2013. *Other People's English: Code-Meshing, Code-Switching, and African American Literacy.* New York: Columbia University Press.

PART II

(Trans)Disciplinarity and Knowledge Building in Graduate Curricula and Mentorship

4

TRANSFORMING GRADUATE EDUCATION IN RHETORIC AND COMPOSITION
Toward a Transnational and Translingual Revaluation

Bruce Horner

Work in transnational composition and translingual approaches to composition is growing.[1] Collections (like this one) are being published, journals are devoting special issues to matters of transnationality and translinguality in composition, and monographs are appearing addressing one or both of these. Many of these publications have been honored with awards by professional organizations, a sign the disciplines these organizations serve are increasingly recognizing the significance of attention to these matters. And the pace of all this growth and recognition appears to be increasing.

From one perspective, this recognition cannot but be gratifying to those of us who have participated in efforts to draw the field's attention to these matters. For me, for example, it's intensely pleasing to see that what began in 2009 as a sparsely populated special-interest group on transnational composition, subject to annual questioning by the program chair of the Conference on College Composition and Communication about whether space should be allotted for its meetings, is now a standing group with a large number of members, that sponsors sessions as well as linking many sessions at the organization's annual conference, and has an active social media presence.

At the same time, there is something unsettling about all this attention. There is, first, the danger that these matters will, in the process of becoming recognized as legitimate, simultaneously become assigned a defined (bordered, restricted) space in the professional imaginary: areas of specialization simultaneously accepted as legitimate and dismissed as, well, "special," in the sense of being marginal. Likewise, there is a sense that these areas (of specialization?) themselves represent something

https://doi.org/10.7330/9781646423262.c004

new—brought about by changes in student demographics, global migration patterns, and the privatization of, and hence global competition among, institutions of higher education (IHE's) for students and, of course, their tuition dollars. For, if these areas are deemed new, they can likewise be dismissed (as new and, it may be hoped or believed, transient), like the literacy crises always imagined as both new and transient and, therefore, meriting little substantive attention or permanent forms of support (see Rose 1985). Or, they can be reformulated into projects consistent with neoliberalism's tenets of friction-free exchange between, and capitalization of, differences (see Canagarajah 2017; Flores 2013; Kubota 2016; Molina 2011). This is not to deny the newness of the enterprise, as it were. But it is to insist its novelty lies not in the phenomena under study per se but in the form of recognition assigned them (just as the Copernican Revolution constituted not the discovery of a new universe but a reappraisal of the only one we have).

I offer this thumbnail sketch of the current state of attention to transnational and translingual composition from the perspective of someone who might well (with justification) be accused of having attempted to advance attention to these matters in the unsettling ways just described. But rather than rehearse my sins, I want to use the occasion of this chapter to offer an alternative rendering of the emergence of translingual and transnational composition as matters of concern, based on the trajectory of graduate seminars I designed and taught from 2006 on at the University of Louisville. It bears emphasizing that as a condition of my position at that IHE, I effectively had carte blanche to design and offer a graduate seminar each year as I saw fit. While on one occasion the course I offered (on translation) did not "make,"[2] all others did. In that sense, I did not design or offer these seminars at the behest of or in response to pressure from any institutional or programmatic curricular exigence.[3]

Here is a list of the graduate seminars I designed and taught during this period, all offered under the umbrella of topics courses:

2006: Basic Writing in History, Theory and Practice

2007: Critical Pedagogy, Its Discontents, and Beyond in English Studies

2008: Writing, Cognition, and Culture in Curriculum Design: Histories, Theories, Practices

2009: Politics of Language in the Teaching and Study of Composition

2010: Outside Composition

2011: Work in English

2012: Academic Writing in Theory and Practice

2014: Writing, Language, Cognition, and Culture in Curriculum Design: Histories, Theories, Practices

2015: Writing Program Administration in History, Theory, and Practice
2016: Mobility Work in Composition
2017: Translingual Writing in Theory and Practice
2019: Writing Program Administration in History, Theory, and Practice

I suspect at least some of the titles and topics listed above resemble those offered at other IHEs with graduate programs in composition—for example, Writing Program Administration. But my interest here is not in using this listing to serve as an index of a general trend in graduate education in composition programs. (I suspect it does not.) Instead, I want to use my inside perspective—that is, inside the experience of designing, offering, and teaching these courses, and of wanting to do so—to explore the tension I've sketched above between the drive to initiate and develop study of the transnational and translingual in composition, on the one hand, and, on the other, the dangers of so doing. And in exploring that tension, I hope also to point to an alternative to how the transnational and translingual might be addressed in graduate education in composition: not as additional but intrinsic to that education—*trans* as perforce demanding revaluation and transformation.

I suspect four of the seminar titles will stand out to readers as signaling something outside the norm of graduate curricula in composition, at least in past iterations of those curricula: Politics of Language, Outside Composition, Mobility Work in Composition, and Translingual Writing in Theory and Practice. I'll begin with the first of these, Politics of Language. That seminar was meant to prepare students to participate actively in the following year's Thomas Watson Conference, held at the University of Louisville every other year, which had as its theme "Reworking English in Rhetoric and Composition." The assigned readings for that seminar suggest I thought of the politics of language as something from outside composition that had to be engaged: as I wrote to students in the course description,

> While we will be exploring some recent critiques of approaches to language in composition, much of our work will involve exploring possible ways to rework scholarship arising outside the discipline of composition "proper" for the uses to which it might be put by compositionists, as well as for what the perspectives of compositionists might contribute to that scholarship. In that sense, this seminar is meant to address lacunae in the work of composition rather than familiarize you with traditions of such work.

But in the seminar I offered the following year (2010), Outside Composition, this view of such matters as "outside the discipline of composition 'proper'" came into question. In the opening statement of the syllabus for that seminar, I announced, "This seminar responds to recent provocations for rethinking the defining boundaries commonly invoked to distinguish composition from other areas of teaching and research—among them, language, education, and political economy." It's clear from subsequent statements in the same paragraph of that same syllabus that I felt the need to hedge. I cautioned that the readings would come from "scholarship on education, extracurricular writing, second-language writing instruction and scholarship, writing instruction and scholarship outside the US, and the 'internationalization' and 'globalization' of education generally and composition specifically." However, I also promised the seminar would prepare students "to pursue relations between the work of composition and at least some of the issues and scholarship on the teaching, study, and learning of writing outside composition that nonetheless intersect with the teaching, study, and learning of writing identified with 'composition.' " Statements later in the syllabus are more furtive. I suggest that

> we will attempt to address that scholarship [intersecting with work "inside" composition] that impinges in ways that, while meriting our attention as directly relevant to work in composition, has at least until recently been kept beyond its conceptual horizon as a consequence of its focus, its language, its writers, and/or the (extra)institutional setting of the writing.

And, finally, I admit, "Necessarily, the seminar puts into question the definition of the field variously identified as 'composition' or 'rhetoric and composition,' or 'writing studies.' And necessarily, in questioning those definitions, we will also be problematizing translations of either what is designated 'outside' to 'inside' composition and the reverse." In retrospect, at least two of the speakers I invited to speak to the class (and whose work I assigned) were and are indisputably established members of composition (Paul Kei Matsuda, Christiane Donahue), and many of the readings would be recognizable as belonging at least as much to composition as to other fields (e.g., Brandt 2001; Gere 1994; New London Group 1996). More important, it's clear that the "outside" in the seminar title increasingly came with an invisible question mark: work that addressed the globalization of education, L2 writing, studies in postsecondary writing education outside the United States (e.g., Ivanič 1998), as well as studies of writing outside IHEs (in K–12 education and in the extracurriculum), could no longer be kept outside composition, nor composition outside these otherwise other realms. The subtitles assigned in the syllabus to readings and discussions for specific weeks make clear that boundaries of nationality and discipline are porous—for example, "English in the World," "Multilingualism in Writing," "Cross-cultural/

Cross-disciplinary Writing Research," "Distributed Learning and/in the University," "Literacy in Advance of the University," "Geopolitical Economies of Education"—all introduced by a week devoted to "Defining Contexts."

These hedges and admissions suggest that the revaluation of the transnational and translingual in composition may be best understood not as requiring we import some new other outsider to what has been an entirely insular, discrete, internally uniform field called *composition* but, instead, as rethinking what we have been led to believe that field is. This parallels how we think of the transnational and translingual more broadly. In globalization studies, it has now become an accepted truism that globalization is not new but rather a longstanding, even unending process of migration of peoples (as well as, of course, other life forms) across continents and oceans extending well into "prehistory." Likewise, the transnational movement of knowledge and goods is not new but longstanding. It is what our nationalist—for lack of a better term—framework has precluded us from recognizing. In the same way, translinguality does not name a new phenomenon. What is new about translinguality is, instead, the framework it offers for how we understand languages, language relations, and the relations of these to language users—a framework at odds with the dominant ideology of monolingualism and what that ideology has occluded.

This reevaluation does not mean work directly addressing transnational and translingual composition is unnecessary, for recognition of what would otherwise remain occluded effects change by changing the sense of agency, and thereby the tendency to exert that agency, of those experiencing that recognition. As Louis-Jean Calvet (2006) puts it regarding recognition of language(s), "Representations—what people think about languages and the way they are spoken— . . . act on practices and are one of the factors of change. They produce in particular *security/insecurity* and this leads speakers to types of *behaviour* that transform practices" (241). Hence, he cautions, "*the invention of a language* and consequently the *way it is named* constitute an intervention in and modify the ecolinguistic niche" (248). And as Sara Alvarez and I have glossed, "Beliefs about language exist and affect [language] practice, and, hence, affect language" (Horner and Alvarez 2019, 13).

Following these parallels, work explicitly addressing the transnational and translingual in composition can change beliefs about composition, intervening in the practice of composition. We can see something of this effect in the differences between what would otherwise appear to be almost identical iterations of two different seminars I taught:

a course on writing, cognition and culture, and a course on writing program administration. In 2008, I offered Writing, Cognition, and Culture in Curriculum Design: Histories, Theories, Practices, and, in 2014, Writing, *Language*, Cognition, and Culture in Curriculum Design: Histories, Theories, Practices (emphasis added). In 2015 and again in 2019, I offered a seminar titled Writing Program Administration in History, Theory, and Practice. As might be expected, there was significant overlap between both iterations of both seminars. So for example, in both the 2008 and 2014 seminars, seminar members each designed a sequence of assignments for a composition course and provided an explanation of the logic of that design in relation to approaches and issues we'd be considering in response to readings, many of which remained the same across both courses. However, there were also significant, if subtle, differences, signaled by the addition of the term *language* into the title of the 2014 iteration of the seminar. In both iterations, we read works like Lev Vygotsky's (1986) *Thought and Language*, Bill Coles (1970), a chapter of Anis Bawarshi's (2003) book on the genre of writing assignments, Alan France's (1993) "Assigning Places," David Bartholomae's (1983) essay on writing assignments, Bartholomae and Anthony Petrosky's (1986) *Facts, Artifacts, Counterfacts*, and Elizabeth Rankin's (1990) "From Simple to Complex." However, in the 2008 iteration (itself a revision of yet another graduate seminar I had offered at the University of Wisconsin–Milwaukee in 2003, Sequencing in Writing Pedagogy and Curricula), we read William Perry's (1968) *Forms of Intellectual and Ethical Development in the College Years* and debates on cognitive versus social accounts of writing development (Bizzell 1984; Flower 1989; Trimbur 1987; Williams 1989) and on the "contact zone" (Harris 1995; Miller 1994; Pratt 1991). In the 2014 iteration, these disappeared, replaced by works like Jay Jordan's (2012) *Redesigning Composition for Multilingual Realities*, Calvet's (2006) *Towards an Ecology of World Languages*, Claire Kramsch's (1998) "The Privilege of the Intercultural Speaker," Leslie Milroy's (2001) "Language Ideologies and the Consequences of Standardization," Suresh Canagarajah's (2009) "Multilingual Strategies of Negotiating English: From Conversation to Writing," Vershawn Ashanti Young's (2009) " 'Nah, We Straight,' " and several articles by Constant Leung and his coauthors critiquing notions of "communicative competence" and the "native speaker" (Leung 2005, 2013; Leung, Harris, and Rampton 1997).[4] As this change in readings suggests, in the 2014 iteration, language was now given an explicit place of prominence as a subject of inquiry and consideration in the design of writing courses and curricula. But it may be more accurate to say

language was now given explicit recognition as being of central importance in such considerations, rather than being an area to be imported
into the course from somewhere else. However, following the argument
above drawn from Calvet (2006), that recognition itself changed the
course and the courses following from its work.

Both iterations of the seminar Writing Program Administration
(hereafter WPA) carried the same title. That said, transnationality (and
language) came more to the fore in the second iteration. Compare,
for example, the following statements that appeared in the course
descriptions:

> My own current perspective on writing program administration will (inevi-
> tably) be manifest in the selection of course readings. I will be expecting
> your individual projects to revise that perspective, both building and
> moving from and beyond it, in the additional works considered, questions
> posed, and directions pursued. (2015)

> My own current perspective on writing program administration will (inevi-
> tably) be manifest in the selection of course readings—*most explicitly in the
> emphasis on transnational writing program administration.* I will be expecting
> your individual projects to revise that perspective, both building and mov-
> ing from and beyond it, in the additional works considered, questions
> posed, and directions pursued. (2019; emphasis added)

Aside from demonstrating my shameless reliance on the first course description when composing the text of the second, these quoted passages
also show a key difference, one manifested in my addition to the list of
questions I provided in the course description for us to use as guides:
"How does transnationality figure into, or require changes to, writing
program administration and how we think about and practice it?"

But even these changes belie a continuity, or at least intended continuity: in the 2019 seminar, readings from David Martins's (2015a) edited
collection *Transnational Writing Program Administration* figured large.
They did not in the 2015 seminar for a simple reason: the collection,
while appearing in 2015, was not available in print in time for the seminar. Had it been, there would have been greater continuity between the
two iterations. Of course, many of the same readings did appear in both
seminars. Also, and significantly, both included attention to language
difference (with readings from Paul Matsuda, Maria Fruit, Tamara Lee,
and Burton Lamm's [2006] guest-edited special issue of *WPA* on second-
language writing). But the apparent change in the 2019 seminar, in its
readings and questions, can better be understood as rendering explicit
what had already been there, if going largely unnoted. For transnational
relations (versus international, say, or purely national) have always been

present. Their apparent newness attests not to their actual novelty but rather to the new awareness of their presence. Just as, from a mobilities perspective, mobility (e.g., migration) is not new but, rather, a feature sedentarist perspectives have kept us oblivious to, transnationality and translinguality are not new phenomena but rather offer a new perspective—or awareness—of features of human life that have long been obscured. That said, again following from the argument above drawn from Calvet, that new perspective—a new set of beliefs about the transnational character of WPA work—will necessarily change that work, not to address a new phenomenon but instead as a consequence of a new understanding of the phenomenon known as *WPA work*.

In that sense, in retrospect, unlike my explicit change in the seminar title of Writing, Cognition, and Culture in Curriculum Design to Writing, *Language*, Cognition, and Culture in Curriculum Design, my repetition of the title Writing Program Administration for both offerings of that seminar may be more apt than a renaming of the later iteration to incorporate *transnational* (or *translingual*) into the title: the transnational is simply an inevitable feature of writing program administration, acknowledged or not.[5] This does not mean the transnational should not be used as a point of departure for inquiry in a seminar on writing program administration; rather it means any seminar ostensibly focused on writing program administration that does not address transnationality as key is inadequate, just as a seminar on writing-curriculum design that is not attentive to language is also inadequate. Or, to return to the seminar The Politics of Language in Composition, it's clear that, whether the course was new in the sense that I and not someone else was teaching it and giving it a title likely not on the books (it was offered as one iteration of a topics course), clearly there has never not been a politics of language in composition. Significantly, however, just as the ideology of autonomous literacy claims to be nonideological (Street 1984), the politics exercised has often been masked as being apolitical (as in invocations and heraldings of Standard English or good English, and in insistences on what is thereby invoked and heralded).

We can see the inescapability of the politics of language in composition more clearly in the first seminar I offered at the University of Louisville, one whose title will likely not raise as many readers' eyebrows: Basic Writing in History, Theory, and Practice. Those familiar with the readings I included in that course—for example, Mina Shaughnessy's (1977) *Errors and Expectations*, Glynda Hull, Mike Rose, Kay Losey Fraser, and Marisa Castellano's (1991) "Remediation as Social Construct," Bartholomae's (1980) "Study of Error" and "The Tidy House" (1993),

Min-Zhan Lu's (1991) "Redefining the Legacy of Mina Shaughnessy" and "Professing Multiculturalism" (1994), and even Thomas Farrell's (1977) notorious "Literacy, the Basics, and All That Jazz"—will recognize the concern with the politics of language permeating this scholarship, whether or not the politics of language advanced in specific instances are those we might support. Likewise, the seminar I offered on the seemingly unprovocative subject Academic Writing in Theory and Practice involved participants throughout in confronting the politics of language—whether in terms of register, stance, error, style, or named language differences—as we read such works as Bartholomae's (1985) "Inventing the University," Christopher Schroeder, Helen Fox, and Patricia Bizzell's (2002) edited collection on *ALT/DIS*, Peter Elbow's (1991) "Reflections on Academic Discourse," Canagarajah's (2002) *Geopolitics of Academic Writing*, Christine Casanave's (1998) "Transitions: The Balancing Act of Bilingual Academics," Mary Lea and Brian Street's (1998) "Student Writing in Higher Education," and Theresa Lillis and Mary Jane Curry's (2010) *Academic Writing in a Global Context*. And, as the titles of several of these works suggest, we also could not avoid the transnational character of our topic: to study academic writing in theory and practice necessarily raised, and raises, questions of language difference and the transnational relations among and exchanges of language, knowledge, and people.

Of course, syllabi statements and reading lists like those presented above offer at best a sliver of a sense of the work of a seminar, embodied in seminar discussions and writings and in work appearing subsequently that might be prompted by events unfolding during a seminar. And I suspect that, in line with at least one explanation, the increased interest of composition teacher-scholars in matters of translinguality and transnationality could be understood to result from changes to student demographics—the enrollment of more recognizably translingual and transnational students prompting faculty (like me) to offer courses such students are presumed to have an interest in. Or, more broadly, what is viewed as the increasingly superdiverse and migrating character of populations worldwide, and (consequently) an increasingly mixed and mixing linguistic landscape, perforce has necessitated attention to the translingual and transnational conditions now obtaining. In line with this explanation, it is possible to say my courses, and the trajectory they might appear to outline, are in keeping with this growing recognition of the emergence of such conditions. And the publication of works I subsequently assigned indexes such a recognition: Canagarajah's *Geopolitics of Academic Writing* appeared in 2002, his *Translingual Practice:*

Global Englishes and Cosmopolitan Relations in 2013, Horner, Lu, and Matsuda's *Cross-Language Relations in Composition* in 2010, Horner and Karen Kopelson's *Reworking English in Rhetoric and Composition: Global Interrogations, Local Interventions* in 2014, Lillis and Curry's *Academic Writing in a Global Context: The Politics and Practices of Publishing in English* in 2010, Martins's collection on *Transnational Writing Program Administration* in 2015.

But as I've already suggested, these publications, and my subsequent use of them in seminars, is better understood *not* as indexing changing conditions—real as those changes might well be—but as indexing changing understandings of what has obtained all along while previously going unrecognized: giving new names to phenomena for which the available terms have proved to be inadequate (see Horner and Alvarez 2019, 7–8). Actual changes on the ground have served at best as catalysts for that recognition to occur, making what had previously been easier to ignore more difficult to deny, and should not be mistaken for the realities terms like *translingual* and *transnational* have been introduced to name.

We can see this process of groping toward a changed recognition in the course I offered on basic writing. Neither *transnational* or *translingual* appear in the materials for the course I offered on basic writing, nor, so far as I can remember, did they emerge in the writing and discussions produced during the seminar. Nonetheless, I think it fair to say the work of that seminar pressed toward such terms in its interrogation of the inadequacy of the available terms for understanding language, identity, and the relations among these—I'm thinking here of Bartholomae's (1993) caution that "the basic writing program . . . can be seen simultaneously as an attempt to bridge AND preserve cultural difference, to enable students to enter the 'normal' curriculum but to ensure, at the same time, that there are basic writers" (8). Most notably, we came to think of difference in all these differently, even in discussions of such seemingly prosaic issues as error (and its opposing twin correctness), as well as in the pressure basic writers and their writing put on such notions as native versus alien, as well as literate versus illiterate.[6] That is to say, in exploring "basic writing in history, theory, and practice," we found ourselves engaged not in pedestrian matters but, instead, in discovering, in what are commonly believed to be pedestrian matters, challenges to fundamental tenets of what I would now view as the language ideology of monolingualism, with its reified chains linking fixed and uniform languages, identities, and literacy: the basics of writing, indeed, if redefined.

To return to the question of the relation of course offerings to conditions on the ground, as it were, were there changes in the characteristics of the students themselves in my seminars that would account for changes in what I offered—students more translingual and transnational prompting courses addressing these directly? As tempted as I am to offer a thumbnail sketch of the students in these seminars, my short and quick answer is, instead, to reject the premise of the question: neither translinguality nor transnationality is, for me, a characteristic or condition of individuals on the basis of their language repertoires or histories of travel or habitation. As my coauthors Min-Zhan Lu, Jacqueline Jones Royster, John Trimbur and I observe of language,

> Students who are identified by conventional standards as monolingual might take a translingual approach to language difference, as demonstrated by their response to unfamiliar ways of using language, while individuals identifiable by conventional standards as multilingual with regard to their own linguistic resources might well approach language differences in ways at odds with a translingual approach. (Horner et al. 2011, 311–12)

Likewise, one may take a transnational approach to identity and relations while appearing to maintain a single location of residence, just as, conversely, one may take a nationalist (as it were) approach while traveling incessantly around the world and having no fixed place of abode. The difference students made, then, was not as consumers shaping the market for seminars by their demands. Rather, and more significantly, they shaped the seminars—effectively and unavoidably remaking them—through their work with the materials I presented to them for their consideration and with what they brought to those considerations collectively from their previous experiences and thinking and interests—reworking all these in the heat of discussions, weekly response papers, and seminar projects. Thus, as much as I might like to take credit for the significant representation of "my" former graduate students in CCCC's Transnational SIG and its subsequent standing group or for their published scholarship on matters of translinguality and transnationality, the work of these individuals is a consequence of neither their previous linguistic repertoires nor their transnational experience with transnationality per se but rather of their concrete labor with, and remaking of, what they encountered, including but not limited to graduate seminars.

In one sense, then, I am reiterating a point I've made with others regarding translinguality: that transformation is inevitable, including the transformation of graduate education. However, this does not mean we can or should ignore the labor effecting such transformation as irrelevant, nor the conditions in which such labor takes place, to which it responds, and which it shapes. Instead, it means that, while we cannot not produce difference through our work, the kind of difference we make depends on our labor (while keeping in mind Marx's dictum that we do not make history just as we please but rather in conditions not of our making). I argue above that transnationality and translinguality have always been present in graduate education, as well as in our lives more broadly, but that until recently they have gone unrecognized, just as the spherical character of the earth is not a recent development but was not recognized for much of human history. But that recognition itself makes a difference in how we work and live. Adopting frameworks of translinguality and transnationality forces revaluations not of what else we need to add to the graduate curriculum but of how we think about such matters as the design of that curriculum, writing program administration, academic writing, the politics of language, and disciplinary boundaries. While the terms *translingual* and *transnational* by themselves (if one can imagine any such thing) carry no force, compositionists can and have put these to useful work to engage in just such revaluations of the entire curriculum rather than offering competition for courses already on the books. Graduate education in composition provides the occasion for that work to take place.

I am suggesting, then, that rather than seeing the translingual and transnational as add-on areas of concern to a graduate curriculum already straining from competing demands and interests, matters for specialists in translinguality and transnationality, we can understand and address them as intrinsic characteristics of the curriculum that heretofore have gone unremarked and unaddressed to the detriment of graduate education and the discipline the curriculum is meant to sustain. We need to adopt the frameworks those terms pose to rethink, and direct, the work we and our students set out to accomplish. In practice, this means not merely, or only, courses on translinguality and/or transnationality per se, as helpful as these might be in providing forums for thinking through the implications of the frameworks they might constitute. Rather, it must also require reimagining and redesigning all our graduate courses in terms of a different understanding of language, language relations, users, contexts of use, and the relations among these, and a different understanding of the transnational location and movement of work in and on composition: both broadening and deepening the conceptual horizon into which we place that work locally and globally. Like Molière's (1670) character Monsieur Jourdain, delighted to learn that all his life he has been speaking prose, we can learn to take delight in this new understanding of what we have been doing in order that we may do it differently.

Others in this collection pose specific kinds of changes to pedagogical practice, whether in terms of changing from a pedagogy of transmission to one of dialogue and openness to difference (Lerma et al.; Zaleski and You) or in terms of including more coursework on language knowledge (Pawlowski and Tardy). My own sense is that a dialogic approach to teaching would be appropriate regardless of matters of language or nationality. While translinguality's foundation in a respect for opacity mandates such an approach (see Horner and Alvarez 2019), there are other paths, many of them well trod, by which educators have come to this same view. The argument for courses and course requirements intended to provide students with what Madelyn Pawlowski and Christine Tardy in their chapter for this collection identify as "pedagogical language knowledge (PLK)—a knowledge of language and its pedagogical relevance to and role in the writing classroom" (chapter 7) runs counter to this insistence on opacity and dialogue, as it seems to require a stable body of knowledge to be transmitted to students. It also appears to run counter to the "panoramic ethos" Corina Lerma, Moisés García-Rentería, Patricia Flores, Kate Mangelsdorf, and Lucía Durá Lerma argue for, given Lerma et al.'s emphasis on the inevitability of deficits, as well as resources, among both students and teachers, an emphasis that appears to level the playing field. That said, the translingual perspective for which I argue might well resolve conflicts among these positions by emphasizing the inevitability not so much of resources and deficits but rather of the reworking of any language knowledge and its pedagogical relevance for the writing classroom that anyone and everyone—teachers and students, and later versions of these same teachers and students—might believe they have: a reworking that takes place as that seemingly same knowledge is mobilized insofar as any mobilization of knowledge subjects it inevitably to transformation.

Beyond the level of individual courses, how might programs redefine their missions to address the transnational and translingual character of writing and writing programs in ways governing all course offerings so course syllabi, examinations, and dissertations assume, as a matter of course, a transnational and translingual framework in their design, in the same way that, once upon a time at least, graduate courses and exams and syllabi in musicology, say, were expected to engage with materials from a range of languages and locations? My sense is that this kind of programmatic change is, in fact, a sea change—one in which we fish come to recognize the water in which we've been swimming and thereby learn to swim differently. But despite the image we might have of recognition as sudden realization—the electric bulb suddenly turning on in our minds—my sense is that these kinds of changes are ideological and therefore take place slowly and insidiously (like climate change). So, for example, persuading a graduate program's faculty to revise their program missions in these ways, and to revise the curricular and other requirements and resources to align with those revised missions, itself requires faculty committed to making those persuasive arguments, which itself requires hiring new graduates of programs who recognize the always already transnational and translingual character of work in composition (and, of course, in related areas of study in literature, creative writing, and linguistics). Such faculty may be more persuasive insofar as they are perceived as asking not for something new or an add-on but for recalibrating the program to take into account what has previously gone unrecognized.

What forms any such recalibration might take are bound to be local rather than systemic, taking into consideration a particular IHE's faculty and student resources and departmental and college politics while adopting the kind of "panoramic ethos" toward these Lerma et al. argue for: a revolution that does not so much breach the ramparts as insidiously infect those residing within their circuit, invading the seemingly secure meaning of terms like *language, language learning,* and *translation* so that the "keep" of the concepts to which these terms refer is undermined, their retaining walls sagging as their foundations crumble. Courses might contribute to this kind of viral infection by taking seemingly standard or ordinary topics but approaching, even infusing, these from a foundation in translingual and transnational tenets. This approach might be more effective, too, than either requirements for courses on language purporting to provide students with PLK, on the one hand, or one-off courses (like mine) by lone faculty (like me) on what seem like idiosyncratic or special topics—for example, a course on translingualism for those graduate students hoping to cash in on the current exchange value for "experts" on it, but at the risk of being marginalized as the "translingual" person if and when hired as exactly that (see Shuck 2006). The more insidious approach would, instead, insist on the opacity of governing terms like *language* and, therefore, the need to keep reworking their meanings (as well as, of course, the meanings of terms like *translingualism* and *transnationalism*). Programs designed by faculty committed to such reworkings might then produce graduates who do not so much earn certificates in translingualism or transnationalism as bring to their consideration of all matters an ethos founded on the recognitions these represent and committed to rethinking curricula and program requirements in light of those recognitions.

I can't claim the courses I've offered, described above, constituted that kind of insidious work toward such ends graduate education might undertake. And in fact, the title of at least one—Translingual Writing in Theory and Practice—seems close to offering precisely the niche specialty knowledge about which I've expressed skepticism. But what I and my colleagues can hope for is that our course—whether marked as "special" (as in special topics) or generic (as in Composition Theory)—will be occasions for students, as future faculty, to work with and on the translingual and transnational and to grow more adept at and more acclimated to doing such work so it is the normal work in composition and rhetoric rather than a deviation from the norm.

NOTES

1.   I use *composition* as my preferred term to name what also goes by various other terms and collections of terms—for example, *writing studies, rhetoric and composition* (or the reverse), *language and literacy studies,* and so forth—to give emphasis to the study of writing that incorporates the teaching and learning of writing as intrinsic to that study (see Horner 2016).

2.   .Any number of factors might account for why that course didn't make, from the mundane (scheduling) to the local (competing seminars) or even personal ("I don't want to work with him!"); it's also possible students did not enroll because of the lack of currency for translation as a topic in composition, a sense of the difficulty translation might pose for students, and the lack of clarity about whether the course would fulfill the language requirement then in force for our graduate program. That is to say, a view of it as addressing concerns outside the norm may have condemned it.

3.   Thus I cannot address the challenges faced by those interested in offering similar courses who lack the privileges my own institutional position afforded me.

4.   I had also invited Leung to the university to deliver a lecture and meet with seminar members.

5.   Recall here David Martins's (2015b) report of his discovery, early into his position as WPA, that the program he directed included courses taught in Croatia.

6.   Recall Mina Shaughnessy's (1977) paradoxical identification of basic writers as students from New York City who nonetheless seemed "to have come from a different country," "strangers" (2, 3), her account of teachers' discovery of the diversity of language practices among students and the prejudice against these (1980b, 112–13), and her acknowledgment that basic writing teachers came to know through their students that "the uses of literacy in this society need to be re-examined, [and that] the possibilities of a much richer definition of literacy exists alongside the thread of a more and more exclusive cultivation of that power" (1980a, 93).

REFERENCES

Bartholomae, David. 1980. "The Study of Error." *College Composition and Communication* 31 (3): 253–69.

Bartholomae, David. 1983. "Writing Assignments: Where Writing Begins." In *Forum,* edited by P. Stock, 300–312. Montclair: Boynton/Cook.

Bartholomae, David. 1985. "Inventing the University." In *When a Writer Can't Write: Studies in Writer's Block and Other Composing Process Problems*, edited by Mike Rose, 134–65. New York: Guildford.

Bartholomae, David. 1993. "The Tidy House: Basic Writing in the American Curriculum." *Journal of Basic Writing* 12 (1): 4–21.

Bartholomae, David, and Anthony Petrosky. 1986. *Facts, Artifacts, and Counterfacts: Theory and Method for a Reading and Writing Course*. Upper Montclair, NJ: Boynton/Cook.

Bawarshi, Anis S. 2003. *Genre and the Invention of the Writer: Reconsidering the Place of Invention in Composition*. Logan: Utah State University Press.

Bizzell, Patricia. 1984. "William Perry and Liberal Education." *College English* 46 (5): 447–54.

Brandt, Deborah. 2001. *Literacy in American Lives*. Cambridge: Cambridge University Press.

Calvet, Louis-Jean. 2006. *Towards an Ecology of World Languages*. Translated by Andrew Brown. London: Polity.

Canagarajah, Suresh. 2002. *A Geopolitics of Academic Writing*. Pittsburgh: University of Pittsburgh Press.

Canagarajah, Suresh. 2009. "Multilingual Strategies of Negotiating English: From Conversation to Writing." *JAC* 29 (1/2): 17–48.

Canagarajah, Suresh. 2013. *Translingual Practice: Global Englishes and Cosmopolitan Relations*. London: Routledge.

Canagarajah, Suresh. 2017. *Translingual Practices and Neoliberal Policies: Attitudes and Strategies of African Skilled Migrants in Anglophone Workplaces*. Springer.

Casanave, Christine Pearson. 1998. "Transitions: The Balancing Act of Bilingual Academics." *Journal of Second Language Writing* 7 (2): 175–203.

Coles, William. 1970. "The Sense of Nonsense as a Design for Sequential Writing Assignments." *College Composition and Communication* 21 (1): 27–34.

Elbow, Peter. 1991. "Reflections on Academic Discourse: How it Relates to Freshmen and Colleagues." *College English* 53 (2): 135–55.

Farrell, Thomas. 1977. "Literacy, the Basics, and All That Jazz." *College English* 38 (5): 443–59.

Flores, Nelson. 2013. "The Unexamined Relationship between Neoliberalism and Plurilingualism: A Cautionary Tale." *TESOL Quarterly* 47 (3): 500–520.

Flower, Linda. 1989. "Taking Thought: The Role of Conscious Processing in the Making of Meaning." In *Thinking, Reasoning, and Writing*, edited by Elaine P. Maimon, Barbara F. Nodine, and Finbarr W. O'Connor, 185–212. New York: Longman.

France, Alan. 1993. "Assigning Places: The Function of Introductory Composition as a Cultural Discourse." *College English* 55 (6): 593–609.

Gere, Anne Ruggles. 1994. "Kitchen Tables and Rented Rooms: The Extracurriculum of Composition." *College Composition and Communication* 45 (1): 75–92.

Harris, Joseph. 1995. "Negotiating the Contact Zone." *Journal of Basic Writing* 14 (1): 27–42.

Horner, Bruce. 2016. *Rewriting Composition: Terms of Exchange*. Carbondale: Southern Illinois University Press.

Horner, Bruce, and Sara Alvarez, 2019. "Defining Translinguality." *Literacy in Composition Studies* 7 (2): 1–30.

Horner, Bruce, and Karen Kopelson, eds. 2014. *Reworking English in Rhetoric and Composition: Global Interrogations, Local Interventions*. Carbondale: Southern Illinois University Press.

Horner, Bruce, Min-Zhan Lu, and Paul Kei Matsuda, eds. 2010. *Cross-Language Relations in Composition*. Carbondale: Southern Illinois University Press.

Horner, Bruce, Min-Zhan Lu, Jacqueline Jones Royster, and John Trimbur. 2011. "Language Difference in Writing: Toward a Translingual Approach." *College English* 73 (3): 303–21.

Hull, Glynda, Mike Rose, Kay Losey Fraser, and Marisa Castellano. 1991. "Remediation as Social Construct: Perspectives from an Analysis of Classroom Discourse." *College Composition and Communication* 42 (3): 299–329.

Ivanič, Roz. 1998. *Writing and Identity: The Discoursal Construction of Identity in Academic Writing.* Amsterdam: John Benjamins.

Jordan, Jay. 2012. *Redesigning Composition for Multilingual Realities.* Urbana, IL: CCCC.

Kramsch, Claire. 1998. "The Privilege of the Intercultural Speaker." In *Language Learning in Intercultural Perspective: Approaches through Drama and Ethnography,* edited by Michael Byram and Michael Fleming, 16–31. Cambridge: Cambridge University Press.

Kubota, Ryuko. 2016. "The Multi/Plural Turn, Postcolonial Theory, and Neoliberal Multiculturalism: Complicities and Implications for Applied Linguistics." *Applied Linguistics* 37 (4): 474–94.

Lea, Mary, and Brian Street. 1998. "Student Writing in Higher Education: An Academic Literacies Approach." *Studies in Higher Education* 23 (2): 157–72.

Leung, Constant. 2005. "Convivial Communication: Recontextualizing Communicative Competence." *International Journal of Applied Linguistics* 15 (2): 119–44.

Leung, Constant. 2013. "The 'Social' in English Language Teaching: Abstracted Norms versus Situated Enactments." *Journal of English as a Lingua Franca* 2 (2): 283–313.

Leung, Constant, Roxy Harris, and Ben Rampton. 1997. "The Idealised Native Speaker, Reified Ethnicities, and Classroom Realities." *TESOL Quarterly* 31 (3): 543–60.

Lillis, Theresa, and Mary Jane Curry. 2010. *Academic Writing in a Global Context: The Politics and Practices of Publishing in English.* New York: Routledge.

Lu, Min-Zhan. 1991. "Redefining the Legacy of Mina Shaughnessy: A Critique of the Politics of Linguistic Innocence." *Journal of Basic Writing* 10 (1): 26–40.

Lu, Min-Zhan. 1994. "Professing Multiculturalism: The Politics of Style in the Contact Zone." *College Composition and Communication* 45 (4): 442–58.

Martins, David, ed. 2015a. *Transnational Writing Program Administration.* Logan: Utah State University Press.

Martins, David. 2015b. "Transnational Writing Program Administration: An Introduction." In *Transnational Writing Program Administration,* edited by David S. Martins, 1–18. Logan: Utah State University Press.

Matsuda, Paul Kei. 2006. "The Myth of Linguistic Homogeneity in U.S. College Composition." *College English* 68 (6): 637–51.

Matsuda, Paul Kei, Maria Fruit, Tamara Lee, and Burton Lamm, eds. 2006. "Bridging the Disciplinary Divide: Integrating a Second-Language Perspective into Writing Programs." Special issue, *WPA: Writing Program Administration* 30 (1/2).

Miller, Richard E. 1994. "Fault Lines in the Contact Zone." *College English* 56 (4): 389–408.

Milroy, Leslie. 2001. "Language Ideologies and the Consequences of Standardization." *Journal of Sociolinguistics* 5 (4): 530–55.

Molière, [Jean-Baptiste Poquelin]. 1670. *Le bourgeois gentilhomme* [play].

Molina, Clara. 2011. "Curricular Insights into Translingualism as a Communicative Competence." *Journal of Language Teaching and Research* 2 (6): 1244–51.

New London Group. 1996. "A Pedagogy of Multiliteracies: Designing Social Futures." *Harvard Educational Review* 66 (1): 60–92.

Perry, William. 1968. *Forms of Intellectual and Ethical Development in the College Years: A Scheme.* New York: Holt, Rinehart, and Winston.

Pratt, Mary Louise. 1991. "Arts of the Contact Zone." *Profession* 91: 33–40.

Rankin, Elizabeth. 1990. "From Simple to Complex: Ideas of Order in Assignment Sequences." *Journal of Advanced Composition* 10 (1): 126–35.

Rose, Mike. 1985. "The Language of Exclusion: Writing Instruction at the University." *College English* 47 (4): 341–59.

Schroeder, Christopher, Helen Fox, and Patricia Bizzell, eds. 2002. *ALT/DIS: Alternative Discourses and the Academy.* Portsmouth: Boynton/Cook.

Shaughnessy, Mina. 1977. *Errors and Expectations: A Guide for the Teacher of Basic Writing*. New York: Oxford University Press.

Shaughnessy, Mina. 1980a. "The English Professor's Malady." *Journal of Basic Writing* 3 (1): 91–97.

Shaughnessy, Mina. 1980b. "The Miserable Truth." *Journal of Basic Writing* 3 (1): 109–14.

Shuck, Gail. 2006. "Combating Monolingualism: A Novice Administrator's Challenge." *WPA: Writing Program Administration* 30 (1–2): 59–82.

Street, Brian V. 1984. *Literacy in Theory and Practice*. Cambridge: Cambridge University Press.

Trimbur, John. 1987. "Beyond Cognition: The Voices in Inner Speech." *Rhetoric Review* 5 (2): 211–21.

Vygotsky, Lev. 1986. *Thought and Language*. Translated by Alex Kozulin. Cambridge: MIT Press.

Williams, Joseph. 1989. "Afterword: Two Ways of Thinking about Growth." In *Thinking, Reasoning, and Writing*, edited by Elaine P. Maimon, Barbara F. Nodine, and Finbarr W. O'Connor, 245–55. New York: Longman.

Young, Vershawn Ashanti. 2009. "'Nah, We Straight': An Argument Against Code Switching." *JAC* 29 (1/2): 49–76.

5
TRANSLATION AND TRANSLINGUAL COMPETENCE IN GRADUATE TRAINING

Nancy Bou Ayash

As a translingual turn continues to shape US composition studies, translation is receiving increased attention as a valuable translingual meaning-making practice and pedagogical resource for rethinking writing and its learning (Bou Ayash 2020, 2019; Horner and Tetreault 2016, 2017; Gonzales 2018; Wang 2020). Expounding the principles upheld by translingualism and their implications for various stakeholders, Bruce Horner, Min-Zhan Lu, Jacqueline Royster, and John Trimbur (2011), in "Language Difference in Writing," call for introducing "more multi- and cross-language work into graduate curricula" with a "greater attention to the problematics of translation" in teaching, studying and practicing writing (309). Translation, posited as the "new frontier" for translingualism, also plays a key role in Guillame Gentil's approach[1] to fostering cross-language relations in academic graduate writing and learning in the disciplines. Counteracting the compartmentalization of academic knowledge construction in higher education more broadly, and the humanities in particular, into separate and bounded languages, disciplines, and departments, Gentil (2018) argues for offering graduate students curricular and pedagogical opportunities "to learn to translate and translate to learn across languages" (126), thereby "foster[ing] self-awareness in one's strategies, resources, and challenges" in writing across "disciplinary, professional, and social contexts and genres" (120). In a pilot study on the pedagogical possibilities of translation as a form of inter- and intralingual textual creation in first-year writing classrooms, I have argued in *Toward Translingual Realities* (2019) that the goal of developing translingual competencies for navigating the complex realities of translation across "meanings, interpretations, texts, identities,

https://doi.org/10.7330/9781646423262.c005

languages, discourses, and Englishes" must be fully integrated into the preparation of the current and future generation of writing scholars and teachers (173, 179–85).

Though laborious, time consuming, and still novel to graduate faculty, program administrators, and their students, such substantive training in translation is necessary for all to "better understand and participate in negotiations of difference in and through language, including those leading to the position that no translation is possible" (Horner et al. 2011, 308). However, for graduate programs in rhetoric and composition to take up such difficult yet necessary work, they "need to take more seriously, and be more ambitious in making use of, what is now all too often treated as a token second language requirement of its graduates," as Bruce Horner and colleagues argue (Horner et al. 2011, 309). After all, at a moment in which the field is showing a greater interest in language matters and in valuing and harnessing student writers' language resources, the persistence of monolingualist practices of devaluing, reducing, and even eliminating the language-proficiency requirement in many of its graduate programs (Kilfoil 2015) seems contradictory and counterproductive. As Christine Tardy (2017) puts it, "It should be a significant concern to faculty and students in these programs that serious attention to language study has virtually disappeared just as" (186) our own disciplinary community and the community of writers we support have become more linguistically and socioculturally diverse.

In this chapter, I emphasize the pivotal role translation can and must play in graduate rhetoric and composition programs to foster translingual competence in the strategic deployment of available linguistic resources and the negotiation of the complex language ideologies affecting such deployment in diverse academic writing situations. Using the English department's graduate program at the University of Washington (UW) as a case in point, I describe an introductory translation seminar designed for training rhet/comp graduate students in the basics of translation and its potential value for teaching and research. I specifically reflect on the possibilities and challenges associated with implementing this translation-oriented pedagogic initiative, developed as a response to the pressures the program's language requirement has placed on graduate students and their academic trajectories. The insights offered throughout this chapter suggest a deliberate, sustained emphasis on translation in graduate education can open up opportunities for re-envisioning language-requirement structures that facilitate translingual awareness and inquiry.

EPISTEMOLOGIES OF TRANSLATION AND TRANSLINGUALISM: PRODUCTIVE SYNERGIES

Among the first efforts to bring translation and translingualism together, the 2007 report of the MLA Ad Hoc Committee on Foreign Languages advocated the explicit teaching of translation and interpretation in undergraduate and graduate language curricula to develop "deep translingual and transcultural competence" (Modern Language n.d.). As seen from the perspective of the report, translingual competence places value on agility and resourcefulness in "operat[ing] between languages" (237) as conventionally defined, negotiating the power inequalities and ideological complexes that constrain specific linguistic choices and meanings, and "consider[ing] alternative ways of seeing, feeling, and understanding things" in and through language (238). In this section, I explore some of the synergies between translation and translingualism to reveal the potential inherent in aligning them in mutually transformative ways to promote and strengthen the kind of graduate cross-language work I'm arguing for here. In fact, the common prefix *trans* locates both translation and translingualism at a remove from a monological, monolingual mindset in the direction of a transformative rewriting of norms, beliefs, and practices. I particularly address the following questions: What insights can a way of looking at language and its use in writing through the prism of an emerging research niche like translingualism contribute to engagements with translation? What possibilities could be opened up when theories and practices in the more established field of translation studies inform discussions on language and language difference in written texts?

Translingualism in composition studies redefines the very way we conceive of language, its use and learning in academic writing contexts. Translingual scholarship rejects monolingualism's powerful fiction that languages function as closed, homogeneous, and autonomous entities preexisting their performance in time and space and instead foregrounds their dynamic, situated, and emergent character. Translingualism's reinvention of languages as repeated, agentive practices of identity (re)construction is advantageous for interrogating our basic conceptions about what it really means to engage in translation. A translingual-oriented take on the nature and workings of languages helps us move beyond traditional views of translation as the linear, one-way process of conveying the same meaning expressed in one linguistic code by means of a different code. These views assumed one-to-one mapping of textual aspects (e.g., content, style, form, function, etc.) is reliant on clear distinctions between the original and the translated text, distinctions only possible if the languages in which these texts are written continue to be viewed as fixed and insulated from one another. In his reflection on the subject, Anthony Lewis (2005) points to the "deficiency inherent in [such] conventional conceptions of translation" (16) in that the underlying "separation of 'languages'" (21) and the related "existence of (relative) linguistic stability" (19) is the "only framework within which a valid notion of translatability can be formulated" and imagined (21). In contrast, a translingual conception of named languages involved in translation as fluid, mobile, and inherently heterogeneous rather than static, separate, and hermetically sealed systems has very specific implications for theorizations of translation and its practice. Under the project of translingualism, translation involves much more than the transposition of the syntactic, structural, discursive, and design features of a text from one language into another. Given the pronounced attention translingualism affords the (re)localized rather than the universally reproducible in language forms and usages, it is the resonances, intersections, entanglements, fractures, and frictions in cross-language work, their histories, politics, and asymmetries, that should matter in our understandings of translation.

Critical translation theories, particularly anticolonial approaches to translation (Bassnett and Bush 2007; Bassnett and Trivedi 1999; St-Pierre and Kar 2005; Venuti 2002), are uniquely effective in making the "transformative action of translation" more visible (St-Pierre 2005, 6). Translation, as Susan Bassnett and Peter Trivedi (1999) note, is never "an innocent, transparent activity but is highly charged with significance at every stage; it rarely ever involves a relationship of equality between texts," conventions, writers, readers, languages and cultures (2). Translation is, therefore, perceived as "a social, political, cultural, and ethical act, which, in the process of reconstituting its origin(al)s, leaves them other than what they were" (St-Pierre 2005, 6). This understanding of translation necessitates a shift away from a preoccupation with the most fundamental concepts—such as source versus target text/language/culture/context, original writing versus translation, equivalence versus nonequivalence in meaning, faithfulness versus infidelity to a putatively superior and sacred original. Such hackneyed binary oppositions, as St-Pierre (2005) explains, begin to "point to the *disturbing difference* introduced through translation, but in the end, only to deplore and deny it" (6; emphasis added). In the context of language difference, a break from such traditional translation-based rhetoric not only allows no invisibility to translators and their concrete labor but also potentially illuminates the range of appropriations, accommodations, and compromises they actively make in negotiation with the changing ideological, social, and aesthetic expectations of their audiences. Bringing about the true character of translation as a form of translingual writing and rewriting has the potential to challenge the imposed separation between the roles of the translator and the writer. To talk about a continuum of translating and translingual-oriented writing is not to suggest both practices are the same and interchangeable but rather that it is worth exploring the range of (implicit or explicit) meanings, effects, feelings, and identities that get produced in texts when the boundaries of translation and writing practices overlap and are tested.

As I have tried to demonstrate, brought together as trans concepts and modes of thought and conduct, translation and translingualism can open up the multiple, layered dimensions of power and difference—linguistic, social, cultural, racial, and (geo)political—that get erased, overlooked, or covered up under a dominant English-only monolingual ideology. This organic linkage of translingualism and translation as theoretical-pedagogical responses to a monolingual orientation to language and language difference, therefore, prioritizes the diversity of conceptualizations and "social, cultural, historical, and aesthetic meanings" that get (re)produced, subverted, transformed and "infiltrated by other meanings when in contact with other languages" (Kramsch 2010, 18) and knowledges.

An example that sets this qualitative approach to difference in high relief is the significance and force assigned to particular meanings surrounding translations of the word *translation* itself but not others. The *Oxford English Dictionary* (2004) defines translation as "to carry across" and "to convey in a different language." The word *translation* in Latin means "to carry across." The supposed commonality of the spatial sense of the English/Latin word *translation* has mainly shaped dominant models of translation as the transparent, neutral transfer of meaning. In the Indian tradition, however, the notion of translation takes on different meanings and is hardly a monolithic expression. For instance, the word for translation in Sanskrit and many modern Indian languages is *anuvad*, which etymologically means "to resound"; "saying after or again; repeating by way of explanation; explanatory repetition or reiteration with corroboration or illustration" (Bassnett and Trivedi 1999, 9). Another term for translation is *bhavanuvad*, "to repeat, not merely at the syntactic level, but in a way suggestive of the symbolic, material, and emotive" (Menon 2016, 116). Interestingly, the majority of meanings from the Indian context suggest a temporal, not only a spatial, emphasis, thereby constituting a serious challenge to the dominant Western sense of translation.

The distinguishing temporality underlying non-Western understandings of translation is very reminiscent of translingual conceptualizations of language use in writing as *fertile mimesis*, or the kind of repetition of something already written "that is something else, of sameness that is difference" (Pennycook 2010, 37) and closely relates to the idea of transformation as already inherent in translation practice I discuss earlier.

What is important to our discussion is that what begs uncovering is the charged politics of translation that conceals from purview such counterhegemonic nuances and sensibilities and their direct implications for our collective knowledge-making processes. As far as graduate education is concerned, the pedagogical implication is that we must start socializing students about how (overt and/or covert) systems of domination and subversion manifest themselves through the traffic of translation at the core of all meaning making but also about how their own subtraffics can and must be firmly embedded in the distinct yet connected translingual and anticolonial logics. It is to this decentering and broadening of the notion of translation, and the diversification of its integration in graduate rhetoric and composition studies, that I turn to next.

TEACHING TRANSLATION AS TRANSLINGUAL COMPETENCE IN RHET/COMP COURSEWORK

Probably due to my research and teaching-related focus on language politics in various aspects of higher education, I have usually been the go-to person for complaints or advice about the dreaded language requirement in the English graduate program. During my first year at UW, I was approached by a third-year PhD student in the rhetoric and composition track who was struggling to pass her Spanish-language exam though she believed she had advanced competence in Spanish after studying it in high school and for four years as an undergraduate. Expected to demonstrate her knowledge in near-impossible testing conditions—from translating a random seventeenth-century Spanish text (which can produce an estranging effect upon the most proficient of contemporary Spanish-speaking readers) to being prohibited from consulting electronic or traditional bilingual dictionaries—this student was bound to fail. Unsolicited accounts of similar struggles from numerous graduate students were a clear indication that the program's language requirement was hindering progress toward their degrees, especially given its complete dissociation from their professional interests and goals. As an attempt to address this disconnect between (cross)language work and disciplinary knowledge, the translation seminar was conceived.

In 2014 and 2018, I designed a special-topics graduate seminar to familiarize students with current trends and debates in translation and offer hands-on individual and collaborative experiences with translation activities, projects, and workshops. As its title indicates, Cross-Disciplinary Perspectives on Translation: Theory, Practice and Pedagogy, the ten-week seminar offered students basic training in translation theories and practices while also encouraging them to think carefully about their pedagogical applications. The course's tripartite focus was developed with a firm commitment to foregrounding the intellectual value of cross-language work in graduate education.

Given the transdisciplinary nature of translation, the seminar attracted students from the department's three graduate-degree concentrations—rhetoric and composition, literature and cultural studies, and TESOL—as well as from outside the traditional boundaries of the English department, namely economics, education, comparative literature, French and Italian studies, and Slavic languages and literatures. None of the students enrolled in the course had any training in translation studies. Those with extensive literary training were only tangentially exposed to issues of language difference and translation, if at all. Students were expected to have a reading knowledge of but not perfect competence in (if at all attainable) at least one written language other than English. Though the course design did not require advanced prior language knowledge, the majority of the students had varying relations with a broad range of languages. There were three native Mandarin Chinese speakers, one native French speaker, two native Arabic speakers, and several students with intermediate or advanced competence in Spanish, French, Russian, or German.

The first few sessions were dedicated to exploring critical perspectives on language and translation as practices of textual creation in what Mary Louis Pratt (1991) calls the "contact zone." As I indicated in the syllabus, the course's underlying premise was that "all interpretive and communicative acts are essentially acts of critical translation, in that the very medium that makes textual transactions possible—language itself (and English in particular)—is in constant state of translation" and transformation. To guide us there, I adopted selections from Susan Bassnett's *Reflections on Translation* (2011), Lawrence Venuti's (2002) *Scandals of Translation*, Basil Hatim and Ian Mason's (1997) *The Translator as Communicator*, and Alastair Pennycook's (2010) *Language as Local Practice*, which were helpful in taking up translation in this expansive, transdisciplinary sense. Gradually sensitizing students to the alternative ways of understanding language use and translation these readings advanced provided an important basis for interrogating and complicating the agreed-upon meanings of notions like authorship, agency, originality, (inter)textuality, accuracy, acceptability, and adequacy in writing and translation practice. Because some of the theoretical pieces in this course required some degree of familiarity with discipline-specific concepts the majority of students did not have, Mark Shuttleworth's (2017) *Dictionary of Translation Studies* was a great resource for grounded definitions and examples of key terms and phrases like *equivalence, domesticating versus foreignizing strategies, (un)translatability*, and so forth.

Weekly individual or group presentations focused on explorations of the affordances and limitations of a range of translation theories and strategies, and ensuing student-led discussions explored their concrete applications. One of the first presentations examined how narrative theory serves as a useful approach in producing and analyzing written and screen translation. Drawing on various texts (e.g., opinion pieces and analyses, news articles, interviews, press releases, testimonies, etc.), this presentation exposed the class to a range of rhetorical strategies (such as omission, addition, explication, substitution, and compensation) available for situating and framing individual translations in subtle or radical ways in relation to wider sociohistorical and political contexts. This deep focus on the political and ideological in narrative approaches was a great way to transition into the importance of the linguistic aspect of translation.

Another student presentation provided a detailed overview of past and more contemporary approaches to translation borrowed from different strands of linguistics, such as contrastive linguistics, critical discourse analysis, stylistics, and pragmatics-oriented approaches. Discussions on translating variations in linguistic features (e.g., tense, definiteness, voice, collocation, reiteration, idioms, register) highlighted, as Hatim and Mason (1997) observe, "the ideological consequences of a translator's choices and . . . the linguistic minutiae of text-worlds in transition" (143). To encourage further explorations of the important nexus of language theory and translation, I introduced into the 2018 section materials on linguistic landscaping research, with a focus on studying translation activity in urban spaces. Insights from a translation practitioner in American Indian studies inspired vibrant discussions on the complex politics and stakes involved in translations of Indigenous languages and their representations in public signage and on building walls (see photographs taken by author in figures 5.1, 5.2, and 5.3) in and around the UW Seattle campus, situated on the ancestral homelands of the Coast Salish Peoples.

Aimed at making exclusionary racial, cultural, and linguistic ideologies and their operation visible in written and translated texts, another

Figure 5.1. Translations on the walls of a remodeled Starbucks café

presentation introduced postcolonial translation theory based on Bassnett and Harish Trivedi's (1999) and Paul St. Pierre and Prafulla Karr's (2001ƽ) work. Accordingly, students pondered how and why specific relations of power, domination, and privilege are manifested in translation or nontranslation decisions (i.e., moments in which traditionally named languages coexist without visible translation practice), and relatedly, the ways specific (non)translation choices actively intervene in power imbalances among sociocultural identities, languages, cultures, and interpretive systems. The final set of presentations invited explorations of the ways the diverse translation strategies and techniques introduced in previous sessions apply to multimodal texts, such as graphic memoirs, comics, subtitling, and audiovisuals. Taken together, these presentations helped students conclude that one theory or approach alone cannot account for the full complexity of translation phenomena.

Spread throughout the course and paired with the core readings were analytical essays by translators critically reflecting on a range of micro- and macrolevel translation decisions while unpacking the challenges the translators had to grapple with and the diverse ways they approached them. The pairing of these narrative-based pieces with the

Figure 5.2. Phrase in Southern Lushootseed language welcomes visitors to the university graduate library

Figure 5.3. English translation displayed on adjacent wall space

theoretical readings worked very well, making palpable the complex realities of the writing of translations: How did translators manage to attend to the contours of how texts spoke to their first readers while gauging the needs of new translated readers? What kind of problems did they have to wrestle with and resolve along the way? What (aesthetic, linguistic, and/or cultural) compromises did they have to make in the face of conflicting demands and allegiances and on what (ideological and epistemological) grounds?

To jumpstart these discussions, I selected several essays from Bassnett and Peter Bush's (2007) *The Translator as Writer* and the *Translation Studies* journal. Juan Guix's (2007) commentary on his Spanish translation of *Alice in Wonderland* was a good example of the whole array of choices, judgements, and adjustments translators must make, especially when translating for a Spanish-speaking readership who already had the experience of more than forty other translations of Carroll's book. Guix described a succession of forked lexical, semantic, and syntactic paths he had to confront before making nonstandard translation choices that set his version apart from previous translations. For instance, the popular title *Alicia en el país de las maravillas* (retranslated as *Alice in the Land of Marvels*), according to Guix, placed emphasis solely on the marvels Alice discovered underground and completely erased her other kinds of wonderings and curiosities that captured "the freshness of a gaze which [wa]s surprised by otherness and [wa]s able to subvert the logic of language and the adults' world" (99). Tracing the etymological root of the name Alice to the notion of truth, Guix argued that the socially sanctioned Spanish title was "misleading" and that the "hidden title" would be *Truth in the Land of Inquiry*. Constrained by the "automatism of the traditional title," however, Guix chose to uncover this crucial aspect of the work in a translator's note added to the translation rather than changing a title that has become a "cultural cliché or fetish" (99). These and other instances of actively negotiating language norms in Guix's essay led to stimulating conversations on how translation can play an "active and enriching role" (97) as a rewriting practice in or around the translation and "way of questioning a work" and releasing its interpretive possibilities (96).

Other essays inspired valuable discussions about the complex workings of language, power, ideology, and difference in the production, interpretation, and reception of translations. Deep reflections on the tension-filled negotiations of revisions imposed, for example, by the press and the novel's writer on Marilyn Booth's translation *The Girls of Riyadh* of Raja' al-Sani's *Banat al-Riyadh* and by a Penguin Classics copyeditor on John Rutherford's translation of *Don Quixote* offered useful insights into how multiple and conflicting ideologies of writing and translation are constantly at play and in a relationship of tension. To elaborate, we extensively discussed commentaries on translations in which some translators' active resistance to dominant translational interventions was made visible to readers (as in the case of Rutherford) as well as other self-reflective commentaries on published translations in which the translator's agency was regrettably questioned and undermined by both the press and the original text's author (as in the case of Booth). These ideological differences in the work of translation helped reveal the varied responses to hegemonic demands in the global English marketplace for standardized translation practices that produce the illusion of transparency, unambiguity, and translator invisibility. In this sense, the wide range of translators' commentaries we read together helped generate an awareness among students of the "ongoingly negotiable" nature of translators' positionings in relation to their texts, readers, dominant ideologies, and a host of institutional gatekeepers (e.g., publishers, editors, proofreaders, reviewers, authors, etc.) and "embed [these positionings] in concrete political reality" (Baker 2007, 152, 167).

Building on the nuanced attention to the politics and problematics of translation these practice-oriented commentaries inspired, we conducted close readings of a selection of primary life-writing texts that could not be identified as belonging to one specific nation and using one specific language/variety, and hence did not fit into neat dichotomies of monolingual versus bilingual, trilingual or multilingual, local versus global, domestic versus foreign, eastern versus western. Profoundly varied in thematic breadth, linguistic choices, stylistic patterns, historical purviews, and ideological positions, these translations helped broaden our discussion of the complexities of translating translingual and transnational experiences and ways of knowing for an Anglophone readership: What theories of the trafficking of language(s) and meaning(s) did these texts tap into, whether directly or tacitly? How did the translators navigate the copresence and clash of geopolitical, historical, ideological, economic, and sociocultural forces? How did they represent conflict, movement, and change in time and space? To what extent and in what ways did they refract the range of voices and experiences of peoples, communities, and cultures historically Othered by Western-centric viewpoints without running the risk of diluting their impact or of romanticizing and exoticizing them?

These discussions were considerably enhanced as we delved into the thick, multilayered translations across generations (from the late nineteenth to the early twentieth and twenty-first centuries), geographic locations (Cuba, Lebanon, United States, and France), writing genres (letters, photographs, genealogical research, political speeches, newspaper clippings, notarized deeds, poems, etc.), languages and language practices (French, English, Spanish, Castilian Spanish, Modern Standard Arabic, and colloquial Lebanese Arabic) in Catherine Temerson's translation of Amin Maalouf's *Origins* (2008). Deborah Smith's award-winning yet controversial translation of Han Kang's *The Vegetarian* (2016) invited deeper considerations of the political implications of the translation process and pushed students to ponder possible evaluative criteria in assessing works of translation, particularly in relation to issues of representation and the kinds of misunderstandings and mistranslations that might arise. Based on these discussions, we reached a consensus regarding the need to reorient discourse and inquiry from the perceived quality of translations (e.g., good, accurate, stylistically favorable, readable, etc.) to the kind of (linguistic, ethnic, and racial) ideologies, cultural frames, historical mentalities, values, and knowledge systems that get activated, reinforced, muted, or erased and, more important, the effects these translations had on the individuals, communities, and contexts they engaged with and emerged from. This heightened sensitivity to the social materiality of translation choices and the need for more nuanced reader response came in handy in the final translation workshops that required students to constructively critique one another's work.

After developing a better understanding of the discursive negotiations necessary for making particular translation choices and the stakes involved, students were ready to try their hands at translation. Over the course of the quarter, students engaged in short in-class translation activities in pairs or small groups and then reported to the entire class. These exercises progressed from exploring the nuanced meaning beneath the apparent simplicity of words or phrases central to students' pedagogical and/or scholarly interests to crafting translations of journal-article abstracts into the languages students were comfortable with to conducting comparative analyses of brief passages from competing English translations. These translation activities were an opportunity for students to synthesize their growing theoretical and practical knowledge of translation while honing their language competence. Along with the discussion of course readings and in-depth analyses of translations and translators' commentaries, these workshop-style activities offered preparation for a more complex undertaking, an article-length English translation of a non-English work of scholarship (or literature).

For their final project, students composed a substantial translation of research in their specialization area published in a language other than English and a robust translators' commentary (2,000–2,500 words). In addition to explaining the significance ([socio]historically, generically, theoretically, geographically, etc.) of the chosen work for their field of study in the written commentaries on their work, students retraced the pathways of decision-making and closely analyzed the translation approaches and strategies they adopted in response to specific moments of translatability and untranslatability. Aside from my Arabic and French language abilities, I did not share many of the languages in my students' repertoires, so the translation commentaries—often used as learner-centered and process-based assessment tools in many translation degrees and programs at European universities (Shih 2018; Venuti 2017)—were extremely informative. In fact, as hybrid writing genres involving both reflective narration and persuasion, these commentaries helped make visible students' dynamic identities as novice translators and their micro- and macrolevel negotiations of the norms and conventions of language, writing, and translation.

There was considerable leeway with regard to the scope and focus of the accompanying commentaries. For instance, two students who produced translations of Spanish scholarship emerging from Colombia and Brazil respectively on diverse issues pertaining to writing education focused more narrowly on the translation challenges presented by discipline-specific and context-specific terminologies, their definitions, uses, and theoretical groundings. Another student, who translated one of Bruno Perreau's book chapters, framed his translation conceptually in the way it identified a "transatlantic resonance" between US and Francophone queer studies scholars and at times deliberately intervened in the "exclusionary politics" that privileged the ideas and perspectives of "queer theorists over queer of color critiques," thereby "broadening the scope of Perreau's claims within the framework of a US-based context." Other students attempting more literary-oriented renderings (e.g., Palestinian novelist Jabra Ibrahim Jabra's *Al bi'r* [*The First Well*] from Arabic, Marie Ndiaye's French play *Papa doit manger* [*Papa Must Eat*], Judith Hermann's short story "Rote korallen" ["Scarlet Coral"] from German, and Anton Chekhov's "Дама с собачкой" [Lady with a Dog] from Russian, to name a few) found tackling their analyses from a comparative angle useful, thereby highlighting intersections and divergences with other translations in global circulation.

The final week of classes was dedicated to interactive translation workshops. Students were asked to read working drafts of one another's translations at home and offer in-depth feedback. Once again, following a translingual approach to translation, I instructed students to withhold judgements in their written and oral feedback about the quality of the translations and focus instead on translation choices and their rhetorical function. Though demanding and time consuming, these workshops turned out to be very productive. Students greatly appreciated the multiple perspectives and constructive discussions of their translations. After peer and instructor feedback, students were ready to take a stronger hand in the translation process, making necessary modifications, additions, deletions, and clarifications in the translation itself, or, alternatively, in supplementary textual materials, such as footnotes, explanatory notes, or the translator's commentary. It is through this immersive learning experience, which at times intensified moments of friction, uncertainty, and untranslatability, that students started to recognize that achieving equivalence, superior accuracy, and perfection was an unattainable ideal since, in the words of Indian and postcolonial translation theorist A. K. Ramanujan (1985), "translations . . . are never finished, only abandoned" (quoted in Dharwadker 1999, 116).

Some of the most productive conversations in this seminar were surrounding the potential value and place of translation practice in the teaching of writing, language, rhetoric, and/or literature. Since the majority of the seminar participants were current or past TAs in the department or its writing program, I dedicated several sessions throughout the quarter to investigating how some of the translation competencies developed in this class might connect to the specific outcomes of the undergraduate courses they taught. We discussed how samples of their teaching materials (e.g., writing-assignment or project prompts, in-class activities, syllabi, lesson plans, etc.) might serve as fertile grounds for incorporating translation-related components. Some of the difficult questions we tackled together were, What are the risks and rewards for teachers and students interested in enacting readings/teachings/compositions of translated texts that foreground the material labor of translation? What locally specific political, socioeconomic, cultural, ideological, and pragmatic considerations might influence one's decision to fully pursue this line of thinking and work? In the context of one's academic life and work, what available and/or possible resources, collaborations, and partnerships at a local, regional, national, and/or international level might one capitalize on to help materialize and enhance translation-oriented pedagogical initiatives?

I designed this graduate seminar as a hub for the dialectical dynamic among translation theory, practice, and pedagogy, but in retrospect, I realize the crucial aspect of publishing in relation to this structure was an unfortunate omission. As this course piqued students' interests in translation, some of them reached out for guidance on where they might take their nonprofessional translations next. Reworking the current curriculum with an eye toward the nature and demands of the translation publishing market would surely be beneficial in future course offerings.

Needless to say, one of the challenging aspects of teaching this seminar was scaffolding translation practices in a way that accommodated students' vastly different linguistic backgrounds and levels of preparation while at the same time facilitating interactions surrounding these practices in the pursuit of mutual intelligibility, whether in small-group or whole-class discussions. Since the majority of the class (myself included) were not familiar with one another's linguistic resources, but still needed to make sense of one another's work and engage with it at a deep critical level, I presented the technique of *back translation* usually adopted in translation textbooks targeting the wider, nonprofessional audience. As a basic form of rewriting deliberately utilized to make foreign-language usages more comprehensible and aid with cross-lingual comparisons at the morphological, lexical, and/or syntactic level, back translation refers to loosely approximate word-for-word translation into English, the global lingua franca. Though "theoretically unsound and far from ideal" (Baker 2018, 7), back-translation was a necessary and practical compromise in our coursework. For instance, in their translator's commentaries, students provided specific examples from their non-English-language texts immediately followed by their English back translations to better illustrate intermediary steps as they moved between their chosen texts and translations of them.

Another language-related constraint I had to come to terms with was the hypercentrality of English as the default translating or translated language in the field of translation studies more broadly and in a course housed by the English department. These unavoidable contradictions in matters of curriculum design became the topic of open explorations: the ways the readings and coursework favored a counterhegemonic translingual stance that foregrounded the multidirectionality of translation within and across languages other than English while, paradoxically, still affirming the hegemonic status of English as the metalanguage for translation. In fact, the seminar's necessary focus on translation from or into English allowed students to develop a nuanced sense of the complex institutional hierarchies and arrangements that factored into Anglophone translation.

Despite these challenges and the compartmentalizations of "disciplines, languages and programs" (Gentil 2018, 119) we were all navigating in this course, it is through the crosspollination of translation that we realized how much our shared interests in the politically and ideologically laden composition, evolution, and movement of texts across real or imagined borders brought us all together. Several seminar participants indicated in their coursework, unsolicited email correspondences, and/ or final course evaluations how a strong focus on translation theory and practice in this course contributed significantly to their learning and development as writers and teacher-scholars. The exceptionally complex negotiations this course demanded of students in both coursework and discussions helped foster their metalinguistic awareness and offered a unique chance for them to tap into and develop their existing language resources with increased confidence and in ways they had not thought about formally in the context of their research and teaching. In a way, this class enabled some students to confront a lingering attitude—that may well be unconscious—toward their foreign-language competence as imperfect, insufficient, or irrelevant to what truly mattered in graduate study. As one student wrote in an anonymous end-of-the-course evaluation, "This course allowed me to revisit my language skills and draw upon my own research interests, in addition to learning a great deal from the incredible readings that attend to translation from a variety of disciplinary perspectives." "I am walking away from this class with a richer understanding of translation, language, and writing among other things. My thinking was very stretched," read another student evaluation. In a written rationalization of his translation processes, a second-year PhD student who had studied French for four years in high school and completed a minor degree in French during his undergraduate studies described how "incredibly surprised" he was by his "reading comprehension skills" and writing abilities across national, disciplinary, and linguistic contexts, especially knowing he "had not utilized [his] linguistic resources in the language for nearly five years prior to signing up for this course." As I have tried to illustrate, coalescing around the centrality of translation theories and practices to the labor of producing, interpreting, and circulating writing helped facilitate translingual awareness and positioning, irrespective of whether or not everyone in this seminar shared the same repertoire of disciplinary and linguistic knowledge.

REWORKING TRANSLATION IN GRADUATE STUDIES: ONGOING CHALLENGES AND OPPORTUNITIES

The complex cross-language work that evolved out of the translation seminar served as an opportunity to gradually bring a translingual mindset to the attention of several directors of graduate studies (DGS) and help consolidate the elusive and contested relationship between the program's language requirement and its core curricula. Like most English graduate programs at peer institutions, the UW PhD language requirement has become a box to check off on degree audits rather than a crucial component of graduate students' academic preparation.

At the end of the 2014 translation seminar, though I had hoped for an "in-house" acknowledgment of the value of the translingual-oriented translations students produced, the then DGS agreed to reassess several students' final translation projects in consultation with colleagues in modern-language departments and decide on a case-by-case basis whether or not these translations demonstrated sufficient language competence to satisfy the requirement. I continued conversations on the need to strengthen the language requirement with the succeeding DGS, but dedicating time and resources for reforming other curriculum benchmarks like exams and the dissertation took precedence. A few weeks before I taught the translation seminar again in winter 2018, the acceptance of my proposal by another DGS to count a grade of A- or higher for the seminar as equivalent as fulfilling the language requirement came as an unexpected but much welcome surprise to me and my students.

In the following year, as rethinking the language requirement was among the new DGS's top agenda items, I helped reveal the many problematic manifestations of a monolingualist paradigm in its structure, such as the idealization of native-like proficiency in another language, a before-comprehensive-exams policy that inhibited sophisticated language knowledge, and the mechanical view of translation the language exams adopted and reinforced. After introducing colleagues on the graduate studies committee to recent scholarship in foreign-language education and translingual writing,[2] I presented examples from the translation seminar discussed above to demonstrate how translation practice can contribute to broadening conceptualizations of language learning and competence and activating the PhD language requirement's potential value for graduate research and teaching. What began as an individual effort to address the real problems with meeting the language requirement a considerable number of graduate students were experiencing has now turned into a program-wide initiative to mobilize graduate students' existing linguistic and epistemic resources. It took seven long years and persistent negotiations with different DGSs and graduate faculty to finally prove the worth of this endeavor.

The revamped language requirement on the program website is currently framed using translingualism as an organizing principle under which language learning and translating are conceived of as closely "intertwined and mutually enriching" practices (cf. Kramsch 2010; Laviosa 2014, 89):

> The UW Department of English language requirement reflects the importance of translingual, cross-cultural competencies to academic work. . . . [which] invite . . . both second (and sometimes third) language knowledge and, equally important, the ability to work across languages.
>
> We therefore encourage students to consider second language knowledge as something to be *used* in their research and (if applicable) their pedagogy, rather than just something to be *certified*. Increased attention in their research areas to scholarship emerging outside the Anglo-American sphere and published in languages other than English can indeed enrich intellectual debate and engagement in the humanities. (University of Washington n.d.)

The revised policy offers students the opportunity to explore how their evolving language knowledge and translation practices can shape and take shape within the growing translingual and transnational connections in various domains of their academic career. In this sense, students can meet the requirement through the successful completion of an individualized translation project either as an independent study, under the supervision of their doctoral committee, or as part of the translation seminar, which is now offered biannually. Reflecting and advancing students' scholarly and/or pedagogical interests, these translation projects are evaluated on the basis of demonstrating

- comprehension of texts and their specific (ideological, [geo]political, historical, economic, and sociocultural) contexts
- awareness of and sensitivity to linguistic elements (syntax, diction, ambiguity, idiomatic expressions, register, cultural references, etc.) that make literal translation impossible
- ability to identify and critically reflect on one or more of the central problems or challenges posed by the task of translation and the ways the translator opted to resolve them.

In its current form, the language requirement engages the friction between the translingual orientations it aspires to and the persistent monolingualism that continues to guide its structure and define graduate English studies. Paradoxically, the newly revised requirement still preserves the conventional options of demonstrating "native-speaker ability in another language" or the language-proficiency exams administered and assessed by modern-language departments that have turned the requirement into a nuisance in the first place in the eyes of students and their supervising faculty. Though my colleagues and I were not entirely successful in changing the monolingual straitjackets of the conventional options of satisfying the language requirement, the translingual-oriented translation work the current requirement promotes moves in that direction. After all, the postmonolingual condition of twenty-first-century academic work and life we and our graduate students are constantly operating under is "full of contradictions and does not proceed smoothly" (Yildiz 2012, 201) towards a translingual paradigm in which the languages and knowledges in one's repertoire may be dynamically interwoven in meaningful, sustained ways. However, the unique logic and labor of translation that might (and should) be accentuated and disseminated in graduate education can help to begin imagining this different structure.

Ideally, as Bruce Horner notes in his contribution to this collection, translingual engagements with language and language heterogeneity in academic writing would not take place solely through separate, supplemental projects, courses, or special-topics graduate seminars in one's own or allied department. After all, such structures create a false sense among students that the translingual competence and language relations these alternative options strive to promote are distinct from "the 'real work' of graduate studies" (Kilfoil 2015, 437). Translation must be a constant and integral component of the graduate rhetoric and composition curriculum in order to successfully work to "problematize [and transform] taken-for-granted assumptions that devalue" students' working language knowledge and cross-language capabilities, construct those as having no effect on their identity formation as writing researchers and teachers, and contribute to "the privileging of English and knowledge in that language" (Singh 2020, 24).

Working on this chapter amidst cascading crises—from a global COVID-19 pandemic to manifestations of systemic anti-Black racism and other sociopolitical challenges to US-American democracy—has brought to the fore the importance of linguistic and cultural mediation with the intention of textual, intertextual, and interpersonal meaning construction. In this globalized yet conflict-ridden world where lives, voices, and ways of knowing and being in and through language are increasingly at stake, where appealing to single, local, and mainstream constituencies alone is no longer enough for socially just and peaceful relations, translingual-oriented translation across opaque relations of difference must become central to our and our graduate students' research, teaching, administration, and public engagements.

NOTES

1. Despite foregrounding a translanguaging model and emerging from the Canadian context, Gentil's work intersects with the tenets of translingualism and resonates well with the US experience.
2. I am indebted to Carrie Kilfoil for suggesting readings successful in gaining uptake from faculty outside rhetoric and composition proper.

REFERENCES

Baker, Mona. 2007. "Reframing Conflict in Translation." *Social Semiotics* 17 (2): 158–69.

Baker, Mona. 2018. *In Other Words: A Coursebook on Translation.* London: Routledge.

Bassnett, Susan. 2011. *Reflections on Translation.* Bristol: Multilingual Matters.

Bassnett, Susan, and Peter Bush. 2007. *The Translator as Writer.* New York: Continuum.

Bassnett, Susan, and Harish Trivedi, eds. 1999. *Postcolonial Translation: Theory and Practice.* London: Routledge.

Booth, Marilyn. 2008. "Translator v. Author." *Translation Studies* 1 (2): 197–211.

Bou Ayash, Nancy. 2019. *Toward Translingual Realities in Composition: (Re)working Local Language Representations and Practices.* Logan: Utah State University Press.

Bou Ayash, Nancy. 2020. "Critical Translation and Paratextuality: Translingual and Anti-Racist Pedagogical Possibilities for Multilingual Writers." *Composition Forum* 44. https://compositionforum.com/issue/44/critical-translation.php.

Dharwadker, Vinay. 1999. "A. K. Ramanujan's Theory and Practice of Translation." In *Postcolonial Translation,* 114–40. London: Routledge.

Gentil, Guillaume. 2018 "Modern Languages, Bilingual Education, and Translation Studies: The Next Frontiers in WAC/WID Research and Instruction?" *Across the Disciplines* 15 (3): 114–29.

Gonzales, Laura. 2018. *Sites of Translation.* Ann Arbor: University of Michigan Press.

Guix, Juan. 2007. "The Translator in Aliceland: On Translating *Alice in Wonderland* into Spanish." In *The Translator as Writer,* edited by Susan Bassnett and Peter Bush, 95–105. London: Routledge.

Hatim, Basil, and Ian Mason. 1997. *The Translator as Communicator.* London: Routledge.

Horner, Bruce, Min-Zhan Lu, Jacqueline Royster, and John Trimbur. 2011. "Language Difference: Toward a Translingual Approach." *College English* 73 (3): 299–317.

Horner, Bruce, and Laura Tetreault. 2016. "Translation as (Global) Writing." *Composition Studies* 44 (1): 13–30.

Horner, Bruce, and Laura Tetreault. 2017. *Crossing Divides: Exploring Translingual Writing Pedagogies and Programs.* Logan: Utah State University Press.

Kang, Han. 2016. *The Vegetarian: A Novel.* Translated by Deborah Smith. New York: Hogarth.

Kilfoil, Carrie. 2015. "Beyond the 'Foreign' Language Requirement: From a Monolingual to a Translingual Ideology in Rhetoric and Composition Graduate Education." *Rhetoric Review* 34 (4): 426–44.

Kramsch, Claire. 2010. "Theorizing Translingual/Transcultural Competence." In *Critical and Intercultural Theory and Language Pedagogy,* edited by Glenn Levine and Alison Philipps, 15–31. Boston: Heinle.

Laviosa, Sara. 2014. *Translation and Language Education: Pedagogic Approaches Explored.* London: Routledge.

Lewis, Anthony. 2005. "Language and Translation: Contesting Conventions." In *In Translation,* edited by Paul St-Pierre and Prafulla Karr, 15–24. Amsterdam: John Benjamins Publishing Company.

Maalouf, Amin. 2008. *Origins: A Memoir.* Translated by Catherine Temerson. New York: Farrar, Straus, and Giroux.

Menon, Nirmala. 2016. *Remapping the Indian Postcolonial Canon: Remap, Reimagine and Retranslate.* London: Palgrave Macmillan.

Modern Language Association. n.d. "Foreign Languages and Higher Education: New Structures for a Changed World." Report of the MLA Ad Hoc Committee on Foreign Languages. https://www.mla.org/Resources/Guidelines-and-Data/Reports-and-Profes sional-Guidelines/Teaching-Enrollments-and-Programs/Foreign-Languages-and -Higher-Education-New-Structures-for-a-Changed-World.

Oxford English Dictionary. 2014. "Translation." *Oxford English Dictionary.* Oxford: Oxford University Press.

Pennycook, Alastair. 2010. *Language as Local Practice.* London: Routledge.

Pratt, Mary Louis. 1991. "Arts of the Contact Zones." *Profession* 33–40.

Ramanujan, A. K. 1985. *Poems of Love and War: From the Eight Anthologies and the Ten Long Poems of Classical Tamil.* New York: Columbia University Press.

Shih, Claire. 2018. "Translation Commentary Re-examined in the Eyes of Translator Educators at British Universities." *Journal of Specialised Translation* 30: 291–311.

Shuttleworth, Mark. 2017. *Dictionary of Translation Studies.* London: Routledge.

Singh, Michael. 2020. "Migration and Decolonizing Doctoral Education through Knowledge Translation." In *Migration, Education and Translation,* edited by Vivienne Anderson and Henry Johnson, 13–26. London: Routledge.

St-Pierre, Paul. "Introduction." 2005. *In Translation: Reflections, Refractions, and Transformations,* by Paul St-Pierre and Prafulla Karr, 1–10. Amsterdam: John Benjamins Publishing Company.

St-Pierre, Paul, and Prafulla Karr. 2005. *In Translation: Reflections, Refractions, and Transformations.* Amsterdam: John Benjamins Publishing Company.

Tardy, Christine. 2017. "Crossing, or Creating Divides? A Plea for Transdisciplinary Scholarship." In *Crossing Divides,* 181–89. Logan: Utah State University Press.

University of Washington Department of English. n.d. "MA/PhD Degree Requirements: Language Requirement." Accessed September 12, 2020. https://english.washington .edu/maphd-degree-requirements-language-requirement.

Venuti, Lawrence. 2002. *The Scandals of Translation: Towards an Ethics of Difference.* London: Routledge.

Venuti, Lawrence. 2017. *Teaching Translation: Programs, Courses, Pedagogies.* London: Routledge.

Wang, Xiqiao. 2020. "Becoming Multilingual Writers through Translation." *Research in the Teaching of English* 54 (3): 206–30.

Yildiz, Yasemin. 2012. *Beyond the Mother Tongue: The Postmonolingual Condition.* New York: Fordham University Press.

6

COMPARATIVE RHETORIC AND THE TRANSLINGUAL FUTURE OF MENTORSHIP

Michelle Zaleski and Xiaoye You

Transnationalism is a framework within rhetoric and composition that encourages students to transcend linguistic, ethnic, and national boundaries by promoting a view of literacy as a dynamic material social practice. Such a move "from the confines of national borders towards transnational connectivities" requires composition scholars to learn about writing research and pedagogy beyond their national and linguistic boundaries (Horner, NeCamp, and Donahue 2011, 287). In rhetorical studies, the attempt to study less represented rhetorical traditions has constituted a move towards transnationalism. Courses in comparative rhetoric have become one way the transnational framework has been adopted and encouraged within graduate studies in rhetoric and composition. These courses can focus on the act of reading other rhetorical traditions, as well as the methods required by such work. This chapter attempts to suggest how such courses can also become an opportunity for scholars to practice translingual methods of teaching and learning that engage both student and teacher in rewriting the cosmopolitan potential of rhetoric and composition's transnational turn (You 2016, 2018). Translingualism is a practice that breaks down the barriers between languages and peoples by acknowledging communication transcends words and involves diverse semiotic resources in meaning making (Canagarajah 2013a). However, we argue, translingualism must become more than a language practice if we are to overcome the static, national confines of monolingualism. That is, translingual practice is essential to the transnational future of rhetoric and composition, but only when it works at the level of disposition. Translingualism can provide a pathway to transcend the national framework and realize a more dynamic, transnational ideal of interconnectivity when it reframes not only how we use

https://doi.org/10.7330/9781646423262.c006

language but also how we think, act, and respond to each other, that is, when it destabilizes our conception of rhetorical agency and fosters a more cosmopolitan sensibility within ourselves.

This chapter uses the experience of a teacher and student in a graduate course in comparative rhetorics to demonstrate the ways translingual practice mediates the field's movement from the national towards the transnational. Such a course, on the one hand, adopts a transnational framework by including the study of underrepresented rhetorical traditions and cultures in the graduate curriculum (Donahue 2009). Our reflections, on the other hand, demonstrate it is not enough that graduate students alone be exposed to scholarship that transcends boundaries. These courses must also question how it is that we relate to texts and to each other. Rather than focusing on the necessary texts that make up a syllabus on comparative rhetoric, this chapter outlines the relationships to texts, rhetorical traditions, and authority such a course can foster by outlining how practicing translingual mentorship rewrites the relationship between novice and expert in graduate education.

This chapter begins with a review of translingualism and aligns this research with the objectives and methodologies of comparative rhetoric. Then, detailing the experience of a teacher and student in a comparative rhetoric graduate course, this chapter illustrates the possibilities a translingual approach may bring to the study of comparative rhetoric. Bringing these two perspectives together reveals the central role mentorship and collaboration must play in the formation of translingual dispositions that can sustain graduate students as they pursue transnational work. Graduate students must be mentored in new ways, ways that can help them overcome the field's monolingualist and nationalistic history. Such a move necessarily asks graduate faculty to give up the usual flow of authority that comes with this inheritance and equip students with skills that transcend their classroom and sustain work across borders.

THE TRANSNATIONAL IS TRANSLINGUAL

The concept of translingualism emerged out of a desire to destabilize a once tacit monolingual paradigm in rhetoric and composition with an explicit policy of multilingualism (Horner 2010). Unexamined processes of nationalism and colonialism previously erased the complex history of both the English language and English education (Canagarajah 2006; Trimbur 2008). Because language difference is mediated by global capitalism as well as colonialism, the renegotiation of language is one method of resistance to the uneven processes of globalization (Lu

2004). From this perspective, teachers should not only provide students with methods for using language as a resource but should work to create critical writers who understand and intentionally use language to negotiate their position and power (Canagarajah 2002). For student *and* teacher, we argue translingualism can act as a tool to foster a more cosmopolitan disposition within the framework of transnationalism.

A translingual pedagogy of negotiation teaches students to understand language as a process of sedimentation they participate in even when they are acting to reproduce more of the same (Lu and Horner 2013). It asks students to understand and reflect on the process of envoicing, recontextualization, interaction, and entextualization that make a translingual text successful (Canagarajah 2013b). Rather than learning how to reproduce an autonomous form of grammar to control language, which scholars have demonstrated does not translate in transnational, translingual contexts (Baca 2009; Pollock 2006; Pratt 1991), students must learn how to manipulate the resources around them. And as Jay Jordan (2014) suggests, this means students must take into account resources that might not seem readily symbolic. Students and scholars alike must consider what exactly is a resource for communication, or more simply, what makes for communication. Such a reorientation to language rewrites not only how we do language but changes the very way we relate to language.

This reorientation is why scholars like Suresh Canagarajah (2013a) emphasize translingualism as a way to *approach* or *practice* literacy. This is a new kind of literacy that demands performative competencies, as Alastair Pennycook (2010) argues. Literacy as performance means language is made and remade in every new interaction. Literacy is coconstituted by writer and reader within meaning-making ecologies bound by neither time nor space, always in a process of becoming (Guerrattaz and Johnston 2013). As Jan Blommaert's (2013) work on sociolinguistic landscapes suggests, there is no synchrony to be had in this model. Rather, different timescales exist at once as language evolves and meaning is recontextualized from place to place. Such a model of literacy, in which performative competency is measured by the ability to negotiate, values language as an improvised rather than a memorized performance. For rhetoric and composition, this model means not only teaching students how to negotiate meaning making across traditionally recognized sociocultural boundaries but also teaching them to question their reliance upon the security of such constructs for their own rhetorical agency.

This emphasis on literacy as a translingual practice is only the beginning, then. A translingual reorientation to meaning making requires not only a change in approach but also a change of mindset. Bruce Horner, Min-Zhan Lu, Jacqueline Jones Royster, and John Trimbur (2011) write that taking a translingual approach is not about accruing languages or linguistic resources but rather "it is about the disposition of openness and inquiry that people take toward language and language differences" (311). In its emphasis on approach, in its focus on encouraging a particular disposition towards literacy, and in its attempt to foster skills of negotiation rather than the uptake of particular linguistic patterns, translingual literacy is important for the way it reorients our relationship to the outside world and in the process reorients the self in its relationship to the other. This approach "pulls the subjective ground from under composers," rewriting the agency and authority of writers as they begin to understand their relationship to and dependence upon the affordances that make meaning possible (Jordan 2014, 375). Writers must begin to make themselves "permeable" to their surroundings as they learn to negotiate meaning and transform language (375).

By reframing how we understand language, a translingual approach provides concrete ways of thinking, acting, and responding to each other that foster a more cosmopolitan sensibility within ourselves (You 2016). Translingualism provides an avenue for realizing the ideals embodied in transnationalism, deconstructing the national framework that we have come to depend on and that often structures how we approach our students (Lu 1994). The easy translation of a transnational syllabus into student practice cannot be taken for granted (Zheng 2017). Translingual practice is required of teachers as well as students, an important consideration in crafting a more critical graduate education (Micciche and Carr 2011). Even "small, intentional decisions" towards a translingual orientation in education affect student attitude, which in turn is integral to subverting the hierarchy of novice and expert that too often structures both language and school (Kimball 2015). Such teaching rejects indoctrination and instead becomes a practice that depends on collaboration, openness, and a commitment to communication as border-crossing work (79). In its emphasis on the doing of language, in learning and teaching as practice, translingualism gives us the tools to craft such a cosmopolitan orientation towards language that can resist the limitations of a nationalistic framework. In its emphasis on rewriting the rhetorical canon as transnational, the comparative rhetoric course challenges the traditional canon of graduate education. This course is one possible place to realize the cosmopolitan possibility of translingual, transnational graduate education.

REORIENTING COMPARATIVE RHETORIC AS TRANSLINGUAL

While rhetoric has historically positioned itself within the liberal arts tradition of the West, as Roberta Binkley (2009) points out, comparative rhetoric moves beyond the West to embrace rhetoric as a transnational enterprise. By seriously considering the ethical implications of any attempt to represent other cultures and by reflecting on possible methodologies for such a venture, the field of comparative rhetoric has been able to move past initial failed attempts to catalog cultural logics. Over the last two decades, comparative rhetoric has instead emerged as a way to decenter the rhetorical tradition. By revealing blind spots within the canon, it opens up new "ways of seeing, being, and making knowledge" (69). In this sense, comparative rhetoric takes translingualism one step further by questioning how these new definitions of language change the way we see the world. Given this emphasis, comparative rhetoric has the ability to facilitate translingual practice as a method for fostering the cosmopolitan disposition that makes transnational connection possible.

Comparative rhetoric attempts to define the cultural bases of discursive power and acts as a strategy for engaging other cultures and discourses, yet it emphasizes comparing reflexively, dialogically, and openly (Hum and Lyon 2008). LuMing Mao (2013) urges scholars to move beyond the emic and etic in the practice of comparative rhetoric by developing "new terms of engagement that can capture the contested" (214–15). He theorizes incongruity in a way that recontextualizes rhetoric in relation. Other scholars of comparative rhetoric like Scott Richard Lyons, Bo Wang, Xiaoye You, and Keith Lloyd have all anticipated the global turn in rhetoric and composition (Hesford 2006). Each provides important ways of approaching the transnational future of the field by emphasizing the contingency (Lyons 2010), impurity and hybridity (Wang 2013), adaptation and change (You 2010), and ultimately collaborative nature of rhetoric when it is practiced beyond the Western tradition (Lloyd 2011). The work of these scholars is important not just for the new rhetorical traditions they uncover but for the way they challenge our very notion of what rhetoric can be.

It is the transnational work of comparative rhetoric that illuminates how translingual practice changes how we use language and how this change affects us. Calling for a transnational feminist approach to comparative rhetoric, Wang's research (2013) pulls together past and present China to create a place from which to stand, in this case to understand the Chinese women of her past. She interrogates the very link between thought and dwelling to draw attention to the coincidental mimesis with rhetorical history she experienced in a walk through modern China.

Noticing her research in the beauty advertisements that surround her, Wang experiences the same collapse of time and space that anchors Blommaert's (2013) theory of sociolinguistic landscapes and is captured in a similar walk, in this case his walk across a zebra crossing in his hometown of Antwerp, Belgium. When placed alongside one another, both create a way to understand how meaning is reworked across cultures and how space and time reconstitute language as a practice. Each scholar uses their research to change our definition of language or rhetoric. These new definitions depend on the relationship between meaning making and our world. They collapse history into the present and use this different perspective on time to create understanding. This approach changes their relationship to their research and in the process reworks their standpoint, that is, their disposition. They show how translingual and comparative rhetoric scholars are pursuing work, separately, that changes how we think we know meaning making occurs. But both challenge the way we do research. They construct new rhetorics from the ground up that help us understand how language moves across time and space by bringing together history and ethnography, past and present, what is spoken and what is read, and most of all, what is neither. In combination, they reveal the value of bringing together comparative rhetoric and translingualism to challenge not only how we do research in rhetoric and composition but also how we see ourselves.

As this review demonstrates, comparative rhetoric is already translingual. Graduate education in comparative rhetoric first and foremost encourages students to develop an awareness of their limitations and biases. Citing Linda Alcoff, Sue Hum and Arabella Lyon (2008) suggest that those who are interested in doing comparative research must learn to speak *with* rather than *for* others. They encourage scholars to listen first and resist the urge to speak—to interrogate their own position and embrace accountability, weighing the effects of their decision to speak. Hum and Lyon make clear that "the quest for meaning, however, cannot be limited to the standpoints within each disparate culture; pragmatically, they must be in dialogue" (15). Such a change in perspective reorients our independence as scholars and reminds us of our dependence on others. This makes collaboration across contexts imperative and brings us back to cosmopolitanism.

While comparative rhetoric emphasizes self-reflexive research methods to encourage more cosmopolitan research practices in the study of other cultures, practicing translingualism provides another way. Carrie Kilfoil (2015; 2018) advocates for an emphasis on linguistic difference and exposure to other rhetorical traditions in graduate education. In reaching beyond this emphasis on subject matter towards translingual practices, we better face, as a discipline, "the forces shaping current work in rhetoric and composition and the effects of its work in return, globally and locally" (Horner and Lu 2010, 288). We can better foster cosmopolitan dispositions, that is. Translingual practice encourages the same collaborative, decentered, and cosmopolitan approach Hum and Lyon argue for. In order to establish a sustainable transnational future for our field, this approach is required of teachers as well as students. In the next section, we suggest how a return to translingualism as a method in teaching comparative rhetoric provides concrete ways of rethinking scholarly training through transnational coursework.

A GRADUATE SEMINAR IN COMPARATIVE RHETORIC

We were brought together as teacher, Xiaoye, and student, Michelle, by a graduate seminar offered in the spring of 2015. The course identified the emergence of comparative rhetoric as taking place after the Cold War as a response to the transnational flows of people and cultural products in globalization. The emergence was part of general trends in rhetorical studies to interrogate and broaden dominant rhetorical paradigms and to study non-Euro-American rhetorical traditions on their own terms and in their own contexts. As comparative rhetoric engages different, non-Euro-American rhetorical practices across time, place, and space, it shines a new light on dominant rhetorics through a comparative lens. Situated in this context, the seminar aimed to further contribute to this comparative turn by focusing on both the methodologies and practices of comparative rhetoric.

The class began by first connecting comparative rhetoric to contrastive rhetoric and intercultural rhetoric. Thanks to Robert Kaplan's work in the 1960s and, in particular, to his insight that different cultures have different rhetorical tendencies, attention to, and interest in, non-Euro-American rhetorical practices began to emerge in English studies, though the focus then was largely limited to helping understand and improve the discursive practices of ESL students in the United States. The class then explored, among other issues, ongoing tensions underlying the pursuit of comparative rhetoric between the disciplinary desire to search for a "Theory of Rhetoric" (Kennedy 1997) and the need of any comparative endeavor to develop local grids of intelligibility, and between an appeal to the dominant paradigms of logic and a call for aesthetic, analogical, or alternative frames of ordering (Hall and Ames 1995). In class, we investigated what it means to represent "the native's point of view" and to search for a "third" in comparative work (Mao 2003). We considered such questions as (1) How does knowledge get produced and disseminated at points of comparison?, (2) What are the possibilities and impossibilities of studying the Other on its own terms and in its own context?, and (3) How can the art of recontextualization serve as a productive heuristic in the global contact zone where boundaries of all kinds are being blurred, conflated, and/or recreated.

THE GRADUATE STUDENT PERSPECTIVE

I enrolled in Xiaoye's seminar at the beginning of my doctoral graduate coursework. The course began by questioning the field of comparative rhetoric, setting the tone for a semester of inquiry that, rather than taking comparative study for granted, questioned the practical, ethical, and epistemological possibility of such an enterprise. The course encouraged constant reflection on our attitudes as students and researchers with readings that fostered self-reflexivity and a community that practiced mentorship translingually. This course became the foundation of my dissertation, not because we read international texts directly related to my area of interest but because it encouraged a new kind of relationship to my work.

A translingual orientation to mentorship encourages young scholars to explore beyond their expertise and think more creatively about themselves as global citizens. In a course on comparative rhetoric, this kind of mentorship means sitting with students as they grapple with what it means to rewrite the rhetorical tradition and how to account for the boundaries of time and place as they do so. In other words, translingual mentorship seeks to foster a cosmopolitan disposition within both student and teacher (You 2016). It works against assumptions about the Other by destabilizing the center of authority within ourselves. As You demonstrates, such a disposition is necessary for sustaining border-crossing work. It is at the heart of translingual practice in its ability to build these kinds of negotiation skills. Such an approach requires teachers to be open not only to coconstructing meaning but also to giving up a bit of their authority.

Xiaoye's mentorship proved essential to establishing the sincerity required for translingual mentorship. While taking this course, I found myself at a crossroads in my research. I had pursued several different projects during graduate school based on what I saw as my competing interests in qualitative international writing center research and South Asian studies. While these interests had come out of their past convergence in my life before graduate school, my ability to pursue both at the same time while living in central Pennsylvania had become more limited. Because of this, I had recently pursued a new research interest, a project on Jesuit rhetorical education in the United States. Our seminar made me all the more aware of the ways this shift in the direction of my research had drawn me back into a Western framework and seemingly away from what had brought me to graduate school in the first place: my experience teaching in South Asia. Yet it remained true that my research into Jesuit rhetoric had produced genuine, new insights. During another course, I realized my interest in Jesuit rhetoric was rooted in a desire to understand my upbringing. But, I did not yet know how to pursue such a personal subject. It felt like a risk. Xiaoye's guidance became invaluable. When I broached the idea of using this course to test the possibility of a project that bridged my interest in South Asia and the Jesuits, Xiaoye was curious. He questioned the relevance of my new research interest and the kind of contribution it could make to the field. Underneath these difficult questions, however, was a visible interest and "dialogical pedagogy" open to coconstructing meaning (Canagarajah 2013b, 45–46). Xiaoye's questions developed out of a genuine interest in me and my research. He sat. And he listened. His questions were critical but careful. They were invested. They demonstrated engagement and revealed his knowledge of my research and of me. He encouraged me to build on past experience he was already aware of and made connections between this new interest and past projects.

As my example demonstrates, a level playing field is essential to such translingual negotiations because it reconstructs our capacity to make meaning together. Based in a genuine desire to understand and learn from one another, such a dialogic calculus centers the cosmopolitan potential of translingual practice. It opens up the self to "exciting experiments where every normative 'Self' is willing to be rendered vulnerable by the gaze of the 'Other'" (Radhakrishnan 2009, 471). The ability to act differently and effect a change in our relationship to one another demonstrates the transnational potential of translingual mentorship. Translingual mentorship increases our capacity to work across borders. It changes how we relate to our work and how we make meaning *together*. In changing one, it changes the other. Such a change in the position of student and teacher, one that upsets the strict binary between novice and expert, roots collaboration at the heart of a course on comparative rhetoric by emphasizing the ability to learn together in order to build new ways of doing rhetoric. This kind of mentorship is imperative for comparative rhetoric, where new projects are defined by self-awareness and careful dialogue.

A translingual approach, therefore, asks us to understand student success and failure differently. As Lu and Horner (2013) suggest, moments of language use that defy normative standards become useful in the construction of meaning for the ways they encourage deliberate reflection and negotiation. Canagarajah and Yumi Matsumoto (2017) show how a translingual pedagogy requires different models of assessment aimed at fostering this kind of negotiation and rhetorical awareness. The project I turned in at the end of the semester failed in many ways. While I was building on three previous projects on the Jesuits, researching their work in India required me to become familiar with an entirely new geography. In becoming familiar with the terrain, new problems emerged. This project uncovered important points of tension in the Jesuit mission, but it was inconclusive. Instead of providing me with a tidy thesis I could forward in a final draft, this project revealed to me the limits of my perspective and the need to do more research. The project depended on one primary source in translation, and while it was in conversation with the field of comparative rhetoric, it needed to also be in conversation with studies in history, religious studies, and anthropology. Rather than dismissing the project as a failure, Xiaoye encouraged me to see it as a stepping stone. Assessment reframed as reception, a kind of rhetorical listening, is an ongoing process, dependent upon "sustained and protracted negotiations to achieve voice as an affect" (403). Failure, in this case, can be mobilized within graduate coursework to encourage reflection and to widen our framework beyond this one moment, one course—to draw attention to the need for comparative work to draw from other disciplines and a range of courses. I had to see my project as emergent and as in-process as language, and I needed to learn to discover rhetorical affordances that lay beyond the bounds of this one classroom.

Canagarajah's (2016) work emphasizes the ongoing nature of translanguaging, but its discussion of the ecological affordances in the classroom remains limited to familiar textual artefacts like course textbooks. Following the "mobility" turn (Faist 2013), we might seek to also consider how we can utilize translingual mentorship to encourage each other to work with texts beyond the classroom and "increase their [our] sensitivity to the spatio-temporal domains through which texts travel" (Canagarajah 2019, 15). In taking into account an alternative translingual orientation to space and time, these courses might be understood within wider ecologies and a timeline not strictly defined by the academic calendar.

After taking Xiaoye's comparative rhetoric course, I enrolled in a history class on religion and state in the early modern period the next semester. The semester after that, I took a course specifically studying

South Asia and began my study of Portuguese. Eventually, I travelled to archives in Italy, Great Britain, and Portugal, and I also began learning Tamil. These steps allowed me to work with more primary texts. I began to incorporate native voices and understand the ways Jesuit rhetoric converged with other rhetorical traditions in South Asia. That first course provided a way in. This project would take time, but I came to appreciate these preliminary steps for how they contributed to a long-term project. A translingual perspective on language sees the barriers between language as "porous" and "in constant revision" (Horner et al. 2011, 287). Such an orientation to language is built on understanding meaning as interactional. When language is understood to be negotiated, dependent on audience and speaker, meaning is achieved across interactions. Canagarajah (2013b) refers to this as "entextualization," in which a text is shaped in response to continuous negotiations that facilitate alignment between audience and speaker (59). Entextualization not only changes how we understand the role of texts in the production of meaning but also adds a spatiotemporal dimension to translingual practice that challenges how we might conceive of transnational graduate coursework. In my case, this meant being open to developing my project in the liminal spaces between and across courses. It meant identifying affordances—textual, personal and interpersonal, geographic, and financial—that could carry this project forward.

While working on this seminar paper under the guidance of Xiaoye, I began to see the resources in front of me I could use to pursue a transnational dissertation project from central Pennsylvania. The course became an important space for extending myself beyond the known and embracing experience and inexperience. This cosmopolitan attitude shaped the entire course. The class became a community, a place to acknowledge personal limitations and encourage each other to develop new, burgeoning areas of international expertise out of experiences we might have otherwise dismissed on our own. I tentatively began my project on Jesuit rhetoric in India. Another student who was hesitant about drawing from his childhood in Indonesia eventually developed a feminist project that revealed his familiarity with a culture and language yet to be included in rhetorical studies. When practiced through translingual mentorship, comparative rhetoric can open up graduate students to exploring beyond their expertise and thinking creatively about themselves as global citizens. This does not mean ignoring what is around us but instead developing an understanding of how to constructively operate within the limits of time and place to open up more transnational space within rhetoric and composition.

In reorienting me to my work in this way, Xiaoye allowed me to develop hubris in my scholarship. This became an invaluable skill for what later developed into a transnational, translingual project. In the work I later pursued across languages, disciplines, and national borders, I was continually confronted by my own limits. I was able to persist not because of any stubbornness but because of my ability to give in and recognize interdependence. I've now become resourceful in the way I have worked to build bridges. In one instance, this ability meant combining my curiosity over a transcription "error" with the expertise of a classicist scholar. In another instance, this meant recognizing both my privilege as an English speaker working in the international archive and the way such a privilege limited my ability to translanguage abroad with ease instead of embarrassment. This also has meant giving into that embarrassment and brazenly following curiosity that could otherwise be dismissed by an expert as commonplace. Xiaoye's mentorship was important not so much for the knowledge it conveyed as for the cosmopolitan attitude it instilled. His guidance was generative. It allowed me to recognize new translingual affordances and be open to developing still more.

THE TEACHER'S RESPONSE

In my interactions with students like Michelle during the comparative rhetoric seminar, I consciously or unconsciously practiced what we might call *translingual mentorship*. That is, I viewed mentoring as a dialogical process of coconstructing meaning in scholarly contexts as the teacher and student draw on diverse linguistic and cultural resources. As Michelle notes, I already knew something about her when she approached me about her term paper. When she applied to Penn State, I had a chance to read her personal statement. At that time, Michelle was teaching writing and directing a writing center at the Asian University for Women in Bangladesh. In her personal statement, she talked about her experience working there with a keen understanding of the complex relationship between her teaching as a Western-trained American and the region's colonial past. With two years of dedicated work in South Asia, undoubtedly Michelle had developed an understanding of rhetoric beyond the Western tradition. This translingual and transcultural understanding was an asset I believed she could draw on.

When we discussed her term paper, I asked about her dissertation. I understood she had just started her PhD program but thought whatever she produced in the course should be able to contribute to her dissertation. Based on my prior experience as a PhD student, I believed it would be more productive if the student developed a vision for their dissertation project and worked towards that goal through the seminar papers. For completing certain types of dissertations, such as historical studies, the all-but-dissertation period is simply too short. Asking her about her dissertation made sure that whatever I was going to say about her seminar paper would be consequential for her future.

When Michelle talked about a study of the Jesuits' educational work in South Asia, Japan, and South America for her dissertation, I listened, with both concern and excitement. On one hand, I was concerned that religion had not been a central focus in rhetoric and composition. It was often studied in the margins of the political, social, and cultural functions of public speaking and literacy practice. Would a dissertation focused on religion be welcomed in the field? Would Michelle be able to produce worthy scholarship in a less trodden area? On the other hand, I was excited about her topic. First, Michelle was a Catholic. Catholicism might provide her with both insights and impetus for her proposed work. Second, growing up in Communist China as an atheist, I knew very little about Catholicism and nothing about the Jesuits. Interacting with Christian friends over the years convinced me there was much to learn about the religious Other. Learning to speak across religions must be practiced in our scholarship. Third, I had limited knowledge about the South Asian rhetorical tradition, and I wanted to know more about it. My knowledge had mainly come from a few materials I read and taught (such as *The Bhagavad Gita* [Johnson 1994]; Oliver [1971]; Stroud [2004]). These texts examine rhetorical thinking as embodied in ancient Hindu scriptures but say little about rhetoric in secular institutions such as politics and education. My concerns and excitement undergirded my ensuing interaction with Michelle, related not only to her seminar paper but also to her dissertation.

Our further conversations on her seminar paper seemed to help her narrow down the scope of her dissertation. She decided to only focus on the Jesuits' educational work in India. For her seminar paper, Michelle wrote about the missionary work of Francis Xavier in India by examining his letters and instructions. She suggested his work enacts a philosophy of rhetoric, the rhetoric of immanence, both a method and a particular way of being in the world. Xavier's work uses this rhetorical base to adapt his practice to his local contexts and to communicate across cultural difference in a way that maintains the paradox of unity in difference, in which Xavier was able to maintain the core of Christian beliefs as unchanging while using that core to adapt to the local region.

To bring Michelle further into the scholarly conversation, I responded to her paper assuming it was written as an article to be submitted to a rhetoric journal. I asked questions and made suggestions related to language difference, the broad cross-cultural conversations Xavier engaged, and cosmopolitanism, all central concerns in comparative rhetoric and translingualism. I asked Michelle questions on the languages Xavier had to work with when writing his letters and when conducting his missionary work in India. In my feedback, I urged Michelle to consider how Xavier's rhetoric of immanence interacted with local political and religious discourses: "I did not hear the civil or the local sociopolitical discourse that Xavier was engaging. If Xavier's letters do not provide a full picture of the local discourses, you can cite from writings of his contemporaries or from modern, secondary sources. Further, I did not hear how local Christians and non-Christians have responded to Xavier's teaching/practice of rhetorical immanence. I attach an article written by Homi Bhabha on how Indians read the Bible." At the end of her paper, I suggested Xavier's rhetoric of immanence could be examined in light of the current scholarship in religion and cosmopolitanism: "In addition to concluding about the Jesuits' rhetorical practice, connect your findings to the framing that you set up in the introduction, that is, rhetoric is inseparable from religion and the field needs to attend to this relationship in a more profound way. The Jesuits' rhetorical practice, which is cosmopolitan by nature, provides a window to understand the rhetoric-religion relation in globalization." In the end, these comments would shape her dissertation as the seminar paper evolved into one of the chapters.

CONCLUSION

With a translingual and transnational orientation, comparative rhetoric should be a course required of all graduate students entering the field of rhetoric and composition. Unfortunately, this has not been the case. In a 2004 national survey of US graduate programs in rhetoric and composition, Karen Peirce and Theresa Enos (2006) found that while rhetorical theory and history of rhetoric were the most commonly taught courses, they hardly touched upon non-Western rhetorics. An attempt to globalize a graduate curriculum was recently reported by Ghanashyam Sharma (2016), who taught world rhetorics in a writing-teacher certificate program at SUNY Stony Brook. With more scholars joining the research and teaching of comparative and global rhetorics, such as those represented in *The Routledge Handbook of Comparative World Rhetorics* (Lloyd 2020), we are hopeful.

In addition to reading scholarship that transcends linguistic and national boundaries, our experience suggests graduate students must be mentored in ways that could help them overcome the field's nationalist history and develop equal, collaborative relationships. Specifically, students' multilingual/multidialectal and transcultural identities must first be recognized and appreciated. Their language and cultural experiences can be drawn on as resources alongside the reading materials for class discussions and seminar papers. Second, teachers must engage students as peers in scholarly conversations, thus exposing students to ways of academic thinking. To treat the student as a peer also means the teacher must relegate power and admit their lack of knowledge in certain areas. Working in those areas, thus, students gain power and their voices can be encouraged. Third, a comparative lens must be adopted throughout the course. This comparative lens means that, when approaching other cultures and rhetorical traditions, Western concepts must be used with caution and native terms be incorporated into the analytical framework. What a comparative rhetorician achieves is not truths or facts about a rhetorical tradition but creative understandings generated through the art of recontextualization, "negotiating between developing a localized narrative and searching for its new and broader significance within and outside its tradition" (Mao 2013, 220). The comparative lens would push both parties to recognize the limitations of nationalism in their understanding of language and culture; it would encourage them to broaden their linguistic and cultural repertoire and to always examine the other cultures in those cultures' own terms and in their own contexts.

REFERENCES

Baca, Damián. 2009. "The Chicano Codex: Writing against Historical and Pedagogical Colonization." *College English* 71 (6): 564–83.

Binkley, Roberta. 2009. "The Gendering of Prophetic Discourse." In *Ancient Non-Greek Rhetorics*, edited by Carol Lipson and Roberta A. Binkley. West Lafayette, IN: Parlor.

Blommaert, Jan. 2013. *Ethnography, Superdiversity and Linguistic Landscapes: Chronicles of Complexity*. Bristol: Multilingual Matters.

Canagarajah, Suresh. 2002. *Critical Academic Writing and Multilingual Students*. Ann Arbor: University of Michigan Press.

Canagarajah, Suresh. 2006. "The Place of World Englishes in Composition: Pluralization Continued." *College Composition and Communication* 57 (4): 586–619.

Canagarajah, Suresh. 2013a. *Translingual Practice: Global Englishes and Cosmopolitan Relations*. New York: Routledge.

Canagarajah, Suresh. 2013b. "Negotiating Translingual Literacy: An Enactment." *Research in the Teaching of English* 48 (1): 40–67.

Canagarajah, Suresh. 2016. "Translingual Writing and Teacher Development in Composition." *College English* 78 (3): 265–73.

Canagarajah, Suresh. 2019. "Weaving the Text: Changing Literacy Practices and Orientations." *College English* 82 (1): 7–28.

Canagarajah, Suresh, and Yumi Matsumoto. 2017. "Negotiating Voice in Translingual Literacies: From Literacy Regimes to Contact Zones." *Journal of Multilingual and Multicultural Development* 38 (5): 390–406.

Donahue, Christiane. "Internationalization and Composition Studies: Reorienting the Discourse." *College Composition and Communication* 61 (2): 212–43.

Faist, Thomas. 2013. "The Mobility Turn: A New Paradigm for the Social Sciences?" *Ethnic and Racial Studies* 36 (11): 1637–46.

Guerrattaz, Anne Marie, and Bill Johnston. 2013. "Materials in the Classroom Ecology." *Modern Language Journal* 97 (3): 779–96.

Hall, David, and Roger Ames. 1995. *Anticipating China: Thinking through the Narratives of Chinese and Western Culture.* Albany: SUNY Press.

Hesford, Wendy. 2006. "Global Turns and Cautions in Rhetoric and Composition Studies." *PMLA* 121 (3): 787–801.

Horner, Bruce. 2010. "Introduction: Cross-Language Relations in Composition." In *Cross-Language Relations in Composition,* edited by Bruce Horner, Min-Zhan Lu, and Paul Kei Matsuda, 1–4. Carbondale: Southern Illinois University Press.

Horner, Bruce, and Min-Zhan Lu. 2010. "Working Rhetoric and Composition." *College English* 72 (5): 470–94.

Horner, Bruce, Min-Zhan Lu, Jacqueline Jones Royster, and John Trimbur. 2011. "Language Difference in Writing: Toward a Translingual Approach." *College English* 73 (3): 303–21.

Horner, Bruce, Samantha NeCamp, and Christiane Donahue. 2011. "Toward a Multilingual Composition Scholarship: From English Only to a Translingual Norm." *College Composition and Communication* 63 (2): 269–300.

Hum, Sue, and Arabella Lyon. 2008. "Recent Advances in Comparative Rhetoric." In *The SAGE Handbook of Rhetorical Studies,* edited by Andrea A. Lunsford, Kirt H. Wilson, and Rosa A. Eberly, 153–65. Thousand Oaks: SAGE.

Johnson, W. J., trans. 1994. *The Bhagavad Gita.* Oxford: Oxford University Press.

Jordan, Jay. 2014. "Material Translingual Ecologies." *College English* 77 (4): 364–81.

Kaplan, Robert. 1966. "Cultural Thought Patterns in Intercultural Education." *Language Learning* 16 (1–2): 1–20.

Kennedy, George. 1997. *Comparative Rhetoric: An Historical and Cross-Cultural Introduction.* New York: Cambridge University Press.

Kilfoil, Carrie Byars. 2015. "Beyond the 'Foreign' Language Requirement: From a Monolingual to a Translingual Ideology in Rhetoric and Composition Graduate Education." *Rhetoric Review* 34 (4): 426–44.

Kilfoil, Carrie Byars. 2018. "The Postmonolingual Condition and Rhetoric and Composition Ph. D.: Norming Language Difference in a Doctoral Program." *Composition Forum* 40 (Fall). compositionforum.com/issue/40/postmonolingual.php.

Kimball, Elizabeth. 2015. "Translingual Communities: Teaching and Learning Where You Don't Know the Language." *Community Literacy Journal* 9 (2): 68–82.

Lloyd, Keith. 2011. "Culture and Rhetorical Patterns: Mining the Rich Relations between Aristotle's Enthymeme and Example and India's *Nyāya* Method." *Rhetorica* 29 (1): 76–105.

Lloyd, Keith. 2020. *The Routledge Handbook of Comparative World Rhetoric.* New York: Routledge.

Lu, Min-Zhan. 1994. "Professing Multiculturalism: The Politics of Style in the Contact Zone." *College Composition and Communication* 45 (4): 442–58.

Lu, Min-Zhan. 2004. "An Essay on the Work of Composition: Composing English against the Order of Fast Capitalism." *College Composition and Communication* 49 (4): 16–50.

Lu, Min-Zhan, and Bruce Horner. 2013. "Translingual Literacy, Language Difference, and Matters of Agency." *College English* 75 (6): 582–607.

Lyons, Scott Richard. 2010. *X-Marks*. Minneapolis: University of Minnesota Press.

Mao, LuMing. 2003. "Reflective Encounters: Illustrating Comparative Rhetoric." *Style* 37 (4): 401–25.

Mao, LuMing. 2013. "Beyond Bias, Binary, and Border: Mapping out the Future of Comparative Rhetoric." *Rhetoric Society Quarterly* 43 (3): 209–25.

Micciche, Laura R., and Allison D. Carr. 2011. "Toward Graduate-Level Writing Instruction." *College Composition and Communication* 62 (3): 477–501.

Oliver, Robert T. 1971. *Communication and Culture in Ancient India and China*. Syracuse, NY: Syracuse University Press.

Peirce, Karen P., and Theresa Jarnagin Enos. 2006. "How Seriously Are We Taking Professionalization? A Report on Graduate Curricula in Rhetoric and Composition." *Rhetoric Review* 25 (2): 204–10.

Pennycook, Alastair. 2010. *Language as a Local Practice*. Abingdon: Routledge.

Pollock, Sheldon. 2006. *The Language of the Gods in the World of Men: Sanskrit, Culture, and Power in Premodern India*. Berkeley: University of California Press.

Pratt, Mary Louise. 1991. "Arts of the Contact Zone." *Profession*: 33–40.

Radhakrishnan, Rajagopalan. 2009. "Why Compare?" *New Literary History* 40 (3): 453–71.

Sharma, Ghanashyam. 2016. "World Rhetorics." *Composition Studies* 44 (1): 108–26.

Stroud, Scott R. 2004. "Narrative as Argument in Indian Philosophy: The Astavakra Gita as Multivalent Narrative." *Philosophy & Rhetoric* 37 (1): 42–71.

Trimbur, John. 2008. "The Dartmouth Conference and the Geohistory of the Native Speaker." *College English* 71 (2): 142–69.

Wang, Bo. 2013. "Comparative Rhetoric, Postcolonial Studies, and Transnational Feminisms: A Geopolitical Approach." *Rhetoric Society Quarterly* 43 (3): 226–42.

You, Xiaoye. 2010. *Writing in the Devil's Tongue: A History of English Composition in China*. Carbondale: Southern Illinois University Press.

You, Xiaoye. 2016. *Cosmopolitan English and Transliteracy*. Carbondale: Southern Illinois University Press.

You, Xiaoye. 2018. *Transnational Writing Education: Theory, History, and Practice*. New York: Routledge.

Zheng, Xuan. 2017. "Translingual Identity as Pedagogy: International Teaching Assistants of English in College Composition Classrooms." *Modern Language Journal* 101 (S1): 29–44.

7

THE ROLE OF GRADUATE EDUCATION IN BUILDING WRITING TEACHERS' KNOWLEDGE OF LANGUAGE

Madelyn Pawlowski and Christine M. Tardy

Despite a history of language "erasures" in rhetoric and composition studies (Connors 2000; MacDonald 2007), the field has recently demonstrated a renewed interest in exploring the role of language in writing education. The growing body of scholarship on translingualism, for example, has revitalized important conversations about acknowledging and supporting students' linguistic resources. To traverse this "new linguistic frontier" in rhetoric and composition (Matsuda 2013), teacher-scholars of writing are in need of a sophisticated knowledge of language, yet teacher knowledge and teacher education are frequently glossed over in these scholarly conversations.

In this chapter, we explore why teachers' knowledge of language is a relevant concern for rhetoric and composition graduate programs hoping to support more translingual and transnational approaches to the study and teaching of writing. We consider the role graduate education can play in developing pedagogical language knowledge (PLK) for writing education—a knowledge of language and its pedagogical relevance in the academic writing classroom (Pawlowski 2019). We first situate language and PLK within the context of rhetoric and composition scholarship, graduate education, and writing instruction. Next, we share findings from a study of graduate student teachers in one US writing program, indicating the impact graduate education can have on teachers' confidence in and strategies for working with language and language difference in the composition classroom. Finally, we explore implications from this research, suggesting ways rhetoric and composition graduate programs may incorporate language study more robustly. We argue that a broad interdisciplinary knowledge of language paired with practical strategies for incorporating language into writing

https://doi.org/10.7330/9781646423262.c007

instruction can foster development of graduate students' PLK, which in turn can equip them with concrete tools and epistemological understandings necessary for promoting their students' rhetorical flexibility in working across languages, language variations, and genres. In short, supporting graduate students' PLK is imperative for developing scholars and teachers with translingual and transnational orientations to writing research and pedagogy.

LANGUAGE, TRANSLINGUALISM, AND WRITING INSTRUCTION

A fairly strong disciplinary narrative details the history of declining interest in language within rhetoric and composition. Robert Connors (2000), Susan MacDonald (2007), and Laura Aull (2015) all trace this waning attention and demonstrate how disciplinary and institutional structures contributed to the "erasure" of language-related concerns. Somewhat surprising, MacDonald (2007) notes, is that the field's movement away from language came just at the time "a more descriptive, applied, or functional linguistics developed that was relevant to *writers*, not just *speakers*" (609–10). Christiane Donahue (2009, 2018a, 2018b) has also explored composition studies' departure from language, asking, "How did we move from the entrenched trio of literary theory, composition, and linguistics cited by Nystrand et al. (1993, 304) to the 'I am not a language teacher' and the marginalization of linguistics research in writing studies?" (Donahue 2018a, 134). She suggests the field's turn toward social and cognitive processes is one answer to this question but also links inattention to language with a US-centric approach to the discipline. Donahue (2016) laments that "while language is only one aspect of the global/international context we are in, it is indexical of the complex multilayered meaning-making dynamic that defines writing research today" (147). Xiaoye You (2010) has similarly argued that composition studies must look beyond the United States to locales and professionals around the world, fostering an "international alliance" (180) that attends to language use in local environments.

Inattention to language is evidenced not just in scholarship but also in the education of new scholars in rhetoric and composition graduate programs. As Bruce Horner, Min-Zhan Lu, Jacqueline Jones Royster, and John Trimbur (2011) explain, even the foreign-language requirement in such programs is often tokenized and given little more than superficial attention. Carrie Kilfoil (2015) offers an in-depth exploration of this requirement in rhetoric and composition graduate education and argues that such language requirements are often tacitly framed as irrelevant to rhetoric and composition graduate training, "which in turn renders these requirements vulnerable to reduction and elimination in many programs" (427). And, indeed, she does find a decrease in the number of programs with such requirements from 1999 to 2015. Carol Severino (2017) also advocates for the value of teachers studying additional languages. Sharing her own experiences learning Spanish and Chinese, Severino describes how language learning has helped her empathize with the challenges her students experience when writing in English. She sees diary studies of language learning as a valuable learning tool that can "play an essential part in developing composition teachers' language awareness, sensitivity, and empathy" (28), preparing them to work more effectively with linguistically diverse students.

Increased attention to foreign-language study might indeed help one develop language awareness, empathy, or increased fluency in a language, but foreign-language study may not always include preparation for applying this linguistic knowledge to the *teaching of writing*. One might think this teaching-related knowledge could best be supported in rhetoric and composition graduate courses or teacher training. In a survey and interview study with US writing program administrators (WPAs), we asked thirty-one participants where graduate student teachers should develop language-related knowledge; the most common response was that such knowledge should be developed through coursework (Pawlowski and Tardy 2017). The same WPAs noted language was only minimally addressed in their teacher-preparation activities (such as orientations or practicum courses) because of challenges related to time and teacher educators' own language-related knowledge. The assumption may be that students are learning about language in other courses.

Unfortunately, research suggests that such courses are not always available and that there has been a decrease in language-related coursework in the PhD curriculum of rhetoric and composition programs since the late 1980s. Specifically, Kilfoil (2017) found the percentage of programs that included "linguistics"-related courses fell from 89 percent in 1987 to just 25 percent in 2007 and concludes that the loss of such courses has diverted attention away from language and language difference in writing programs. She calls for renewed attention to language in the graduate curriculum, both in separate "linguistics" courses and the incorporation of language-related work into courses like rhetorical history or the teaching practicum. Tardy (2017) also calls for more attention to language in rhetoric and composition graduate education, noting the limited resources for building language-related knowledge in many programs "should be a significant concern to faculty and students in these programs" (186). She argues for greater interactions among graduate programs in applied linguistics and rhetoric and composition, as well as inclusion of applied linguistics scholarship within rhetoric and composition courses—through readings, invited speakers, online discussions with language scholars, and hiring of academics who bring strong backgrounds in language *and* writing studies.

Many of the scholarly perspectives we have recounted so far come in response to the growing interest in and influence of translingualism within rhetoric and composition. As an orientation that views language as fluid and that values linguistic diversity, translingualism, in Donahue's (2018a) words, "begs us to learn much more about (cross) language—for which we must learn more about language" (135). Yet, given the historical departures from language interests in composition studies, some scholars have questioned whether translingualism can be responsibly addressed within the field. Paul Kei Matsuda (2013) argues that "the lack of a community of knowledgeable peers who can ensure intellectual accountability" (132) poses a major concern for the current interest in translingualism. Similarly, Severino (2017) takes the position that translingualism "needs to acknowledge and then learn about the hard work and the long, slow process of learning other languages" (28).

One challenge to raising the status of language within rhetoric and composition relates to disciplinarity. As the field of applied linguistics has grown, it has taken on much of the language-related attention to writing and writing processes. Indeed, much of the work on writing internationally is carried out within the field of applied linguistics. Citing research by Mary Juzwik, Svjetlana Curcic, Kimberly Wolbers, Kathleen D. Moxley, Lisa M. Dimling, and Rebecca K. Shankland (2006), Donahue (2009) notes that "the top three journals publishing research articles [internationally] about writing between 1999 and 2004 were the *Journal of Second-Language Writing, English for Specific Purposes*, and . . . *Written Communication*" (230). Attention to language, then, seems to coalesce with both (inter)disciplinarity and internationalization, leading Donahue to argue that without an effort to internationalize, the field of rhetoric and composition "will remain stuck in a-historical, a-contextual, and highly partial modes of intellectual tourism" (236).

Despite this somewhat bleak view, scholars have identified fruitful areas in which applied linguistics and rhetoric and composition can productively inform one another around language-related issues. One of these areas is the study of genre. Kimberly Costino and Sunny Hyon (2011) reflect on their mutual uses of genre in the classroom and conclude genre "has the potential to break our communicative impasses" (35) by bringing together the many interests and concerns of writing—including language, rhetoric, and sociopolitics. Julia Williams and Frankie Condon (2017) similarly argue genre has the potential to bridge "an alliance" among scholars interested in language, translingualism, and writing instruction (from various disciplinary backgrounds). Additionally, Donahue (2018a) points to research on "transfer" (including transfer of language knowledge) and "code" (including code switching and code meshing) as areas that offer possibilities of "deep exchange" among language and composition scholarship. She contends collaboration in these areas could deepen expertise and, ultimately, help prepare our writing students for today's globalized and superdiverse world. It should be noted that genre, transfer, and code are all part of a teachers' pedagogical language knowledge (Pawlowski 2019) and play an important role in bridging teachers' language-related knowledge and pedagogical knowledge.

PEDAGOGICAL LANGUAGE KNOWLEDGE

Pedagogical language knowledge (PLK) "is not only a teacher's knowledge *of* or *about* language; it is a knowledge of how to navigate a variety of context-specific language-related teaching and learning situations" (Pawlowski 2019, 151). Like Lee S. Shulman's (1987) "pedagogical content knowledge," PLK is a knowledge domain unique to teachers and can be used to illustrate the complexity of what teachers know and do. PLK is particularly useful for considering the kinds of language-related knowledge writing teachers may need—and thus the kind of knowledge development that could be better supported in rhetoric and composition graduate education. PLK includes *language-related subject-matter knowledge*, such as academic discourse, language acquisition, language varieties, structure of English language, register and genre, rhetoric, critical language awareness, history and trajectory of English, and language ideologies. *Language-related pedagogical knowledge* is also part of PLK and includes knowledge of language-related curricula, instructional strategies, assessment practices, and theories of writing development. Furthermore, PLK includes *general pedagogical knowledge* (teaching strategies shared by teachers across subjects) and *contextual knowledge* that includes knowledge of students' linguistic backgrounds, local language policies, and teachers' own linguistic beliefs and biases. Together, these knowledge domains help teachers navigate the many situations they encounter when teaching writing. Important, the PLK framework highlights how awareness—even critical awareness—of language alone is insufficient; teachers also need practical strategies for addressing language with their students. (See Pawlowski [2019] for a detailed discussion of PLK.) In the remainder of this chapter, we use the PLK framework to understand graduate student writing teachers' experiences in the classroom and to suggest how language study might be incorporated into rhetoric and composition graduate curricula.

STUDY

Here, we report findings from a survey of thirty-four graduate teaching assistants (GTAs) and three case studies that are part of a larger research project on locating and supporting writing instructors' PLK (Pawlowski 2019). The GTAs in this study were enrolled in master's or PhD programs in rhetoric and composition (n=14), applied linguistics (n=12), or literature (n=8) at a public US research university. This university is large and diverse, with over thirty-five thousand undergraduate students enrolled at the time of study (2017–2018).

At this institution, GTAs begin teaching as instructors of record in the writing program after a one-week preservice orientation session regardless of their prior experiences and disciplinary backgrounds. They receive additional support throughout their first year in a weekly practicum that introduces basic pedagogical strategies and theories of composition necessary for implementing the local FYW curriculum. Because GTAs are simultaneously teaching FYW, discussions in the practicum are often tailored to their immediate needs. The degree to which certain topics are discussed also largely depends on the practicum instructor. For instance, two of the participants in this study reported having conversations other participants did not have about L2 writers; they credited their practicum mentor, who has a PhD in applied linguistics, for initiating these conversations. The consistency and degree to which all GTAs are introduced to language-related topics is unclear due to these variables. Additionally, the practicum is the only course in which *all* GTAs enroll regardless of discipline; additional teaching or language-related graduate coursework depends on GTAs' course of study.

A survey was distributed to GTAs in the 2017 fall semester. In addition to identifying the participants' personal, educational, and teaching backgrounds, it aimed to understand GTAs' confidence about language-related concepts and their approaches to addressing language and language differences with FYW students. The survey also asked participants to identify influences on their linguistic confidence and teaching practices. Throughout the survey, language was broadly conceived;

participants were asked to consider a variety of language-related concepts and issues ranging from grammar to language policies.

Case-study participants from across disciplines and experience levels were also recruited. Here, we examine the experiences of Maila, Jackie, and Michael, who were all enrolled in the university's rhetoric and composition PhD program. Information about these individuals was gathered through two interviews, reflective narratives, their teaching materials, and feedback on student writing, all collected over a sixteen-week period and subsequently coded and analyzed using an inductively developed coding scheme. We begin our discussion of the research findings with trends emerging from the survey, paying particular attention to the role of graduate education in supporting GTAs' PLK development. Brief profiles of the case-study participants then extend and complicate the survey data.

SURVEY FINDINGS

The survey revealed participants' perceptions about the importance of graduate education in developing writing teachers' PLK. Participants labeled the extent to which various factors influenced their beliefs and understanding of language, ranging from personal-identity markers (race, gender, sexual orientation, religious associations) to professional and educational experiences. The majority of participants, regardless of disciplinary background, agreed the following factors were "very influential": teaching (85.71%), graduate education (75%), learning additional language(s) (67.86%), cultural background (64%), college education (60.71%), disciplinary knowledge (60.71%), and travel (57.14%).

Participants largely agreed GTAs should be required to take a language-related course as part of their graduate education. When asked what kind of language-related courses or course topics should be required, the highest-ranked course topics across all participants included grammar, second-language writing, language-related pedagogies, multilingualism, and translingualism. Whether participants had actually explored such topics in their graduate coursework was highly dependent on their program of study. Table 7.1 shows what topics participants had explored or were currently exploring in graduate-level courses at the time of the study. It should be noted that this table does not list all the course topics participants could have explored but rather the topics participants selected from a much larger list or added to the list based on their experiences. In other words, topics such as psycholinguistics, bilingual education, language policies, and oral language

Table 7.1. Language-related topics explored by participants in graduate courses

	Applied linguistics (n=12)	Literature (n=8)	Rhetoric and composition (n=14)
Grammar (descriptive, functional, pedagogical, or rhetorical)	100% (n=12)	0% (n=0)	14% (n=2)
TEFL	58% (n=7)	0% (n=0)	7% (n=1)
TESOL	66% (n=8)	13% (n=1)	7% (n=1)
First-language acquisition	33% (n=4)	13% (n=1)	29% (n=4)
Second-language acquisition	100% (n=12)	13% (n=1)	7% (n=1)
Second-language writing	58% (n=7)	13% (n=1)	14% (n=2)
Language diversity	17% (n=2)	13% (n=1)	7% (n=1)
World Englishes	33% (n=4)	38% (n=3)	21% (n=3)
Sociolinguistics	92% (n=11)	0% (n=0)	14% (n=2)
Discourse analysis	66% (n=8)	13% (n=1)	21% (n=3)
Genre studies	50% (n=6)	25% (n=2)	43% (n=6)
Translingualism	8% (n=1)	13% (n=1)	14% (n=2)
Phonology	33% (n=4)	0% (n=0)	7% (n=1)
Morphology	42% (n=5)	13% (n=1)	7% (n=1)
Syntax	50% (n=6)	0% (n=0)	7% (n=1)
Semantics	42% (n=5)	0% (n=0)	7% (n=1)
Linguistics (intro or general)	58% (n=7)	0% (n=0)	14% (n=2)
Corpus linguistics	33% (n=4)	0% (n=0)	0% (n=0)
Stylistics	17% (n=2)	0% (n=0)	7% (n=1)
Semiotics	42% (n=5)	13% (n=1)	21% (n=3)
Translation	17% (n=2)	50% (n=4)	0% (n=0)
Multicultural studies	42% (n=5)	63% (n=5)	29% (n=4)
Writing language development	25% (n=3)	0% (n=0)	7% (n=1)

traditions—all explored in courses from 2012–2017 based on the university's course-catalog descriptions—were apparently not addressed to a significant degree in any of the courses taken by participants.

Personal interests, program requirements, and seat availability undoubtedly impact what language-related coursework graduate students are able and desire to complete. In this study, the disciplinary scope and program requirements for the MA and PhD in applied linguistics, for instance, were most aligned with the topics represented in table 7.1. Thus, the percentage of graduate students in applied linguistics who had taken or were enrolled in courses addressing a variety of language-related topics was generally higher than the percentage of students from other programs, with a few exceptions. Literature students, for example, were more likely to have taken a course on translation because it was a programmatic requirement. The extent to which any individual course influenced participants' language-related knowledge was not explored in the survey. However, by looking at participants' self-identified areas of confidence and weakness, we can infer some potential areas of study that could better be addressed through graduate education.

When asked to consider their language-related subject-matter knowledge, the highest percentage of participants across all three programs felt most confident in their knowledge of academic or disciplinary discourse, grammar, and mechanics. Nevertheless, the majority admitted they sometimes (59%) or frequently (22%) faced difficulty when trying to explain why something is "correct" or "sounds right" in English. This perhaps indicates a lack of metalinguistic confidence, or the ability to transform language knowledge for pedagogical purposes. When it came to identifying areas of weakness related to language-related subject-matter knowledge, disciplinary influences were more pronounced. The majority of participants in literature and rhetoric and composition expressed feeling least confident in their knowledge related to language acquisition, second-language writing, World Englishes, and the history of the English language. These participants also found it challenging to design and facilitate lessons for L2 writers; 60 percent of literature GTAs and 75 percent of rhetoric and composition GTAs felt "not very" or "not at all" confident in doing so. Only 17 percent of participants from applied linguistics acknowledged a lack of confidence in any area. More specifically, these participants tended to feel the least confident in their knowledge of style, the history of the English language, and language policy.

Regardless of individual strengths, weaknesses, and disciplinary biases, all participants agreed that having an understanding of language improves their teaching practices, and all but two desired more training or education to further develop their language-related subject-matter knowledge and language-related pedagogical knowledge. This shared desire among participants from across disciplines reinforces the need to acknowledge language as a transdisciplinary knowledge domain.

Survey findings also demonstrate the need to support graduate students in developing their abilities to transform language-related subject-matter knowledge for pedagogical purposes. Though research on teacher knowledge suggests teaching-related knowledge is developed largely through engagement in the "actual activities of teaching" (Johnson and Golombek 2016, 9), participants in this study felt their engagement in graduate coursework was almost as influential. We now turn to looking more closely at the experiences of three of these teachers.

MAILA

At the time of study, Maila was pre-ABD in the university's rhetoric and composition PhD program. Maila felt her cultural background and lived experiences as a multilingual woman of color had the most significant impact on her developing language-related beliefs, knowledge, and pedagogical practices (that is, her PLK), but she also acknowledged the influence of her educational experiences from kindergarten through graduate school.

Maila was born and raised in the United States, where she attended a bilingual Spanish/English school from kindergarten through eighth grade. She spoke Central American Spanish at home, but at school and among her friends, Maila spoke US academic English, a Mexican American variety of Spanish, and a regional English dialect. After losing access to bilingual education in ninth grade, Maila worried about being punished or failing for speaking or writing anything but Standard American English in school. It was difficult for her to imagine Spanish as having a "valid" place in academia until her first semester of graduate coursework when she was introduced to Sor Juana Inés de la Cruz—a Mexican nun, poet, philosopher, and influential figure in the history of rhetorical studies. Reading de la Cruz's writings in Spanish and English shifted Maila's view concerning the validity of Spanish in academic spaces. As Maila remarked in her first interview, "For me, as a person who was raised bilingual to some extent . . . [reading Spanish texts in seminars] was important. I was like, I can do this!"

Reading the work of feminist scholar and cultural critic bell hooks also had a profound impact on Maila's philosophy about the role of Standard English in the writing classroom. More specifically, Maila mentioned reading the essay "Language: Teaching New Worlds/New Words" (hooks 1994), in which hooks argues Standard American English is "the language of conquest and domination" and "the mask that hides the loss of so many tongues" (223). Maila felt her learning objectives, assignment sheets, and assessment practices were potential acts of linguistic violence, as they tended to uphold language standards. At the same time, she viewed it as her responsibility to help students learn academic discourse. In wrestling with these two perspectives, Maila wondered how to respect

students' linguistic choices while also helping them "get the skills necessary to talk in college." Maila often felt she was struggling alongside her
students to achieve this goal due to her own gaps in knowledge.

Maila felt that her metalinguistic knowledge was limited and that
it negatively impacted her teaching effectiveness. "I can write, I can
express myself, but I can't tell you the science and the technical reasoning behind it. . . . Thus, I don't know how to tell my students, 'This is an
independent clause, and this is why it doesn't blah blah blah'" (Interview
1). She also felt her limited knowledge about different language varieties
and the linguistic backgrounds of her students hindered her ability to
discuss or teach about these varieties in the classroom. While she liked
the idea of encouraging code switching or translanguaging in FYW, she
was unsure how to responsibly incorporate these practices, especially in
regards to assessment. When asked about her experiences working with
L2 writers, Maila realized she never consciously shifted her approach
to accommodate their needs. In part, Maila felt as though she never
received the proper training to make such pedagogical adjustments.

Though Maila had only taken two language-related graduate courses,
including courses on literacy and discourse analysis, she showed keen
awareness of the sociopolitical dimensions of language and teaching,
in part due to her own experiences as a multilingual learner. Her
graduate coursework also helped her accept the validity of multilingual
voices—including her own—in academic spaces. Nevertheless, she was
often unsure how to translate this linguistic awareness into pedagogical
practices. She was aware of possible pedagogical approaches, such as
translanguaging, and yet she struggled to engage with such approaches
beyond a theoretical conversation.

JACKIE

Jackie was a second-year PhD student in rhetoric and composition. Born
and raised in a rural US community, Jackie identified as a native speaker
of English. Though she learned Spanish as part of her K–12 and undergraduate studies, she did not identify as a fluent or confident Spanish
user. Jackie, like the majority of participants in this study, felt her experiences in the classroom as both a student and a teacher had the greatest
influence on her developing PLK.

Several negative language-related experiences as a student had
left their mark on Jackie as both a learner and teacher. She recalled
a particularly painful interaction with an undergraduate professor in
which she was told her ideas were adequate despite her having done

"grotesque things to the English language" in writing. This experience coupled with other memorable instances of grammar correction led her to mostly avoid grammar correction with her own students. Jackie recognized her avoidance of direct instruction and feedback related to grammar and other language-related features sometimes made her job feel "easier," but she also felt conflicted knowing many learners benefit from such approaches.

Contradictory messages from Jackie's graduate coursework and professional experiences about grammar and language-related feedback further contributed to her conflicted feelings. During her MA, she learned about Students' Right to their Own Language in a composition theory course and practiced balancing "global" and "local" feedback as a writing tutor. In a PhD course on feminist pedagogies, Jackie encountered Lisa Delpit's (1995) research on the sociopolitical implications of withholding direct instruction of the "codes of power" from minority and low-income students. Yet, Jackie's practicum teacher told her to never comment on students' grammatical or linguistic choices. In practice, Jackie mostly ignored this teacher's advice and relied on the strategies she developed elsewhere. She found ways to integrate language instruction into FYW, but mostly in the form of editing exercises limited to two to three class sessions each semester. Jackie desired more support for designing other forms of language-oriented lessons because "the more I teach, the more I *want* to incorporate language. I just need better ways of doing so."

Like Maila, Jackie felt her metalinguistic knowledge limited her ability to engage in language-related pedagogical practices such as providing feedback and scaffolding language instruction. She also acknowledged having "limited vocabulary for describing grammatical errors or differences" and feeling ill equipped to provide language support. Jackie expressed feeling "not at all confident" in her ability to design or facilitate lessons for L2 writers in particular. She felt empathy for these students, having failed multiple times to pass a Spanish translation exam in graduate school, and while this empathy sometimes helped her anticipate students' language-related challenges, she was often unsure how to meet their needs.

MICHAEL

Michael, an ABD student in rhetoric and composition, was born and raised in the southwestern United States. Michael felt his cultural background and racial identity were most influential on his developing PLK, but he also acknowledged the profound impact of his early educational experiences and graduate studies.

Michael attended a bilingual Spanish/English school from fourth grade until high school. In this environment, the majority of his peers were Latinx, and he was often the only Black student. Learning alongside students from cultural and linguistic backgrounds that differed from his own helped raise Michael's awareness of language varieties and "how they exist in a classroom, and what that means, and why that's okay." Michael attributed his self-confidence in supporting L2 writers to these experiences learning in a multilingual/multicultural environment.

Michael reflected on an experience teaching an FYW course in which multiple students expressed anxieties about how their linguistic backgrounds would affect their ability to succeed in the course. Michael responded to their concerns by explaining that their language choices would be acknowledged and respected and that in his assessments he would focus more on the rhetorical effectiveness of their choices than adherence to language standards. Michael credited his students for creating the space to explicitly discuss language diversity because he otherwise might not have initiated such a conversation.

Early in Michael's graduate studies, he enrolled in a course on global Englishes and critical pedagogies and was introduced to scholarly perspectives, mostly from rhetoric and composition scholars, about code switching, code meshing, translingualism, and linguistic imperialism. This course helped him realize how he had benefited from code switching throughout his life. Code meshing, or bringing AAVE into his academic work, was not something he felt comfortable doing until graduate school. Code meshing and code switching had gradually become part of his writing and teaching identity, but he still felt concerned about the potential for exoticizing himself and his students through code meshing in particular.

In describing his general approach to language in the classroom, Michael stated he generally decenters mechanics and stylistics in part due to previous failed attempts. "I felt like I wasn't teaching these things the way I wanted or intended to. I then thought, 'I don't like this, so let's not do this anymore.'" Michael felt the idea of teaching grammar in a rhetorical way (something he had gained exposure to in an undergraduate linguistics course) was promising, but he was still trying to figure out how to integrate rhetorical grammar in a way that would align with his goals as a teacher to not privilege one language variety over others.

Michael's general approach to teaching could best be described as *responsive* and *negotiable*, which is perhaps best illustrated by his use of contract grading but is also apparent in his philosophy about language instruction in the FYW classroom. Michael generally avoided planned, direct instruction about language but was open to discussing language-related issues when students raised concern. Michael did not use rubrics or leave written feedback on student work, preferring instead to meet with students one on one after each major project. In these meetings, Michael tried to focus on the student's message, purpose, and attention to their audience and context, bringing language into the conversation minimally. Overall, Michael believed students need the space to develop their thoughts before worrying about *how* the thought is communicated through written language. "If I can make sense of what you're saying," Michael explained, "then who am I to say that you're not successful in saying it?"

Though Michael desired better approaches to teaching "languaging" in FYW (i.e., language as negotiation), he expressed "never" having difficulty discussing language-related subjects or issues with students as they arose. He felt confident overall in his language-related subject-matter knowledge, from his grasp of metalanguage to a theoretical and personal understanding of code meshing. His graduate courses had introduced him to an impressive breadth of language-related topics, including syntax, semantics, semiotics, language diversity, multiculturalism, World Englishes, dialects, sociolinguistics, and translingualism, which he credited for playing an important role in his development of language-related confidence.

DISCUSSION

By considering the broad range of language-related needs, abilities, and perspectives of Maila, Jackie, Michael, and their peers, this study affirms the difficulties of designing comprehensive or, at least responsive, graduate programs. Despite individual differences among participants, however, some interesting patterns emerge with implications for designing rhetoric and composition graduate programs that integrate support for PLK development.

The three case-study participants all shared a strong interest in the sociopolitical dimensions of language that was influenced by their personal backgrounds and graduate education. Indeed, their awareness of language diversity and the ideological complexities of language instruction reflect some of the strengths and promises of the "social turn" in rhetoric and composition studies (Rhodes and Alexander 2014). Yet, they all, to a degree, expressed difficulties in developing pedagogical practices reflective of their critical language awareness. Michael largely avoided language-related issues despite the strengths of his language-related content knowledge and the importance of language to his personal identity, whereas Maila implemented language-related teaching practices that sometimes contradicted her personal and scholarly perspectives. Supporting a critical awareness of language is essential for emerging scholars and teachers of writing, but awareness on its own is insufficient for carrying out the work of linguistically aware writing research and instruction. For this reason, we argue rhetoric and composition graduate programs should support students in developing a more robust body of language-related knowledge (their PLK). The findings from our study point to several areas of PLK that deserve greater attention in rhetoric and composition graduate programs, four of which we highlight here.

KNOWLEDGE OF METALANGUAGE

The ability to talk about language with students requires more than just the development of a specialized lexis about grammar. Metalinguistic knowledge also aids instructors in describing language choices writers make in different genres and registers, connecting language choices to rhetorical choices. The majority of participants in this study felt some degree of metalinguistic insecurity. Jackie, for example, felt she had limited vocabulary for talking about language features and language varieties, and Michael was unsure how to talk about language *rhetorically*. We argue that supporting metalinguistic knowledge development should be an integral part of graduate education in rhetoric and composition. Such knowledge may be best developed through the in-depth and sustained attention provided by a full course on language (e.g., sociolinguistics, discourse analysis, pedagogical grammar), though metalinguistic knowledge should also be integrated throughout a program's curriculum.

KNOWLEDGE OF L2 WRITERS AND WRITING

Writing classrooms are often recognized as multilingual spaces, so knowing how to support linguistically diverse students is an integral element of writing instructors' PLK that deserves more attention in graduate education. We found it particularly concerning in our survey data that 75 percent of the graduate students in rhetoric and composition felt "not very" or "not at all" confident in designing and facilitating lessons for L2 writers despite the fact that all these participants had at some point encountered L2 writers in their classrooms. Here again, we believe teachers of writing need sustained and theoretically informed ways of supporting L2 writers that cannot adequately be addressed in single class sessions or one-shot teaching workshops (Tardy 2017). Rhetoric and composition graduate programs and faculty should share in this responsibility by offering courses in L2 writing or building educational partnerships with other units on campus, such as TESOL or applied linguistics programs.

KNOWLEDGE OF LANGUAGE-ORIENTED PEDAGOGIES

Perhaps the biggest area of concern for Maila, Jackie, and Michael was in knowing *how* to integrate language instruction and support in the writing classroom. Though participants were asked to think about language broadly, when asked about their language-related pedagogical approaches, they often assumed the question was about grammar instruction or correction. The collapsing of language and grammar is not uncommon among writing instructors and in public discourse, and many writing instructors, like Jackie's practicum teacher, believe discussions of grammar should be avoided. However, supporting the development of students' linguistic repertoires is far more complex than teaching grammar, and researchers across disciplines have developed more effective (and far more interesting) methods than grammar drills for supporting linguistic development. A well-developed PLK would include knowledge of pedagogical grammar, genre pedagogies, translingual pedagogies, or even pedagogical strategies adapted from related fields such as second-language writing and TESOL.

KNOWLEDGE OF SECOND OR ADDITIONAL LANGUAGE(S)

For most of the graduate students in this study, including the three case-study participants, learning an additional language (or languages) had a major impact on their PLK: Maila's conflicted views on teaching language standards were influenced by her multilingual background; Jackie's struggles to learn a second language helped her empathize with language learners; and Michael's code-switching abilities and experimentations with code meshing shaped his expectations and interactions with students, as well as his research trajectory. These findings support Severino's (2017) assertion that language learning can help develop "language awareness, sensitivity, and empathy" (28) particularly relevant for teachers and scholars of writing in increasingly multilingual learning environments. We strongly believe language-learning requirements should be integrated into rhetoric and composition curricula. Offering credit for traditional language courses is one option; other possibilities include supporting participation in language-immersion programs or translation courses or helping students identify opportunities for international or intercultural research. Explicit reflection on these learning opportunities (for example, through diary studies like Severino's [2017]) can help highlight the relevance of these experiences to writing instruction. Furthermore, embracing a culture of multilingualism at multiple programmatic levels, from advising to curricular design, could help diversify student and faculty perceptions of the value of language. Faculty could be encouraged, for example, to incorporate research from scholars working in multiple languages and language varieties as core course readings, explore or model the affordances of global research and teaching partnerships with advisees, and make cross-cultural connections to course topics. L2 proficiency need not be the goal of language learning at the graduate level; perhaps the experience of language learning could be reframed as valuable in itself.

CONCLUSION

In sum, adopting a translingual and transnational approach to writing research and instruction requires particular knowledge we feel is best supported through interdisciplinary collaboration and a range of learning experiences. Coursework in, for example, second-language writing, pedagogical grammar, genre and discourse studies, sociolinguistics, or second-language acquisition is especially relevant for writing teachers and can help bridge awareness of language issues with strategies for writing instruction. While it is unrealistic to require rhetoric and composition graduate students to take courses in all these areas, programs might require they take one or two language-related courses from across disciplines. In addition, integration of language-related issues into core courses in rhetoric and composition (such as composition theory and the practicum) is also important for helping graduate students situate their understandings of language within writing studies and to help students bridge, synthesize, or contextualize different disciplinary perspectives about language and pedagogy developed through their interdisciplinary coursework. Rhetoric and composition faculty may find it helpful to focus on bridging concepts like genre, transfer, and code, more specifically, as points of entry to interdisciplinary, language-related discussions. While consistently offering a course on translingualism may be feasible in certain institutional settings, we recognize not every rhetoric and composition department has an expert available to teach such a course, and a single course is not necessarily the only or most effective way of supporting PLK development or translingual and transnational orientations to writing studies.

As Donahue (2016), You (2010), and scholars in this volume note, attention to language—including translingualism—is an interdisciplinary endeavor, requiring teachers and scholars to take on "alternative dispositions and to cross disciplinary divides" (Horner et al. 2011, 313). To take translingualism seriously in the study and teaching of writing, we must also take language seriously, and that task can only be accomplished through a more conscious and robust approach to the development of pedagogical language knowledge in graduate education. When graduate courses pair interdisciplinary knowledge of language with practical strategies for incorporating language into writing instruction, they equip future scholars (and current teachers) with resources for promoting the kind of flexible language use needed in today's mobile and globalized world. Without such resources, however, teachers may lack confidence in addressing language in their classrooms and scholarship, potentially perpetuating the field's abandonment of language. It is our hope the translingual turn will lead the field to embrace rather than erase the important role of language-related knowledge in what we do.

REFERENCES

Aull, Laura. 2015. *First-Year University Writing: A Corpus-Based Study with Implications for Pedagogy.* New York: Palgrave Macmillan.

Connors, Robert. 2000. "The Erasure of the Sentence." *College Composition and Communication* 52 (1): 96–128.

Costino, Kimberly A., and Sunny Hyon. 2011. "Sidestepping Our 'Scare Words': Genre as a Possible Bridge between L1 and L2 Compositionists." *Second Language Writing* 20 (1): 24–44.

Delpit, Lisa. 1995. *Other People's Children: Cultural Conflict in the Classroom.* New York: W. W. Norton.

Donahue, Christiane. 2009. "'Internationalization' and Composition Studies: Reorienting the Discourse." *College Composition and Communication* 61 (2): 212–43.

Donahue, Christiane. 2016. "The 'Trans' in Transnational-Translingual: Rhetorical and Linguistic Flexibility as New Norms." *Composition Studies* 44 (1): 147–50.

Donahue, Christiane. 2018a. "'We Are the 'Other': The Future of Exchanges between Writing and Language Studies." *Across the Disciplines* 15 (3): 130–43. http://wac .colostate.edu/atd/trans_wac/donahue2018.pdf.

Donahue, Christiane. 2018b. "Writing, English, and a Translingual Model for Composition." In *Composition, Rhetoric, and Disciplinarity*, edited by Rita Malenczyk, Susan Miller-Cochran, Elizabeth Wardle, and Kathleen Blake Yancey, 206–24. Logan: Utah State University Press.

hooks, bell. 1994. *Language: Teaching New Worlds/New Words*. In *Teaching to Transgress: Education as the Practice of Freedom*. New York: Routledge.

Horner, Bruce, Min-Zhan Lu, Jacqueline Jones Royster, and John Trimbur. 2011. "Language Difference in Writing: Toward a Translingual Approach." *College English* 73 (3): 303–21.

Johnson, Karen E., and Paula R. Golombek. 2016. *Mindful L2 Teacher Education: A Sociocultural Perspective on Cultivating Teachers' Professional Development*. New York: Routledge.

Juzwik, Mary M., Svjetlana Curcic, Kimberly Wolbers, Kathleen D. Moxley, Lisa M. Dimling, and Rebecca K. Shankland. 2006. "Writing into the Twenty-First Century: An Overview of Research on Writing, 1999–2004." *Written Communication* 23 (4): 451–76.

Kilfoil, Carrie B. 2015. "Beyond the 'Foreign' Language Requirement: From a Monolingual to a Translingual Ideology in Rhetoric and Composition Graduate Education." *Rhetoric Review* 34 (4): 426–44.

Kilfoil, Carrie Byar. 2017. "The Linguistic Memory of Composition and the Rhetoric and Composition PhD: Forgetting (and Remembering) Language and Language Difference in Doctoral Curricula." *Composition Studies* 45 (2): 130–50.

MacDonald, Susan Peck. 2007. "The Erasure of Language." *College Composition and Communication* 58 (4): 585–625.

Matsuda, Paul Kei. 2013. "It's the Wild West Out There: A New Linguistic Frontier in U.S. College Composition." In *Literacy as Translingual Practice: Between Communities and Classrooms*, edited by A. Suresh Canagarajah, 128–38. New York: Routledge.

Pawlowski, Madelyn T. 2019. Locating and Supporting the Developing Pedagogical Language Knowledge of College Writing Instructors. PhD diss, University of Arizona.

Pawlowski, Madelyn, and Christine M. Tardy. 2017. "Locating Language in Writing Teacher Education: An Analysis of Trends and Methods." Paper presented at Conference on College Composition and Communication, Portland, OR.

Rhodes, Jacqueline, and Jonathan Alexander. 2014. "Reimagining the Social Turn: New Work from the Field." *College English* 76 (6): 481–87.

Severino, Carol. 2017. " 'Multilingualizing' Composition: A Diary Self-Study of Learning Spanish and Chinese." *Composition Studies* 45 (2): 12–31.

Shulman, Lee S. 1987. "Knowledge and Teaching: Foundations of the New Reform." *Harvard Educational Review* 57 (1): 1–22.

Tardy, Christine M. 2017. "Crossing, or Creating, Divides? A Plea for Transdisciplinary Scholarship." In *Crossing Divides: Exploring Translingual Writing Pedagogies and Programs*, edited by Bruce Horner and Laura Tetreault, 181–89. Logan: Utah State University Press.

Williams, Julia, and Frankie Condon. 2017. "Translingualism in Composition Studies and Second Language Writing: An Uneasy Alliance." *TESL Canada Journal/Revue TESL du Canada* 33 (2): 1–18.

You, Xiaoye. 2010. *Writing in the Devil's Tongue: A History of English Composition in China*. Carbondale: Southern Illinois University Press.

8
A TRANSLINGUAL APPROACH TO TUTORING INTERNATIONAL GRADUATE STUDENTS

Aimee Jones

In many graduate rhetoric and composition programs, graduate students tutor in writing centers, where they engage in meaning-making work with linguistically diverse students. Accordingly, graduate tutor-training courses could be prime settings to professionalize graduate students to work across language and cultural differences since university writing centers are increasingly becoming sites where students with diverse backgrounds, cultures, and language practices come to seek individualized academic writing support (Ruecker 2011; Thonus 2014). Although all writing center clients have complex and shifting motivations and expectations for utilizing the writing center, the current binary model of tutoring (and tutor training) eclipses the language-related motivations and expectations of international multilingual students. The binary model of tutoring is thought to move writing centers away from the stigma of remediation centers for basic writers with its focus on nondirective tutoring strategies that address "higher-order concerns" (HOCs) like rhetorical awareness, organizational strategies, and argument development before bringing attention to "lower-order concerns" (LOCs) or issues at the sentence level such as punctuation, grammar, and word choice (Brooks 1991; McAndrew and Reigstad 2001). The higher-order/lower-order binary model aims to promote the long-term goal of helping students develop as writers, which is emphasized in Stephen North's (1984) famous axiom: "Our job is to produce better writers, not better writing" (438).

A problem with this binary model of tutoring for international multilingual students is that it assigns the status of lower-order concern to language, which minimizes or negates the linguistic needs of these students. Additionally, the binary tutoring model associates rhetorical

https://doi.org/10.7330/9781646423262.c008

awareness with the process-based approach to writing instruction, while language tends to be relegated to product. In this sense, language becomes a commodity students simply acquire, which is akin to the language ideology of monolingualism. According to Bruce Horner and Sara Alvarez (2019), "Monolingualist ideology represents language users as mere 'users' of something given to them, with the responsibility of then having to use it 'correctly' or 'properly' or 'appropriately'" (20). Additionally, "[monolingualism] has contributed to the commodification of language, denying the role played by language users' concrete labor in maintaining and revising language" (21). In this view, assigning language the role of a lower-order concern erases the complex labor processes involved in language use for linguistically diverse students.

A more inclusive model of graduate tutor training could adopt a translingual orientation, which would shift the focus of language use from consumption to production. An important aspect of a translingual approach to language difference is its acknowledgment of labor, the agency attributed to language users, and the kinds of social relations it advances (Horner and Alvarez 2019, 10). According to Horner and Alvarez, translingual theory "takes as its point of departure not particular language practices already marked by the language ideology of monolingualism as 'different' but, instead, all language as labor confronting and producing difference" (10). In other words, a translingual approach sees language difference not as a deviation from a standard that must be corrected; instead, it looks at what writers are doing with language to produce meaning and why (Horner et al. 2011). Therefore, a translingual approach to tutoring would acknowledge the agency of multilingual students' language practices and allow a space for this agency to be consciously and deliberatively negotiated and exercised.

This chapter contributes to research on translingual graduate education in rhetoric and composition by reporting on a case study that mapped the motivations and expectations of four international multilingual graduate students who frequently utilized the graduate writing center (GWC) at an R1 university in Florida. Given chapter length constraints, this chapter focuses on two of the participants. International multilingual *graduate* students were specifically chosen for the purposes of this study because they can illuminate matters of international multilingual student motivation/expectations to enhance tutor training. As Alan Jenkins, Rosanna Breen, Roger Lindsay, and Angela Brew (2003) explain, graduate students[1] are generally more goal directed than undergraduate students and have more specific goals driving their motivations. Additionally, undergraduates are more dependent on their professors to structure their learning and provide motivation for them (33). Graduate students, on the other hand, are generally self-directed and self-motivated and have undertaken graduate study motivated by very specific academic/professional trajectories. They may also have long relationships with the writing center and show strong self-awareness of their writing development and language resources given their maturity and scholarly focus in the context of extended, graduate-level scholarship and training. From interviews with and observations of the international multilingual graduate students, this project mapped the participants' motivations and expectations for utilizing the GWC, which corresponded with their evolving communicative abilities and identities. In analyzing the participants' motivations and expectations of writing center tutors, the chapter also provides insight into how writing center administrators can prepare their graduate tutors to better work across cultures and languages by integrating translingual theories of composition into their graduate tutor-training courses.

RESEARCH QUESTIONS

In order to inform the development of graduate tutor-training pedagogy that better prepares graduate students to serve the writing needs of multilingual students, this chapter focuses on the results of a case study that examined four international multilingual graduate students' sources of motivation and expectations for utilizing the writing center. As mentioned above, given chapter length constraints, this chapter focuses on two of the participants.

The study was guided by three research questions:

1. What are an international multilingual graduate student's motivations for utilizing the university writing center?

     (Here I define motivation as a general phenomenon of expending energy towards a goal.)

2. What does an international multilingual graduate student expect to gain during sessions at the university writing center?

     (Here I define expectation as a specific desire driven by students' motivations in relation to their evolving identities.)

3. In what ways do these sources of motivation and expectations change over time?

The participants were asked a series of interview questions derived from these research questions. Each participant was interviewed twice—once before their tutoring session and once directly following their tutoring session. The pre- and post-interviews were each about thirty minutes long, and the semistructured interview questions included both Likert-survey questions and open-ended questions. Together the interview questions (1) gathered background and demographic information on the participants, (2) inquired into their sources of motivation and expectations for utilizing the writing center, and (3) ascertained the participants' satisfaction with their writing center experiences. The participants' tutoring sessions were also observed and audio recorded.

Upon completing the collection of data and manually transcribing the interviews, I analyzed and interpreted the data using qualitative methods. I coded the transcripts in units of phrases that responded to the overarching research questions. From the data, three themes emerged across the case studies: (1) early motivations: a focus on the product; (2) shifting motivations: from product to process; and (3) incongruity between the participants' expectations and their tutors' practices. Together, these codes helped me understand what motivates international multilingual graduate students to utilize the writing center and their expectations of and satisfaction with their tutoring sessions.

SITE OF THE STUDY

This study was undertaken in the graduate writing center (GWC) at a large R1 public university in Florida. The GWC is a branch of the reading and writing center (RWC) at this institution, and, as the name suggests, only serves graduate students. The rationale behind establishing a writing center site exclusively for and staffed by graduate students was to create a space where graduate students could get assistance with the particular challenges of graduate-level writing assignments. Often graduate students request feedback on long manuscripts such as theses, dissertations, and articles for publication. Graduate tutors typically have more experience with writing these long-form projects than undergraduates and can more effectively contribute to feedback on both form and content. Almost half, 47 percent of 805 appointments conducted at the GWC, were attended by international graduate students in one semester (Florida State University WC Online 2017). Graduate students could sign up for either a thirty- or sixty-minute tutoring session and could attend tutoring sessions for a maximum of 1.5 hours a week. The GWC is staffed by only graduate English majors, and they work ten or twenty hours per week as part of their graduate assistantships.

To prepare to work in the GWC or RWC, graduate students must complete a required six-week tutor-preparation course. At the end of the course, graduate assistants can decide whether they want to work in the reading and writing center, which serves all students and faculty, or the graduate writing center, which only serves graduate students. The tutor-preparation course introduces graduate assistants to general theories of writing center tutoring and practice centered on nondirective, collaborative tutoring approaches that prioritize higher-order concerns over lower-order concerns. In total, out of this larger context of preparation, GWC tutors receive one day of preparation for working with multilingual students and one day for graduate students. Additionally, once the graduate students begin tutoring in the RWC and GWC, they attend biweekly, sixty-minute professional-development meetings throughout the semester that bring in specialists to discuss specific topics; typically, one meeting per semester focuses on working with multilingual students, and one meeting focuses on working with graduate students.

The RWC's and GWC's approach to tutoring writing, according to their website, is to "act as a practice audience for students' ideas and projects," helping them develop their writing in many areas. Among them are:

- **Process**: tutors focus on students' process of writing and support students' composing throughout all facets of that process;
- **Rhetorical awareness**: tutors support students' development of writing expertise in all writing genres and media employed across campus;
- **Reflective practice**: tutors model and encourage habits of reflection that prompt students to be more critically aware of their own writing practices; and
- **Transfer**: tutors foster the use of techniques and strategies students can apply and repurpose in multiple writing contexts. (Florida State University, Writing Resources n.d.)

Since the RWC and GWC promote the goal of helping students develop writing as a process, the centers report not to offer proofreading or editing services, but tutors will discuss grammar rules and help students improve their own proofreading and editing skills. Additionally, the centers encourage a Socratic style of peer response in which the tutor and tutee engage in a nondirective collaborative conversation about the tutee's text. In these conversations, higher-order concerns such as rhetorical awareness, organizational strategies, and argument development are prioritized over lower-order concerns such as syntax, punctuation, and word choice.

Table 8.1. Participants' background information

Name	Major	Stage of PhD program	Country of origin	Languages written	Perceived proficiency in English writing (1–4)
Min-jun (Male)	PhD in instructional systems and learning technologies	Dissertation prospectus, fourth year as a PhD student	South Korea	Korean, English, Japanese	4-native or bilingual proficiency
Valentina (Female)	PhD in international and comparative education	Coursework, second year as a PhD student	Colombia	Spanish, English, French	4-native or bilingual proficiency

PARTICIPANTS

The two participants featured in this chapter demonstrated diversity in regards to their PhD program stages, as each participant was involved in a different stage: coursework and dissertation prospectus. Accompanying their different stages of the PhD, each of the participants had a unique linguistic writing background and could write in at least three languages. Additionally, both of the participants perceived they had native or bilingual proficiency in English writing. The table above identifies the participants in terms of (1) major, (2) stage of PhD program, (3) country of origin, (4) languages they can write in, and (5) perceived proficiency in English writing.

Min-jun

Min-jun was born in South Korea and has lived in the United States for four years; he came to the United States on a student visa. Min-jun's first language is Korean, and he can also speak, read, and write in English and Japanese. Before coming to the United States, Min-jun completed his bachelor's and master's degrees in South Korea. His BA was in Korean language education, which did not require him to use English often. However, once he decided to pursue an MA in educational technology, he found the work very challenging since he had to read and write about journal articles written in English. Despite his challenges with the language, Min-jun pursued his PhD in the United States, and his discipline is instructional systems and learning technologies. At the time of the interview, Min-jun had completed his coursework and was working on his dissertation prospectus. Although he did not have specific plans about where he would work after obtaining his PhD and said he could live and work anywhere, Min-jun added he would prefer to go back to South Korea to find a job. Min-jun initially visited the GWC during the first semester of his PhD program. He learned about the GWC from his Korean friends, who told him there was a center on campus that offered free help with writing. He has been attending sessions at the GWC for four years.

Valentina

Valentina was born in Colombia and has lived in the United States for five years. Her first language is Spanish, and she can also speak, read, and write in English and French. Valentina came to the United States on a student visa and took intensive English classes (noncredit) at the university's Center for Intensive English Studies (CIES) for one year. She then began her master's degree in international affairs and completed her degree in one and a half years. After obtaining her master's degree, Valentina stayed in town to complete one year of optional practical training (OPT), which is a period when undergraduate and graduate international students on F-1 student visas who have completed their degrees can stay and work in the United States for one year to gain work experience that will complement their degrees. Following her OPT, Valentina began her PhD, specializing in international and comparative education. At the time of the interview, Valentina was in the second year of her PhD program and was taking coursework. After completing her degree, Valentina would like to return home to Colombia or another South American country to look for a job. She does not intend to stay in the United States after graduation. Valentina first visited the GWC while she was working on her master's degree. She came to the GWC expecting to have her sentences corrected by the tutors. Valentina explained that although she completed the intensive English course at CIES, she still made a lot of grammar mistakes when writing in Edited American English. Additionally, the writing she did at CIES (mostly narrative writing) did not prepare her for the kind of academic writing she would be required to do in her master's program, which included genres like research essays, article reviews, and literature reviews. Valentina has been attending sessions at the GWC for four years.

EARLY MOTIVATIONS: A FOCUS ON THE PRODUCT

One theme that emerged from the participants' interviews was that during the first year of attending writing center sessions, all the participants were motivated to gain a polished, error-free text in Edited American

English by the end of their sessions. Furthermore, the participants indicated they understood that having their texts proofread by tutors to gain an error-free product by the end of the session was not optimal for long-term learning according to the research-based process approach to writing development. However, given the time restraints of a tutoring session, they prioritized an error-free product over the learning process. For example, in his retrospective interview, Min-jun described his writing as "very bad" during his first year of his PhD program and explained he wanted instruction in the conventions of Edited American English, but he wanted even more for a tutor to review all his sentences before he submitted his texts to his professors. Min-jun explained, "At the beginning of my coursework, I was not sure of my English grammar at all. Whenever I got stuck with my grammar, I needed someone; I needed tutor at every single point of my sentences." Min-jun clarified he had a very specific expectation of the hour-long tutoring session, that his entire assignment would be reviewed and made acceptable for submission in terms of fluency. Min-jun also explained that this expectation was so strong he often felt nervous during tutoring sessions out of fear he would not have an error-free product by the end of the session.

> At the beginning of my coursework, my expectation was mostly to finish what I wanted within the time. For example, the maximum is one hour. So just suppose that I have one-page assignment, and I have one hour with tutor. My expectation is to complete my assignment with editing within the hour. But sometimes, I was very hurried because I expected oh this tutor cannot finish my assignment, and the deadline is tonight. Sometimes I felt very hurried and nervous, so sometimes I just wanted the proofreading and editing. I know that was not good, but sometimes my expectation was exactly proofreading because the time limit.

While Min-jun was taking coursework in his first year of his PhD program, he was motivated to have his weekly assignments edited and to improve his class grade, both of which he said were "highly related to his status"—in terms of his progression as a doctoral student—"in coursework or not." Min-jun explained that "writing in English was not that much important actually," indicating that proficiency in Edited American English was mostly important for obtaining good grades but not necessarily so important for long-term learning. Interestingly, Min-jun added, "I know that was not good, but sometimes my expectation was exactly proofreading," a statement suggesting Min-jun's awareness of the binary model of tutoring. It seems Min-jun was aware of the distinction between the product-versus-process approach to writing development and that, according to the dominant process-based model, short-term proofreading assistance was not optimal for long-term learning. Although he was regretful about choosing the product approach in the first year of his PhD program, it was a necessary choice in order to progress through his program.

Likewise, Valentina indicated in her retrospective interview that her lack of confidence in her writing prevented her from submitting her texts to her professors without having a GWC tutor proofread them during the first year of her master's program. Valentina explained that receiving proofreading assistance, and in turn reassurance her texts were fluent in Edited American English and error free, were her main expectations for using the GWC in the first year of her master's program.

> I remember that I was expecting only to have like grammar corrected. I was just finishing my GRE at [the intensive English school] and there I have like a lot of grammar mistakes so I wanted to have a place to just to check grammar. So I think my main motivation is that I feel better about my work after going there. I always go there for some feedback and corrections. So I feel like I do a lot of grammar mistakes and I'm also insecure. So I feel like if I go there, I'm more relaxed to turn in the papers.

Although Valentina gained confidence in her texts after having a tutor review them, she said gaining this feeling of reassurance made her a little "writing center dependent." Valentina further explained, "I was desperate when the writing center closes or everybody is busy, that is a nightmare for me. If the writing center doesn't exist, I'm lost. You know for example, for finals, sometimes I paid somebody because the writing center is closed or something. So I pay for having my papers edited, and it's so expensive." The act of paying for an error-free text highlights the materiality of the product. It seems apparent that early on in her use of the GWC, Valentina was dependent on the writing center, according to her own account, and expected to gain a polished, error-free product by the end of each session. She also felt insecure if she was not able to receive feedback on her texts before turning them in.

While Min-jun and Valentina were in the first year of their programs, they had what they perceived as low Edited American English writing proficiency levels and several assignments due weekly. Because of these constraints, they often preferred to receive just proofreading assistance, although they knew it was not optimal according to the research-based process approach to writing development. Additionally, Min-jun expressed a sort of remorse for taking the proofreading assistance, but at the same time, he said it was necessary in order to meet his deadlines and produce fluent texts acceptable for submission to his professors. It also seemed he was aware of the difference between product and process and knew a process approach would improve his long-term writing skills more. However, given his needs at the time and the constraints on his learning—English-proficiency level, time, and weekly assignments—Min-jun needed to focus on the product, and not the learning process, in order to progress through his program.

SHIFTING MOTIVATIONS: FROM PRODUCT TO PROCESS

A second theme that emerged from the interviews was that the participants' most recent motivations for using the GWC at the current stage of their PhD programs appeared to be more dynamic, as they expected to improve linguistic and rhetorical aspects of their writing. For example, the participants both mentioned developing a more professional or US sounding "voice," which reflected a change in the perception of their abilities and identities. Min-jun explained that now, during the fourth year of his PhD program, he is "90 percent sure" about his grammar, so he seeks more advanced-level writing instruction, which he described as learning how to "use paraphrasing and other verbs, other expressions with the same meaning." According to Min-jun, "Sentence is fine, the grammar is perfect. But I'm not sure if this is kind of high schooler's writing or more professional writing. [Professional writing] is my goal recently, and it's different." Min-jun explained that although he is confident with Edited American English grammar, he presently struggles with making his essays sound more professional. Therefore, his motivations have shifted from wanting an error-free product to wanting his writing to reflect an assumed identity as an academic and professional and not an ESL student.

As Valentina described her motivations for using the GWC in the second year of her PhD program (which was her fourth year of using the GWC), it was apparent her shifts in motivations and expectations reflected a change in her perceptions of her abilities and her identity as well. Like Min-jun, Valentina indicated she currently wants more than just proofreading assistance and a fluent text from her tutoring sessions. When asked to explain what she most recently expects from her tutors, Valentina outlined a nuanced set of expectations:

> My expectation, like my minimal expectation is to have like the grammar checked, and to check that the essay has like a logic structure. That is the minimum that I expect. . . . I feel like I have a limitation with the language. So it's very poor or very repetitive about the same words or the same kind of things. So sometimes I feel like they could help me to say things in a different way or to sound like more American, not like an exact translation from Spanish to English.

Unlike Min-jun, Valentina still expects to have her grammar checked by tutors, indicating she is not completely confident in her Edited American English writing abilities. Valentina also said she wants to "sound more American," suggesting she has a new motive informing her use of the GWC as her proficiency in US English writing has increased and her identity is in the process of changing from ESL student to emerging professional. Although she still wants her tutors to proofread her writing, she expects them to go beyond just that and, as Min-jun expects of his tutors, help her develop linguistic and rhetorical resources associated with native English speakers and professional communities to accompany her emerging identity as a member of a US discourse community.

INCONGRUITY BETWEEN THE PARTICIPANTS' EXPECTATIONS AND THEIR TUTORS' PRACTICES

A final theme that emerged from the findings centered on the role tutors played in the participants' tutoring sessions and the dynamism of these roles. Despite the shifting motivations, expectations, abilities, and identities of the participants, each of the participants indicated some of their tutors did not perceive these shifts and did not adjust their tutoring practices to support these changes. Instead, the tutors inverted the hierarchy of the binary HOC/LOC model, regardless of context, and proofread the participants' texts. It can be assumed the tutors may have held a monolingual orientation to writing, or the idea that a text should be constructed in one language with standard norms (coming from the so-called native speaker's use of the language), which is thought to be free of influence from other languages (Canagarajah 2013, 1). Another assumption is that the tutors' default approach to solely proofread the participants' texts suggests the tutors were trying to help the participants achieve a monolingual ideal, which the participants did not value as much later in their graduate programs. For example, Min-jun explained how, by the second year of his PhD program, he did not want tutors just to proofread his papers any longer, and he actually became dissatisfied with tutors who only thought he needed to focus on Edited American English grammar. Min-jun recalled one tutor in particular who would only proofread his work and explained, "I just remember one tutor, I met him kind of second year. His strategy is to just proofreading, and to just tell the answers very straightforward. Like he was reading my sentences and check, check, check, and he told me answer. It was not helpful actually, but it was good to finish by the time. But it was not helpful." When asked to discuss how his tutors could more effectively support his needs, Min-jun described tutors who try to fully understand the meaning of his text before negotiating strategies for revision, which was a common practice of his preferred tutor, Sara:[2]

> I prefer tutors who ask what do you mean, and then I would explain or those who really try to answer my questions sincerely or those with a lot of knowledge about academic writing. Most I prefer tutor is um Sara. I like her strategy. Her strategy is very strong. She tends to ask the students, "What are you saying?" "What do you think about?" and just try to make them your own sentences. I was tutored with Sara for two semesters and I realized that my writing skills has been very improved by her.

As he indicated here, Min-jun no longer wanted to be directed in his tutoring sessions in the fourth year of his PhD program but instead preferred tutors who could help him take agency to improve his writing skills rhetorically and develop his own voice. Thus, Min-jun no longer wanted to have his texts merely corrected; instead, he expected his tutors to act as a surrogate for the audience instead of a proofreader. In the fourth year of his PhD program, Min-jun had reached a dynamic benchmark shift in motivations, expectations, and goals, and he expected his tutors to recognize that shift and be dynamic in their tutoring as well.

Likewise, when Valentina discussed her satisfaction with tutors, she explained that while she appreciates tutors who focus on linguistic concerns and understands it may be difficult for some to make suggestions beyond that, she also wants her tutors to help her shape her writing and make sure it is logical and also help her develop a US academic writing style.

> I mean sometimes when I see the tutors, I get that it can be very boring after a while to have one people after the other, but I would suggest like them to do something. I feel like there are some that just if you say, "I want to check grammar," they just check grammar, that's it. So my suggestion will be like just help with the ideas and the style, and not just the grammar. And I feel like for example, when you want to make like suggestions in style and things, that implies more effort because sometimes you have to change a whole paragraph or something like that. So it's hard. It's not like, ok period, or a word here. It's like let's try to say the same, but in another way. It takes like more effort, so I understand that sometimes they just say like, no let's do it simple.

It is apparent Valentina has moved beyond solely expecting Edited American English grammar-based feedback from tutors in the second year of her PhD program. However, her response suggests her tutors often default to proofreading instead of taking the time to understand her evolving needs and expectations. While she appears grateful for the proofreading assistance, she also seems a bit dissatisfied with tutors who only proofread her work. Her motivations have become more dynamic in the second year of her PhD program (and her fourth year utilizing the GWC), and she is now thinking more about how her voice and identity come across to her audience and how logical her writing is.

The incongruity between the participants' needs and their tutors' practices suggests it would have been helpful for their tutors to understand the participants' motivations for utilizing the GWC were dynamic and not fixed. Although the participants were highly motivated to gain an error-free text from their sessions in the first year of their programs, these motivations shifted over time in relation to their abilities, tasks, progress in their programs, and identities. The participants' motivational shifts followed a sequence that began with meeting basic needs, such as producing fluent texts in Edited American English acceptable for submission to their professors. Once these basic needs were met and the participants' writing proficiencies increased, the participants' motivations shifted. The participants' needs, which were driven by their motivations, became centered more on the linguistic and rhetorical aspects of their texts and how their texts reflected their emerging or perceived identities. Likewise, they expected their tutors to perceive these shifts and better support their needs and motivations for utilizing the GWC.

IMPLICATIONS FOR GRADUATE STUDENT TUTOR TRAINING

As mentioned previously, the hierarchy of the binary model of tutor training (HOCs versus LOCs) presents problems for tutoring multilingual students, as it risks erasing matters of language through their association with lower-order concerns. Although several of the tutors described by the participants in this study inverted the hierarchy and only focused on language matters, in the act of doing so, they assigned a fixed, monolingual identity to multilingual graduate student clients and thus preserved the myth of linguistic homogeneity. The clients' accounts, on the other hand, show awareness of their dynamic, shifting language resources and identities and evidence frustration with the tutors based on how the tutors approached them. Given the monolingual orientation of the traditional binary model of tutoring, a translingual approach to tutor training would better prepare tutors to see multilingual students in a more productive way that aligns with the clients' motivations and expectations. Two ways of incorporating a translingual orientation into graduate student tutor training would be to rethink the HOCs versus LOCs binary to focus on language from a productive viewpoint and to replace nondirective tutor/client communication with dialogue and negotiation.

Rethinking the HOCs versus LOCs Binary: Language as Production

The hierarchy of the HOCs versus LOCs binary assigns all language matters to the status of a lower-order concern, which negates the linguistic needs of multilingual students. As lower-order concerns, matters of language difference are an afterthought in the writing process and are simply addressed as matters that can be fixed according to a presumed monolingual ideal. A problem with the monolingual orientation to writing; as Suresh Canagarajah (2013) explains, is that it assumes the proficiency of a so-called native speaker was developed in a homogeneous environment. However, written and spoken communication do not feature one language at a time; instead, text and talk are influenced and mediated by diverse codes, which may not always be evident on the surface. Therefore, languages are always in contact and influencing each other (6). Since aiming to achieve a monolingual ideal is problematic, it would be helpful for graduate tutors to rethink language matters that arise in tutoring sessions through a translingual orientation that focuses on the productive value of language difference instead.

As mentioned in the introduction to this chapter, an important aspect of a translingual orientation to language difference is its focus on labor and the productive value of language difference. Instead of looking at language as something a language user attempts to acquire and use correctly and appropriately, a translingual perspective shifts the focus to language as a resource for producing meaning in writing (Horner et al. 2011, 303). Therefore, when confronting language difference, instead of looking for the possibility of error, a translingual approach would raise questions such as, "What might this difference do? How might it function expressively, rhetorically, communicatively? For whom, under what conditions, and how?" (303–4). Thus, a translingual approach would allow language users the agency to shape language for specific purposes and asks readers, or in the case of this chapter graduate tutors, to read with patience and with deliberative inquiry.

In order to incorporate a translingual orientation into graduate student tutor training, it is first important to engage graduate students in conversations about translingualism as an approach to language difference. This can be done by exposing graduate students to literature focused not only on translingual approaches to language difference and literacy education but also on the full trajectory of literacy education, from monolingual, to bilingual, to multilingual, to translingual approaches. As Juan Guerra explains in "Cultivating a Rhetorical Sensibility in the Translingual Writing Classroom" (2016), it is important to engage students "in the process of explicitly demystifying the various approaches to language difference—including the translingual—by inviting our students to consider how each of them influences the choices they make in the writing classroom" (232). Bruce Horner et al.'s (2011) "Language Difference in Writing: Toward a Translingual Approach," and the selected bibliography included at the end of the article, offer valuable resources for introducing graduate students to a full trajectory of debates over language difference and literacy education. After familiarizing students with the literature, graduate tutor-training instructors can assign reflective writing or a visual mapping activity to summarize the key takeaways from the various approaches and explain how they relate to their own beliefs about language difference and literacy education. Familiarizing graduate students with the various approaches will enable them to navigate and evaluate the competing ideologies, which is important for informing their future teaching and tutoring practices.

Replacing Nondirective Communication with Dialogue and Negotiation

Another necessary step in incorporating a translingual orientation to graduate tutor training is to help tutors create a space where their international multilingual clients can negotiate language difference and exercise agency over their choices. In order to establish such a space, we must rethink the way tutors communicate with their clients. The traditional binary model of tutor training encourages tutors to use nondirect communication strategies wherein the tutor exerts less dominance over the feedback they give. When tutors use nondirective tutoring methods, tutors are thought to empower students by allowing them to discover answers about their writing through questioning and nondirective responses (Brooks 1991). Jeff Brooks (1991) explains that nondirective tutoring methods are favored in tutoring sessions since they help move the writing center away from the fix-it-shop mentality and encourage students to have agency over and responsibility for their revision choices. Although nondirective tutoring methods can give some students more agency over their writing, these tutoring methods produce problems for international multilingual graduate students. Specifically, these methods only succeed if the writer has some sort of prior knowledge of the target language and its rhetorical conventions (Powers 1993). Additionally, as this study highlights, tutors may default to directive communication strategies when working with international multilingual students, which also diminishes the agency of international multilingual students in a tutoring session.

A translingual orientation to communication between tutor and international multilingual client must focus on dialogue that invites collaboration and negotiation. Canagarajah (2013) explains how dialogue invites collaboration, which allows multilingual students to coconstruct meaning in contact zones, which are defined by Mary Louise Pratt (1991) as "social spaces where cultures meet, clash, and grapple with each other, often in contexts of highly asymmetrical relations of power" (34). For the most part, and as the case studies demonstrate, international multilingual graduate students come to the writing center asking tutors to become practice audiences for their work and are looking for collaborative feedback, not indirect questioning.[3] Thus dialogue with negotiation, instead of directive or nondirective feedback, could prove to be more beneficial for tutoring sessions with international multilingual students. As Canagarajah explains, negotiation allows multilingual students to work through language differences with native English-speaking students to come to an agreement on successful communication. Negotiation looks past grammatical competence of a monolingual paradigm and instead allows multilingual students to have agency and a voice in shaping their communicative practices. An example of dialogue and negotiation arose while observing Valentina's tutoring session. Valentina and her tutor engaged in a moment of dialogue and negotiation when discussing word choice for a survey Valentina was creating.

> TUTOR: How do you think civics classes impact students' thinking . . . knowledge. Why do you have "knowledge" in parentheses?
>
> VALENTINA: Because I don't know if it's better to ask how do you think civics classes impact students' knowledge or students' thinking. They are different things right?
>
> TUTOR: Ya, the way I read it, if I hear "impact students' thinking," I think of the way they are gonna form thoughts in the moment. If I hear "impact students' knowledge," I think like their base understanding. I'm not sure which one you want.
>
> VALENTINA: Ok. So I guess I prefer "knowledge" because I want to know if civics is impacting the way the students will think, but not only in that precise moment, but after the class.
>
> TUTOR: Ya "knowledge" to me implies a core understanding.
>
> VALENTINA: Ya, okay.

In this exchange, instead of directly telling Valentina the more appropriate word, her tutor engaged in dialogue with her to better understand what the purpose of Valentina's survey question was. Then her tutor explained the differences between the two words, and the two of them negotiated the best choice, which gave Valentina agency over her writing. In the end, Valentina made the final decision based on what she was trying to convey in the sentence. Therefore, dialogue and negotiation are important for tutor/client communication because they give multilingual writers agency to shape meaning from their own perspectives and gain reassurance from their tutors that their writing is understood. Additionally, negotiation helps tutors understand the communicative goals of multilingual writers and helps tutors think more critically about helping them fulfill their specific needs and expectations.

CONCLUSION

From this study, we know the international multilingual graduate students' motivations for utilizing the GWC were dynamic. The participants exhibited motivations that shifted between desires for an error-free product to engaging in a process of rhetorical and linguistic development. This knowledge is important because it suggests a translingual approach to tutoring practices could be valuable in rethinking the hierarchy of HOCs versus LOCs by assigning rhetorical power to navigating and negotiating language difference. Additionally, flexible strategies focused on dialogue and negotiation for international multilingual graduate students could be more effective than directive versus nondirective communication for helping them navigate language differences in order to produce meaningful texts. I urge readers who are interested in exploring questions like the ones taken up in this study to undertake longitudinal research projects to investigate whether the participants' shifting motivations are typical of other international multilingual graduate students who attend writing center sessions. By understanding these motivations, we can work to evaluate whether developing a translingual approach to graduate student tutor training is more responsive to the dynamic motivations international multilingual graduate students bring to the university writing center.

NOTES

1. The category of graduate students here includes domestic and international graduate students.
2. The pseudonym Sara was used to protect the tutor's identity.
3. Seeking direct feedback is not exclusive to international multilingual writers. Native English-speaking writers often want direct feedback on their writing as well (Straub and Lunsford 1995).

REFERENCES

Brooks, Jeff. 1991. "Minimalist Tutoring: Making the Student Do All the Work." *Writing Lab Newsletter* 15 (6): 1–4.

Canagarajah, Suresh. 2013. *Translingual Practice: Global Englishes and Cosmopolitan Relations.* London: Routledge.

Florida State University WC Online. 2017. "System Statistics Report." https://fsu.mywc online.com/demographic.php, accessed May 2017; site inactive on April 5, 2020.

Florida State University, Writing Resources, English Department. n.d. "Reading and Writing Center." Last modified 2021. http://wr.english.fsu.edu/reading-writing-center.

Guerra, Juan. 2016. "Cultivating a Rhetorical Sensibility in the Translingual Writing Classroom." In "Translingual Work in Composition," special issue *College English* 78 (3): 228–33.

Horner, Bruce, and Sara P. Alvarez. 2019. "Defining Translinguality." *Literacy in Composition Studies* 7 (2): 1–30.

Horner, Bruce, Min-Zhan Lu, Jacqueline Jones Royster, and John Trimbur. 2011. "Language Difference in Writing: Toward a Translingual Approach." *College English* 73 (3): 303–21.

Jenkins, Alan, Rosanna Breen, Roger Lindsay, and Angela Brew. 2003. "Academic Research and Student Motivation in Higher Education." In *Reshaping Teaching in Higher Education: Linking Teaching with Research,* edited by Alan Jenkins, 31–54. New York: Kogan Page.

McAndrew, Don, and Tom Reigstad. 2001. *Tutoring Writing: A Practical Guide for Conferences.* Portsmouth, NH: Boynton/Cook.

North, Steven M. 1984. "The Idea of a Writing Center." *College English* 46 (5): 433–46.

Powers, Judith. 1993. "Rethinking Writing Center Conferencing Strategies for the ESL Writer." *Writing Center Journal* 13 (2): 39–47.

Pratt, Mary Louise. 1991. "Arts of the Contact Zone." *Profession* 91 (1): 33–40.

Ruecker, Todd. 2011. "Improving the Placement of L2 Writers: The Students' Perspective." *WPA: Writing Program Administration* 35 (1): 91–117.

Straub, Richard, and Ronald F. Lundsford. 1995. *Twelve Readers Reading.* New York: Hampton Press.

Thonus, Terese. 2014. "Tutoring Multilingual Students: Shattering the Myths." *Journal of College Reading and Learning* 44 (2): 200–213.

PART III

Responses

9

SHIFTING THE PARADIGM OF TRANSLINGUAL AND TRANSNATIONAL GRADUATE EDUCATION

Amy J. Wan

In the introduction of this volume, Nancy Bou Ayash and Carrie Byars Kilfoil describe how "translingual theory unsettles a monolingual understanding of languages as discrete, static entities" and how such unsettling requires "engagements" that are "deliberate and visible," including both cross-language work "and/or [work that] involve[s] analysis of literacy practices easily identifiable as translingual in historically complicated geopolitical networks of dominance and resistance." The chapters that follow trace a number of possibilities of what these kinds of engagements could be in graduate education in rhetoric and composition—the successes but also the frustrations—while working to integrate translingual and transnational perspectives. The authors offer concrete practices, approaches, and examples of what graduate education influenced by transnationalism and translingualism might look like, such as Michelle Zaleski and Xiaoye You on mentorship, Aimee Jones on writing centers, and Bou Ayash on translation and language requirements, to name just three of the rich chapters found here.

What can and should graduate programs take from this volume? What can be learned and, most important, what kind of action can readers take, particularly in light of varying institutional statuses and positionalities? And as readers consider what implications these examples might have on their practices, I want to underscore how the collection of voices in this volume asks us to recognize that translingual and transnational graduate education is not just an acceptance of people who speak languages other than English or who come to the United States to study from other countries. Rather, it is, or should be, a paradigm shift, one that questions whose knowledge is privileged and why. As Corina

https://doi.org/10.7330/9781646423262.c009

Lerma, Moisés García-Rentería, Patricia Flores, Kate Mangelsdorf, and Lucía Durá describe in their chapter, graduate students "know how language works and how it connects to power, resistance, and invention. Yet their expertise is often invisible, ignored, [or] exoticized" (see chapter 1). How can students' existing expertise influence how our graduate programs work?

In this response, I take the opportunity to collectively consider a number of the chapters to work towards a broader understanding of the actions needed to engage with this potential paradigm shift in our thinking about language and knowledge beyond these specific examples. I write this from the perspective of a midcareer, Asian American tenured faculty member who is both a WPA for a first-year writing program that employs graduate instructors and a faculty member in a PhD program. I came to these chapters with the hope of gaining ideas and inspiration for how to reconcile a commitment to change and my own institutional status/power, as both someone who actively works towards dismantling the white listening subject and someone who must decide whether or not to admit particular students, pass a student's doctoral exams, approve a dissertation. I recognize my own institutional power and status while I strive to make things different. To that end, I also reflect on what is described in these chapters to consider how change happens within university structures—what contexts shape this kind of change making and how transnationalism and translingualism in graduate education are inextricably intertwined with other movements toward equity in higher education. I urge readers of this volume to think about the transformative potential of what's being proposed here and their own possible roles in enacting that transformation, recognizing the change we seek is not just about changing curriculum but about changing our approaches, our attitudes and ideologies, and our structures.

This process can be messy and necessitates the visible engagement Bou Ayash and Kilfoil describe in the introduction. The chapters in this volume provide guidance and examples of how we might take these up in our own local programs, whether the integration of issues of language diversity into graduate education (Horner; Lerma et al.), curricular and policy decisions (Bou Ayash; Tardy and Pawlowski), or ways we might shape our program communities (Zaleski and You). But these are not and cannot be isolated decisions; we must contend with the less tangible or less immediate—the ideological, dispositional, and structural changes that must be made alongside them. In "On Nonscalability: The Living World Is Not Amenable to Precision-Nested Scales," Anna Lowenhaupt Tsing (2012) calls our attention to the violence in scalability, the expansion of an idea reproduced without recognizing what is obscured, or even repressed or eliminated, in that expansion. For Tsing, "Nonscalability theory requires attention to historical contingency, unexpected conjuncture and the ways that contact across difference can produce new agendas" (510). These new agendas are not always visible, but if we want to make the kinds of changes described in this volume to sustain and have impact, we must consider any new practices in concert with how the whole system must change.

In his chapter on graduate seminars, Bruce Horner calls this process "dialogic" (a process of shifting and adjusting and integrating the changing contexts around him that might end up "recalibrating the program to take into account what has previously gone unrecognized)" (see chapter 4). While one might read these chapters and recognize that many of these changes happened because of the "faculty committed to making those persuasive arguments," we cannot rely only on individual shifts in what graduate faculty teach for programs to commit to such changes. Or rather, instead we must recognize that the decisions and practices that make up the chapters in this book rely on individuals to work hard against the ideologies of their institutions.

Horner describes how such "recalibration" is "bound to be local rather than systemic," but I want to make explicit what he implies, that the local is what can change the system and is reflective of the system. He writes, "A revolution that does not so much breach the ramparts as insidiously infect those residing within their circuit, invading the seemingly secure meaning of terms like *language, language learning,* and *translation.*" But while the process he describes is essential to change and for these terms to become unsettled, the hold of traditional norms about language and what it means to build knowledge within the institution of higher education—who gets certified, who is gatekeeping, what language is seen as "appropriate" (Flores and Rosa 2015)—remains strong. They remain deeply ingrained in our policies, systems, and epistemologies. Our discourses and policies about racialized language differences, such as the Students' Right to their Own Language statement, written in the early 1970s, and its most recent, still-relevant iteration, "This Ain't Another Statement! This is a DEMAND for Black Linguistic Justice!," tell us this is the case. While some might be drawn by genuine intellectual curiosity or an activist imperative to the questions posed by this volume, the gravity center of the field and, more important, the structures that surround it, must be changed with deliberate action. For every one of the success stories included here, there are invisible frustrations, failed attempts, and struggles, sometimes by faculty and graduate students who are already multiply marginalized within their institutions and the field, that did not make it into print.

The graduate student chapters in this volume confirm this Is the case. Joseph Franklin, Emily Yuko Cousins, and Alex Way argue "[translingual and transnational] frameworks help us look inward to recognize our complicity in reinforcing monolingualist values and practices that commodify certain competencies and uncritically emphasize marketability" (see chapter 2). The authors say these frameworks make these mechanisms visible, that these frameworks help us recognize our complicity but also show recognition does not always mean agentive and is not always a signal of transformative lasting change. In the *Reorder of Things*, Roderick Ferguson (2012) warns that the circulation of power often yields a substitution of "redistribution for representation" (8), that in the face of struggles over minority difference, one can easily mistake the redistribution of power within an institution for representation. The chapters here should not be mistaken for simply an argument for more representation—a different. course, some requirement changes—but rather ask us not to compartmentalize translingual and transnational theory in order to pay close attention to the framing of such content as structural critique (Franklin, Cousins, and Way, chapter 2). Bou Ayash's chapter about translation and the language requirement provide a great example of how this is at work, how deep engagement with student knowledge can drive the transformation of the structure of our departments such as requirements to better reflect this necessary paradigm shift (see chapter 5).

In their chapter (see chapter 1), Lerma, García-Rentería, Flores, Mangelsdorf, and Durá argue for this necessary expansiveness by proposing a panoramic ethos to expand "complex negotiations of language use and identities from what is often perceived as a single category, that is, the transnational student, to everyone in the classroom" (see chapter 1). They advocate for the necessity of multiple perspectives to create an "intersubjective ongoing dialogue in which the result is a widening of the horizon for both student and teacher." Graduate students are not just there to receive knowledge from faculty members, but instead, we can work together to create a space where we learn together.[1] And faculty do not have to let students lead the way in making these changes. Allowing graduate students to take the lead is an ugly truth, and those of us with more institutional power must do something to change it. This process of making change doesn't need to be painful in the way graduate students describe in this volume and in the hallways of our programs. As Bou Ayash and Kilfoil describe in the introduction, "Graduate students are positioned in the front lines of these ideological tensions largely not of their own making and are most burdened with the task of confronting them." As readers reflect on how this volume can influence what they do in their own programs, those of us with tenure and institutional stability must stand up. Creating space for graduate student knowledge is not just about programs recognizing them but also about fighting to change how programs work. This is how we might influence monolingual and by extension white-supremacist dispositions and structures.

Recognizing the influence of racialization, not always explicitly mentioned in the preceding chapters, alongside translingualism and transnationalism plays an important role in this process. If one is to think in binaries (cautiously), one must recognize that the opposite of translingualism and transnational are monolingualism and nationalism, both rooted in white supremacy. Within this shift in paradigm is the connection to current antiracist work being taken up in our field, and programs must be particularly cautious not to use the diversity of international students as a cover for the equity issues that have plagued the United States. Transnational and translingual perspectives must be held together with antiracist approaches and linguistic justice or else we are only submitting to the optics of "diversity" rather than thinking through what it would mean to change.

For instance, if we understand the influence of racialization and its attendant privilege on the tenor of our programs, we must always be questioning who is not there, probing the absences (such as students from the global south) to understand how we might address them. Programmatic considerations such as admissions, recruitment, and funding are at the core of who is able to enter graduate programs. In order to take seriously a commitment to translingual and transnational perspectives, we can't just change the curriculum. The people who are in the room and the structures themselves also must change. Zaleski and You talk about the necessary "change of mindset" and the "small, intentional decisions" that can get us there (quoting from Kimball 2015) (see chapter 6). They advocate "translingual mentorship," which is another form this kind of work can take. But this change can only happen if, in addition to thinking about who our graduate students are, graduate programs prioritize the hiring of faculty who can do this kind of mentorship[2] and then create workplaces where they can be more than just employed but can thrive.

Additionally, building on Jones's chapter (see chapter 8) on writing center practice, we must address the problem of what Nelson Flores and Jonathan Rosa (2015) describe as the "white listening subject," which is so deeply part of how we assess and understand writing. While Jones gives us an essential understanding of what it means for a graduate student to be assured of the value of their language, there's an opportunity to recognize the influence of the white listening subject on teachers and their expectation of error-free prose. Kilfoil's research on attitudes toward language difference in graduate programs demonstrates the hazards of an "add-on" approach, which is taken by people who see translingualism as something that happens outside of the center, upholding the "continued dominance of monolingualist ideology" (see chapter 3). The persistence of deficit thinking among graduate students, rather than a shift in disposition about language, demonstrates how easy it is to keep this matter contained as a teaching matter, rather than an ideological one. If you believe in the white listening subject and the ways it's constructed through white supremacy, capitalism, and racialization, then it's not that far a journey to recognize how the institutional structures in which we are employed are also part of this process, and that includes writing and graduate programs themselves. Transnationalism and translingualism in graduate education must be taken up in terms of equity and justice, not just an isolated language requirement or course content. We must make the necessary connections between what we do and those formations.

By paying attention to these terms of engagement, the movement towards this paradigm shift must also consider concrete action within our structures and what those of us with more power can do to change them. This necessitates a layering of local approaches, like how graduate student knowledge is valued, the mentoring relationships, and the institutional and program resources available to students, along with larger structural issues such as how graduate students are recruited, supported, and compensated. Some of these issues are beyond a writing program or department—the political economy of the university, systemic racism, racial capitalism, and immigration—but that doesn't mean we don't need to grapple with them, that they don't filter into our work. They are always present and part of the ecology. How does the work we do, the choices we make in classrooms, the policies we support reflect both the values and shortcomings of these larger structures?

None of what has been proposed can be sustained in isolation, tied to one faculty member, a cohort of graduate students, or a single course. Seeing these chapters together, trying to understand the breadth and depth of the work that must be done, is overwhelming. This is why we must find our accomplices and allies, work with people who have been thinking about and acting on language and race, and move forward together.

NOTES

1. For example, I realized that in the course of writing this response, my thoughts were being heavily influenced by Lindsey Albracht's dissertation on abolitionist transliteracies ecologies (2021), which she had defended right before I started reading this volume. It would be disingenuous to look at her work and not acknowledge the influence her work has had on my own thinking.

2. With contingent faculty making up approximately 50–75 percent of the faculty in the United States (Betensky et al. 2018), the viability of sustained mentorship rests, of course, on the hiring practices and structures within higher education more broadly. The American Federation of Teachers' *Promoting Racial and Ethnic Diversity in the Faculty: What Higher Education Unions Can Do* (AFT 2010) reports that "of 10.4 percent of faculty positions held by underrepresented racial and ethnic groups in 2007, 7.6 percent are contingent positions—which means 73 percent of underrepresented faculty hold positions that do not give them adequate wages or benefits, job security, or meaningful academic freedom" (13). Programs must be aware and attentive to these trends when hiring, as well as to protecting those faculty members once they are on campus. Sheila Carter-Tod (2021) describes the "normal" hiring practices that lead to the systemic exclusion of Black writing program administrators and adds that the "false assumption of neutrality will mean hiring practices will continue to be systemic barriers" (51).

REFERENCES

AFT Higher Education. 2010. *Promoting Racial and Ethnic Diversity in the Faculty: What Higher Education Unions Can Do.* https://www.aft.org/resolution/promote-aft-report -racial-and-ethnic-diversity-higher-education.

Albracht, Lindsey. 2021. Beyond Authorization: Toward Abolitionist Transliteracies Ecologies and an Anti-Racist Translingual Pedagogy. [Doctoral dissertation, CUNY Graduate Center] CUNY Academic Works. https://academicworks.cuny.edu/gc_etds/4285.

Betensky, Carolyn, Seth Kahn, Maria Maisto, and Talia Schaffer. 2018. "Common Good, Not Common Despair." Profession (Fall). https://profession.mla.org/common-good -not-common-despair/.

Carter-Tod, Sheila. 2021. "Why So Few of US: Addressing Larger Issues of Systemic Exclusions That Limit the Numbers of Black Writing Program Administrators." *WPA: Writing Program Administration* 44 (3): 49–55.

Ferguson, Roderick A. 2012. *The Reorder of Things: The University and Its Pedagogies of Minority Difference.* Minneapolis: University of Minnesota Press.

Flores, Nelson, and Jonathan Rosa. 2015. "Undoing Appropriateness: Raciolinguistic Ideologies and Language Diversity in Education." *Harvard Educational Review* 85 (2): 149–71.

Tsing, Anna Lowenhaupt. 2012. "On Nonscalability: The Living World Is Not Amenable to Precision-Nested Scales." *Common Knowledge* 18 (3): 505–24.

10

TRANSLINGUALISM AND TRANSNATIONALISM AS DECOLONIAL RECOVERY

Anselma Widha Prihandita

Like many occasions of theorizing, transnationalism and translingualism emerge from wounds and the need for healing. Or at least that is how I see it—and that was what drew me the most to these theories and approaches throughout my graduate studies. In this volume, for example, Corina Lerma, Moisés García-Rentería, Patricia Flores, Kate Mangelsdorf, and Lucía Durá's theorization of panoramic ethos begins with the often uncomfortable and alienating experiences of students who, for the sake of their education, had to cross national and cultural borders (see chapter 1). In addition, Joseph Franklin, Emily Cousins, and Alex Way's work is founded on how transnational experiences in teaching and learning often do not seem "legible" to the field, and how graduate students' exhaustions often go untreated and normalized (see chapter 2). Like the graduate students who share their experiences in these chapters, I too came to translingualism and transnationalism because of the discomforts I have felt from the earliest days of my graduate school trajectory.

As a woman of color, an international graduate student, and a nonnative English speaker, I am what people would call a minority, an outsider, a guest in the majority-white US higher education institution I found myself in. I have often felt I could not see myself, my people or our problems, interests and sensemaking practices in the issues I studied and read about. Everything was American all the way down—which I thought made sense. After all, I was now studying at a US university. As a result, I spent hours upon hours in my first quarter of graduate school googling what Jim Crow was, why the *Brown v. Board of Education* (1954) ruling was important, what a community college was, what exactly a writing center did or didn't do, how first-year composition worked, and a hundred

https://doi.org/10.7330/9781646423262.c010

other little things that might be taken for granted but were vitally important pieces of historical context I, as a foreigner, was missing.

In my second quarter in graduate school, I decided to write a paper on an issue from home, namely the use of hardline Islamic rhetoric in a series of elections in Indonesia. I thought it would be nice to speak about something I was familiar and deeply concerned with, using some knowledge I had brought with me from "the time before." I was worried I had been spending too much time thinking about US issues and not about my own people. After I had finished the paper, I met with my (white American male) professor for a one-on-one conference. My professor thought my analysis in the paper was insightful, but he also then said I needed to make connections to US culture if I wanted to be seen as relevant in the scholarly community. He asked me how the understanding I had gained from looking at this Indonesian case could help other scholars understand how religious rhetoric worked elsewhere. He suggested maybe I could compare the Indonesian case with Evangelist rhetoric in the United States. He also couldn't understand why there was such contention between Muslims and Christians in Indonesia and recommended I try to explain that better for a US academic audience.

I walked out of his office with a sense of discomfort that took me a long time to unpack: Why was being useful to "other scholars"—and I read that as US scholars, given the context of the question and the de facto US-centrism of rhetoric and composition as a field—more important than making sense of my and my people's own experiences? Why was it taken as a given that I must learn about US history to make sense of my course materials (no professors have ever asked me if I had difficulties with the US context undergirding the issues we read and discussed in class), but when I—the Other, the non-American—talked about my own context, I had to explain everything in detail? Why was the labor of negotiating transnational academic knowledge expected of me, an international female graduate student of color, but not my white American professor and the "other scholars" who eventually may or may not read my essay about my homeland? Does this not imply that the "other scholars" representing academia in its entirety are to be seen as a hegemonic, monolithic entity that takes US and Western contexts and conventions as universal but other peoples and locations as anomalies or foreign objects that must be constantly explained, as the hegemons deem it too troublesome to learn about these anomalies or foreign objects by themselves?

My experiences, along with those described in Lerma et al.'s and Cousin et al.'s chapters, are examples of the many wounds and discomforts resulting from hegemonies and exclusions that invalidate the legitimacy and equality of marginalized individuals and communities based on the specific ways their practices intersect with certain cultures, traditions, locations, and identities outside of "the norm"—broadly construed as the university-educated white male middle-class American/ European. In a way, my professor's feedback was well intentioned and due to no fault of his own; it was a product of much larger structures at work: of Eurocentrism and the Westernized university, of coloniality at large. His advice was expected given the way academia is set up, with its canon, traditions, interests, and valued language and literacy practices.

To borrow from Latin American decolonial theory, Boaventura de Sousa Santos (2014) describes forms of exclusions and invalidations that come as a result of the hegemony of a certain form of knowledge as "epistemicide," or "the murder of knowledge" (92), characterizing it as one of the symptoms or effects of coloniality. Santos makes visible how the world operates on Eurocentric colonial logic and how such epistemic dominance works to murder, erase, silence, or delegitimize other forms of knowledges, existences, and experiences. When it comes to language and rhetoric, epistemicide can materialize, for example, in the form of Standard English policies and the exclusiveness of academic English (Smitherman and Villanueva 2003; Young 2009), the predomi-nance of classical Western rhetoric and alphabetic literacy (Alvarez 2016; Baca 2008), as well as raciolinguistic ideologies (Flores and Rosa 2015), all of which theories like translingualism and transnationalism work hard to critique and undo.

Taking such wounds and discomforts and their connections to colo-niality as points of departure, I have come to hope translingual and transnational graduate education can be an occasion for *decolonial*[1] *recovery*—for healing. Certainly there are plenty of ways to heal, just as there are plenty of ways coloniality has hurt the world. But if one func-tion of coloniality is erasure—epistemicide—then a part of the healing process is necessarily the reclamation of what is lost or erased. Walter Mignolo and Catherine Walsh (2018) propose that decoloniality "does not imply the absence of coloniality but rather the ongoing serpentine movement toward possibilities of other modes of being, thinking, know-ing, sensing, and living; that is, an *otherwise in plural*" (81; emphasis added). A decolonial project involves building a variety of options, of worlds other than the colonial norms that have been enforced on us—whiteness, Eurocentrism, monolingualism, and so forth.

Translingualism and transnationalism speak directly to the manifes-tation of coloniality Santos emphasizes: that of epistemicide and the bracketing of things outside the Eurocentric norm. Furthermore, these theories can contribute to decoloniality's goal for an "otherwise in plural," as Mignolo and Walsh (2018) discuss. Translingual and transnational education starts us on this path by fostering a "disposition of openness" (Horner et al. 2011) and by "[encouraging] students to transcend linguistic, ethnic, and national boundaries to foster a cosmopolitan disposition" (Zaleski and You, this volume, chapter 6). Translingualism and transnationalism both emphasize the normalcy of contact and fluidity in and between entities/differences, and the scholars in this volume clearly illustrate the interventions translingualism and transnationalism can bring into graduate education: the norming of language differences and cross-language work (Bou Ayash, chapter 5, and Kilfoil, chapter 3, this volume), the productive recognition of transnational connections (Horner, chapter 4, and Cousins et al., chapter 3, this volume), and the need for a diversity of knowledges and perspectives (Jones, chapter 8, Lerma et al., chapter 1, Pawlowski and Tardy, chapter 7, and Zaleski and You, this volume). These interventions and their desire for openness and plurality clearly show how translingualism and transnationalism are aligned with epistemic decolonization efforts in that they are driven by the desire for plurality instead of monoculture, for fluidity and connection instead of borders and exclusion, for openness and equality instead of hegemony and hierarchy.

To truly counter epistemicide, dispositions of openness and a cosmopolitanism alone, I argue, are not enough. As rhetoric and composition graduate students, we must also examine, along with our professors—those from both dominant and historically marginalized cultural positions—the extent to which we are working to actively manifest and elevate different knowledges, rhetorics, and ways of seeing and being instead of merely working across the existing differences coloniality has worked to erase over time. As Romeo García and Damián Baca (2019) say, decolonial works in writing and rhetorical studies should function to "delink [the field] from the colonial legacies that authorize capital [R]hetoric and lowercase [r]hetorics" and, in working toward an otherwise-in-plural, "build a foundation, a history, of local knowledges and meaning-making practices that break from such Western hegemonic models" (3). Thus, a decolonial approach to translingualism and transnationalism in graduate education must also make the commitment to build an otherwise-in-plural by materializing in an equal status the non-Western rhetorics, literacies, language practices, writing traditions, knowledges, and subjectivities marginalized graduate students and scholars bring with them but that get treated as nonexistent, noncredible, or nonrelevant in academia.

Translingualism has contributed to making more visible a diversity of languages, language practices, and the knowledges that can come from those through the cross-language relations it advocates for. Bou Ayash's chapter in this volume is an example of this (see chapter 5). As for transnationalism, Zaleski and You in this collection show how "the attempt to study less-represented rhetorical traditions has constituted a move towards transnationalism. Courses in comparative rhetoric have become one way the transnational framework has been adopted and encouraged within graduate studies in rhetoric and composition" (see chapter 6). Ideally, however, the teaching of rhetorics beyond the Western tradition and the English language shouldn't be confined to specialized courses like comparative rhetoric or translation. All teachings of rhetoric and all academic labor should instead be informed by traditions beyond Aristotle and other thinkers emerging from Europe or North America, as well as ways of doing language beyond monolingualism—but as it is now, because of how the field is still rooted in Greco-Roman rhetoric, Eurocentrism, and English, special subjects like comparative rhetoric and translation are needed to train us to look elsewhere and otherwise.

The realization of an otherwise-in-plural within graduate education also depends on what Zaleski and You call "translingual mentorship." This kind of student-teacher relationship demands the fostering of negotiation skills, requiring teachers to "be open not only to coconstructing meaning but also to giving up a bit of their authority," while at the same time "[encouraging] young scholars to explore beyond their expertise and think more creatively about themselves as global citizens" and "sitting with students as they grapple" with that (see chapter 6). Resisting hegemonies, delinking from colonial structures and epistemes, and imagining an otherwise-in-plural often require acts that at first may seem like a mistake, an affront, a breach of conventions, an unnecessary risk, a weakness in argument, a baseless contribution to the field, and so on—simply because these acts are not geared towards the usual end goals and terms of teaching, learning, and research. Graduate faculty and advisors must be more cognizant of when, how, and why their students are performing such acts and be ready to support them accordingly. Conversely, graduate students must negotiate for better support and know how to rhetorically explain their choices (and, when applicable, to refuse to explain and negotiate, or to carry on even without support).

Bruce Horner in his chapter (see chapter 4) and Amy Wan in her response essay (see chapter 9) have spoken of a "revaluation" (Horner) and "paradigm shift" (Wang) to describe the work of incorporating translingualism and transnationalism in graduate education: this is not merely about creating new materials and/or courses and so on ("add-ons," in Horner's words), but rather a new way of seeing and approaching what we already know and the way we already do things. What I am proposing here is that translingualism and transnationalism in graduate education must be understood first and foremost on the basis of their potential for *recovery from coloniality*, from epistemicide. This potential means taking seriously the task of manifesting diversity, including the recovery of knowledges and experiences previously erased by coloniality, and the carving of spaces within graduate-level classrooms and curricula for students from marginalized communities to thrive through finding their own voice(s); setting their own teaching, research, and/or administrative interests and agendas; studying and exploring in their own ways solutions to problems that matter to them the most.

We all must always be on our toes, always vigilant, always questioning how our practices can be, intentionally or not, complicit in the retainment of hegemony. This vigilance necessitates perpetual "structural critique" (as Lerma et al. mention in chapter 1) to expose the way coloniality works in our teaching and learning, and the prioritization of "culturally sustaining" pedagogies, which, according to Django Paris (2012), aim to "maintain heritage ways and to value cultural and linguistic sharing across difference," thereby supporting and ensuring the "continuing presence" of students' own linguistic, epistemic, and cultural practices (96).[2] It is no easy feat to see the structures that trap us and simultaneously work to dismantle and move beyond them, but it is only when graduate students and faculty alike are already in the habit of always looking beyond what they are used to seeing and hearing that translingualism and transnationalism truly function as recovery in both senses of the word: healing in the form of recognition and cultural sustainment for individuals and communities whose traditions, values, knowledges and practices have been sidelined; and recovery in the form of reclamation of traditions, values, knowledges, and practices that have been lost due to coloniality.

NOTES

1. Here I am mostly talking of decolonization in its epistemic sense—epistemic decolonization, following Boaventura de Sousa Santos's (2014) assertion that "there is no global social justice without global cognitive justice" (viii), as well as Walter Mignolo's (2011) "epistemic disobedience."

2. Though Paris advocates for such pedagogies largely in the context of K–12, they can also positively impact learning and knowledge production at the graduate level.

REFERENCES

Alvarez, Steven. 2016. "Literacy." In *Decolonizing Rhetoric and Composition Studies: New Latinx Keywords for Theory and Pedagogy*, edited by Iris D. Ruiz and Raul Sanchez, 17–29. New York: Palgrave Macmillan.

Baca, Damián. 2008. *Mestiz@ Scripts, Digital Migrations, and the Territories of Writing*. New York: Palgrave Macmillan.

Flores, Nelson, and Jonathan Rosa. 2015. "Undoing Appropriateness: Raciolinguistic Ideologies and Language Diversity in Education." *Harvard Educational Review* 85 (2): 149–71.

García, Romeo, and Damián Baca. 2019. *Rhetorics Elsewhere and Otherwise: Contested Modernities, Decolonial Visions*. Urbana, IL: NCTE.

Horner, Bruce, Min-Zhan Lu, Jacqueline Jones Royster, and John Trimbur. 2011. "Opinion: Language Difference in Writing: Toward a Translingual Approach." *College English* 73 (3): 303–21.

Mignolo, Walter. 2011. *The Darker Side of Western Modernity: Global Futures, Decolonial Options*. Durham, NC: Duke University Press.

Mignolo, Walter, and Catherine E. Walsh. 2018. *On Decoloniality: Concepts, Analytics, Praxis*. Durham, NC: Duke University Press.

Paris, Django. 2012. "Culturally Sustaining Pedagogy: A Needed Change in Stance, Terminology, and Practice." *Educational Researcher* 41 (3): 93–97.

Santos, Boaventura de Sousa. 2014. *Epistemologies of the South: Justice Against Epistemicide*. Boulder, CO: Paradigm.

Smitherman, Geneva, and Victor Villanueva. 2003. *Language Diversity in the Classroom: From Intention to Practice*. Carbondale: Southern Illinois University Press.

Young, Vershawn Ashanti. 2009. " 'Nah, We Straight': An Argument Against Code Switching." *JAC* 29 (1/2): 49–76.

11
DISTRIBUTING THE LABOR OF TRANSLATION IN THE CONTEXT OF GRADUATE EDUCATION IN WRITING STUDIES

Joe Wilson

I encountered transnational and translingual orientations to composition early in my graduate education by way of rhetorical genre studies (RGS), as I was drawn to how both bodies of scholarship center a dynamic understanding of translation as relational, negotiated, often messy, and transformative work.[1] For those of us in RGS, translation is a critical metaphor for understanding the mobility of writers' knowledge of/across genres, as well as the mobility of genres themselves across contexts and participant networks. Similarly, Nancy Bou Ayash's synthesis in this edited collection illustrates how translation epistemologies have also become central to translingual thought, highlighting for students "the labor of producing, interpreting, and circulating writing" (see chapter 5) in authentic contexts of inquiry. In foregrounding labor here, Bou Ayash taps into the broader epistemological break with monolingualist assumptions embedded in writing studies many authors have called for in this collection as we tighten the definition of what constitutes a translingual orientation: a recognition of students' "concrete labor" in all languaging practices, including translation across and within named languages. Many scholars have begun to serialize this phrase, most explicitly in Bruce Horner and Sara Alvarez's (2019) definitional piece, and I myself have begun to refer to students' "concrete labor" in conversations with other instructors and administrators. Moreover, "concrete labor" has been used by some authors to refer to a range of practices in addition to translation, from textual revision in a writing center (Jones, chapter 8, this volume) to graduate students' seminar engagement (Horner, chapter 4, this volume).

. It is not surprising that those of us interested in linguistic mobility and friction have been so intentional about sedimenting in the professional

https://doi.org/10.7330/9781646423262.c011

literature *labor* as a term to describe our own work and theoretical orientations, and while translingual/transnational writing scholarship covers a diverse range of foci, I have found grappling with questions of labor in translation essential for my graduate research, teaching, and administrative work.[2] This is because labor signals for many translingual-oriented scholars a threshold concept with which writing studies must grapple to more dynamically conceive of writers' agency in revising languages and genres always in translation (Bawarshi 2016; Pennycook 2008). This response subsequently puts into conversation the perspectives on labor espoused by this collection (and the larger translingual literature it evokes) with the work on genre and translation theorized by RGS to reveal how such a dialogue can expand how we conceive of and locate translational labor.

As my work centers the circulation of writing in borderland spaces, questions of genre and translation have foregrounded my research on how writing moves and is recontextualized across modalities, language representations, and national borders. Scholars in RGS have accounted for such generic mobility and translations primarily through the research and a robust theoretical vernacular on *uptake*, or "the interconnections, interplays, and transactions between genres" (Reiff and Bawarshi 2021, 1). Attention to uptake allows us to look horizontally at translation, accounting for the conditions, forces, and relationships that mediate how an illocutionary force, for example "we find the defendant guilty," elicits a perlocutionary effect, such as a judge disseminating sentencing instructions. Uptake accentuates the translations between genres as sites where language and literacy learners broker histories of power and materiality to integrate or intervene in the performance of genres. While this process at times appears instantaneous and intuitive, it actually involves a complex negotiation of power relations dependent on both the relational contingencies of the immediate context and past serializations of the genre serving as the illocutionary act. Such an approach to translation shares a translingual orientation's understanding of the inherent mobility and transformations embedded in the inevitable reworking and revision of languages and literacies in every communicative situation.

Despite these similar theoretical underpinnings, work in RGS and translingual and transnational writing pedagogy and research seems to begin from starkly different methodological points of departure when seeking to research and recognize translations. RGS hinges inquiry on Carolyn Miller's (1984) groundbreaking text on genre as social action to propose genres *as* illocutionary acts: genres as more than just tools or heuristics but instead, as Miller (2015) later affirms, as actions themselves rather than singularly consequences of one's action. So an RGS scholar begins with genre as social action and the agency of genres when examining the work of translation, then accounts for uptake as "selection and translation" (Emmons 2009, 139). Conversely, translingual scholars begin with agency of humans, drawing from a Marxist, social-historical perspective to understand labor as the active work of individuals, although always in collaboration with others. Under translingualism, the material social conditions that mediate how a language user revises and (re)produces language are recognized, but that individual's agency serves as the point of departure for understanding their "concrete labor." While scholars such as Jay Jordan (2015) have called for translingualism to move beyond human agency alone, room afforded for nonhuman agents, such as genres, bodies, technologies, and so forth, in discussions about translingual labor, still often extend only as a byproduct or extension of this initial, human-centered orientation to agency. This germinal incommensurability in terms of agency has forced RGS to grapple with the ways it understands genre, and Bawarshi (2016) has called for RGS scholars to consider translingual orientations to complicate uptake theory by paying attention "not only to the relations between genres but also to how individuals move and translate across genres" (246). Such a translingually informed approach to genre moves to establish a more distributed notion of agency in translation—foregrounding genres as social action while further focusing on the labor of language users translating across genres and actively negotiating such translation practice with others.

Throughout my doctoral studies, I have taken up such a translingual approach in RGS, and such an approach has allowed me to more fully understand the conditions of power that shape translation practices in geopolitical and sociolinguistic borderland spaces where mobility and stasis (of people, literacies, etc.) cannot be ignored. As a doctoral candidate, I have specifically focused my research on the literacy practices of migrant writers in two contexts: at Seattle area community colleges and at Kazakhstani universities in the Altai Region that extends across Eastern Kazakhstan, Siberia, Mongolia, and Xinjiang. In one project, for example, I analyzed how self-identifying ethnic Kazakh and Tatar students leveraged the multimodal affordances of translation to resist restrictive ethnopolitical assumptions about their identities during public-speaking events such as conference presentations. In that study, a recognition of the agency of different modes—from an Instagram hashtag with multiple orthographies to gestured speech and other embodied modes—was vital for understanding how Kazakhstani students leveraged the distributed nature of translation to force their audiences to engage in the laborious, hermeneutical work of translating multiple language representations and ideologies in the uptake of the presentation. In one particularly compelling example, a self-identifying Kazakh student, Zhannat, presented her project's qualitative results through Russian Sign Language, forcing her audience members to engage in two forms of translation: a translation of her research findings through engagement with Zhannat's written transcription of those findings in Russian on a PowerPoint slide, and translation of clan and ethnically inflected language representations in a context where linguistic identity and ethnic identity are often conflated. Analyses of translations such as these calls for a more dynamic understanding of labor than seems present in current translingual and transnational scholarship. In other words, how can we understand the concrete labor of genres, bodies, modes, ethnolinguistic language representations, and other multisemiotic communicative practices in distribution with the concrete labor of language users?

Keeping the above question in mind allowed me to locate instances of concrete labor of translation illustrated across this collection to further complicate moments emphasized by individual authors. Horner's reflections on his syllabi (re)design offer one tangible example of a professor's labor in writing a syllabus operating in tandem with the concrete labor course syllabus as a genre performs in/beyond the classroom (sese chapter 4). For instance, when Horner describes the readings he includes for a class titled Academic Writing in Theory and Practice, he notes how the copresence of texts as seemingly disparate as David Bartholomae's (1985) "Inventing the University" and Theresa Lillis and Mary Jane Curry's (2010) *Academic Writing in a Global Context* on that syllabus meant he and the graduate students in the seminar "could not avoid the transnational character of [their] topic," yet surely not all encountering Bartholomae's chapter do so with a nuanced eye toward transnationalism. Instead, the copresence of this text with others such as Lillis and Curry's in the course readings/schedule syllabus section helped foster an opportunity for the renegotiation of language knowledges to such an extent that in hindsight such transformation seemed unavoidable. This is an example of distributed labor. A syllabus functions as a social action: a section on course readings communicates to students that such texts belong in conversation and collectively speak to the course description and objectives. A syllabus also necessarily displaces other texts and their concatenated ideologies and research findings by limiting course readings to the scope of a single semester. However, as Anne Freadman (2012) reminds us, "No genre can do more than predict the kind of uptake that will make it happy, and no speaker or writer can completely secure an uptake" (560). So while this syllabus as a genre guides students to specific texts analyzed through the tacit translingual and/or transnational lens of its course objectives, it is graduate students' prior experiences with the seminar syllabus genre that (likely intuitively) attune them to search for such connections across their readings in the uptake of the syllabus. So in the case of Horner's syllabi, an accounting for genre and uptake makes visible the concrete labor of students and their professor in translating theories, praxis, and terminologies (such as *translingual* and *transnational*) across texts that may not even use such terms, while also necessarily illuminating the work of the syllabus genre and the readings themselves as the illocutionary actions of such translations.

This latter form of generic work has a history of interrogation by diverse lines of research, including actor-network theory, technical writing, queer/trans approaches to translation and multimodality, and postprocess and postpedagogical approaches to composition/second-language (L2) writing, in addition to RGS. Engaging these bodies of research would require the mapping of new genealogies for translingual orientations to research beyond those such as basic writing and other primarily US-centered composition movements commonly associated with translingual and transnational research's origin story (Horner 2020) to understand labor. As the current collection attests, at the present moment it often seems as though concrete labor remains individualized and exclusively understood through a Marxist perspective, such that terms like *monolingual* and *capitalism* have become interchangeable and synonyms. Certainly they are interrelated, yet this singular view of individual agency that begins and ends with social class both limits our ability to dynamically and linguistically perceive the mobility and actions of genres and precludes opportunities to understand how linguistic and cultural diversity develops and intersects with other conditions of diversity, including racial, sexual, and ableist positionalities.[3] A more distributed understanding of agency, and therefore labor, opens up translingual and transnational orientations to research to engage with these diverse bodies of research through an intersectional lens, foreground questions of race and embodiment, and more fully account for genre and other actants even as we necessarily maintain an emphasis on social class.

Following Bou Ayash's lead from her chapter in this collection, we may also consider what a translingual orientation to genre offers us as we rethink the work of departmental gatekeeping genres, from the uptake of programmatic language requirements to the actions performed and displaced by the genres our departments select for doctoral students' qualifying exams. How might these genres serve as agentive allies, rather than obstacles, toward the goal of helping graduate students navigate the work of translating their rhetorical, linguistic, and disciplinary knowledges while simultaneously cultivating a deeper translingual ethos? This was a primary question my PhD exam committee considered with me as they helped me move from the construction of exam reading lists to the exams themselves. Unlike some of my graduate student friends at peer institutions who must stressfully isolate themselves in their offices for a weekend to respond to high-stakes exam questions, my department made the move to include syllabi design in the qualifying exams' research statement and oral component so as to offer graduate students an opportunity to both demonstrate a breadth of knowledge and begin thinking about how they might engage their own future graduate students. So, like Horner in this collection, I have been thinking a lot about how translingual and transnational work can transform a syllabus as broad in disciplinary scope as composition theory and pedagogy, as well as the labor the syllabus genre conducts in contrast to that of a traditional research paper or exam-response genres. Simply placing texts such as Catherine Kell's (2017) sociolinguistic research on the multisemiotization and translation of meaning across genres in a housing community in South Africa alongside Horner's (2017) theorization of translation in North American composition contexts in one week's reading on this sample syllabus allowed for a new way of demonstrating knowledge. Rather than answering a question, accounting for the uptake of the syllabus allowed me to ask what kinds of renegotiation of knowledge might happen by placing these two theorists and the contexts of their work in dialogue. How might I grapple with the two different disciplinary genealogies they evoke to show points of overlapping discourse on translation not immediately apparent, and how might that dialogue be generative within the context of qualifying exams or discussions about translation in a future graduate seminar? Here, my program's change in assessment genre to include a syllabus helped facilitate a move toward the kinds of "panoramic ethos" Corina Lerma, Moisés García-Rentería, Patricia Flores, Kate Mangelsdorf, and Lucía Durá describe in their chapter (see chapter 1), as I was not only tapping into prior knowledge but also grappling with theoretical and methodological terminology alongside my committee members in productive dialogue. As we continue to think about how translingual/

transnational orientations to research might transform our graduate programs, I hope we can more dynamically identify and leverage the labor of the many genres acting in these programs to resist assimilation into monolingual ideologies.

NOTES

1. This theoretical approach to translation as a critical metaphor contrasts with views of translational praxis as neutral, quantitatively measurable movement between two named languages.

2. The distinction between *labor* and *work* is worth noting here, as *labor* has been taken up most consistently by translingual/transnational scholarship through the lens of Marxist and activity theories that understand labor as inherently productive on the one hand and work as involving all activity regardless of its reproductive potential on the other. Through a translingual, social-materialist perspective, languages are fluid, and language users engage in the work of maintaining and revising language through social relations, so all language practice ought to be understood as labor (Horner 2016). Posthuman and political-rhetorical orientations to work are rarely included in translingual/transnational distinctions between labor and work.

3. As queer of color critique of Marxist philosophy has demonstrated, Marx's perspectives on labor hinged upon notions of the individual read through the "naturalization of gender, sexuality, and race . . . by posing capital as the social threat to [inherently raced] heteropatriarchal relations" (Ferguson 2004, 14). Instead, many queer and trans scholars, and especially those who engage with translation, argue for attention to the agency of bodies in the transformation of meaning and of situated perspectives (Bassi 2017; Haraway 1988; Stone 1987) toward resistance to such violence via naturalization.

REFERENCES

Bartholomae, David. 1985. "Inventing the University." In *When a Writer Can't Write: Studies in Writer's Block and Other Composing Process Problems*, edited by Mike Rose, 134–65. New York: Guilford.

Bassi, Serena. 2017. "Displacing LGBT: Global Englishes, Activism, and Translated Sexualities." In *Feminist Translation Studies: Local and Transnational Perspectives*, edited by Olga Castro and Emek Ergun, 235–348. London: Routledge.

Bawarshi, Anis. 2016. "Beyond the Genre Fixation: A Translingual Perspective on Genre." *College English* 78 (3): 243–49.

Emmons, Kimberly. 2009. "Uptake and the Biomedical Subject." In *Genre in a Changing World*, edited by Charles Bazerman, Adair Bonini, and Débora Figueiredo, 134–57. Fort Collins, CO: The WAC Clearinghouse.

Ferguson, Roderick A. 2004. *Aberrations in Black: Toward a Queer of Color Critique*. Minneapolis: University of Minnesota Press.

Freadman, Anne. 2012. "The Traps and Trappings of Genre Theory." *Applied Linguistics* 33 (5): 544–63.

Haraway, Donna. 1998. "Situated Knowledges—The Science Question in Feminism and the Privilege of Partial Perspective." *Feminist Studies* 14 (3): 575–99.

Horner, Bruce. 2016. *Rewriting Composition: Terms of Exchange*. Carbondale: Southern Illinois University Press.

Horner, Bruce. 2017. "Writing Language: Composition, the Academy, and Work." *Humanities* 6 (2): 11.

Horner, Bruce. 2020. "Language Difference, Translinguality, and L2 Writing." In *Reconciling Translingualism and Second Language Writing*, edited by Zhaozhe Wang and Tony Silva, 55–66. New York: Routledge.

Horner, Bruce, and Sara Alvarez. 2019. "Defining Translinguality." *Literacy in Composition Studies* 7 (2): 1–30.

Jordan, Jay. 2015. "Material Translingual Ecologies." *College English* 77 (4): 364–82.

Kell, Catherine. 2017. "Tracing Trajectories as Units of Analysis for the Study of Social Processes: Addressing Mobility and Complexity in Sociolinguistics." *Text & Talk* 37 (4): 531–51.

Lillis, Theresa, and Mary Jane Curry. 2010. *Academic Writing in a Global Context: The Politics and Practices of Publishing in English.* New York: Routledge.

Miller, Carolyn. 1984. "Genre as Social Action." *Quarterly Journal of Speech* 70 (1): 151–67.

Miller, Carolyn. 2014. "The Fact That I Could Write About It Made Me Think It Was Real: An Interview with Carolyn R. Miller." *Composition Forum* 12. https://compositionforum.com/issue/31/carolyn-miller-interview.php.

Pennycook, Alastair. 2008. "English as a Language Always in Translation." *European Journal of English Studies* 12 (1): 33–47.

Reiff, Mary Jo, and Anis Bawarshi. 2021. "How to Turn Accumulated Knowledge into Action: Uptake, Public Petitions, and the Climate Change Debate." In *Genre in the Climate Debate*, edited by Sune Auken and Christel Sunesen. Warsaw, Poland: De Gruyter.

Stone, Sandy. 1992. "The Empire Strikes Back: A Posttranssexual Manifesto." *Camera Obscura: Feminism, Culture, and Media Studies* 10 (2): 150–76.

12

TRANSLINGUAL AND TRANSNATIONAL GRADUATE EDUCATION FOR THE LOCAL PUBLIC GOOD

Brice Nordquist

On January 1, 2019, I assumed the position of graduate director for the composition and cultural rhetoric doctoral program at Syracuse University. I was an assistant professor on the eve of my tenure-decision year, and I had significant reservations about the kinds of disciplinary commitments and allegiances graduate programs typically ask their directors to uphold through the administration of course requirements, qualifying exams, admissions processes, prospectus and dissertation hearings, and more. In other words, I was afraid of falling into practices of disciplinary boundary making and parochialism critiqued throughout this collection. And I've always been skeptical of justifications for educational structures that rely solely on projections of the future; in this case, on the demands and promises of professionalization in the field of rhetoric and composition. As the year progressed, I found it more and more difficult to describe, to myself and to others, the collective work of graduate students, faculty, and staff in terms of requirements for and contributions to an academic field of study.

By March of 2019, more than two million students across 135 countries were participating in school strikes inspired by Greta Thunberg's climate campaign (Elks 2019). In April, police shot and killed seventeen-year-old Isaiah Lewis as he was fleeing custody in my birthplace of Edmond, Oklahoma, and more than one hundred Black Lives Matter protestors marched from Lewis's high school to the steps of the Edmond City Police Department (Associated Press 2019). In September, the US House of Representatives began the process of Trump's first impeachment trial. In the first seven days of the same month, 8,373 fires burned in Brazil's portion of the Amazon rainforest. Eighty thousand fires were set in the

https://doi.org/10.7330/9781646423262.c012

Brazilian rainforest over the course of the year (Spring 2019). French President Emmanuel Marcon tweeted in response, "Our house is burning. Literally." In November, Trump initiated the process to withdraw the United States from the 2015 Paris Climate Accord (Tollefson 2019). From April to December, hundreds of people were killed, and thousands were wounded and imprisoned, during mass protests for government reform in Sudan, Hong Kong, Moscow, Iraq, Iran, Chile, Nicaragua, and Bolivia (Yi and Caryl, *Washington Post*, December 10, 2019).

By the start of the new year, the World Health Organization (WHO) announced a coronavirus-related pneumonia in Wuhan. On January 15, 2020, the CDC confirmed the first known case of this novel virus in Washington State. In early March, COVID-19 reached pandemic status, and the United States went into a state of national emergency (AJMC). Like most every school in the country, SU ended residential instruction and transitioned to online learning. We slipped into isolation and disquiet. And then on May 25, George Floyd was murdered by Minneapolis police officer Derek Chauvin, and the nation erupted.

Over a year later, as I draft this essay, United Nations Secretary General António Guterres addresses the 2021 UN General Assembly:

> I am here to sound the alarm: The world must wake up. We are on the edge of an abyss and moving in the wrong direction. Our world has never been more threatened. Or more divided. We face the greatest cascade of crises in our lifetimes. The COVID-19 pandemic has supersized glaring inequalities. The climate crisis is pummeling the planet. Unheaval from Afghanistan to Ethiopia to Yemen and beyond has thwarted peace. A surge of mistrust and misinformation is polarizing people and paralyzing societies, and human rights are under fire.

None of Guterres's remarks strikes me as hyperbolic. And, yet, for the most part, we are going about our business, holding out for signs of normalcy. By and large, we are still framing, pursuing, and sharing our work as scholars, teachers, and students according to status quo structures and strictures of disciplinary professionalization. Our teaching and research agendas may be responsive to the conditions and needs of our time, but our productions and applications of knowledge—at least the ones our institutions most value and reward—are stuck in fixed tracks of professional preparation and performance. What else can we do? What would it look like to wake up?

I appreciate that Nancy Bou Ayash and Carrie Kilfoil conclude their introduction with a reflection on the relevance of the work collected here in the context of this "cascade of crises." They suggest translingual and transnational orientations can help us work across disciplines to reimagine educational practices and structures and make productive changes to rhetoric and composition, improve the lives of the many people this field touches, and reassert the immense social value of graduate education in the humanities. I agree, and I want to think through two interconnected ways translingual and transnational praxis can help graduate faculty and students respond concertedly and effectively in our age of continuous crisis.

The first involves an orientation and attentiveness to local conditions, needs, and opportunities, and specifically to language as local practice (Pennycook 2010). As the authors in this collection assert, translingual and transnational orientations are orientations to spatial and temporal practices. As people interact in and with space and through time, they make and remake languages. Min-Zhan Lu and Bruce Horner (2013) explain: "[Languages] are constantly in movement and rebirth through the labor of those recontextualizing them" (599). This labor is habituated and/or devalued and, thus, often rendered invisible. Consequently, one of the greatest challenges of and opportunities for translingual and transnational praxis is learning to pay attention to the work of recontextualization and to the ways this work is taken up by people with different histories, bodies, expectations, and desires (Gilyard 2016).

In their chapter in this collection, Corina Lerma, Moisés García-Rentería, Patricia Flores, Kate Mangelsdorf, and Lucía Durá suggest attention to and critical reflection on translingual practice should be the collective, panoramic work of a graduate program. The testimonios they offer model this consideration and valuation of local practice and, in doing so, reveal and honor labors of recontextualizing languages, identities, subjectivities, needs, and desires. Their accounts also reject boundaries between academic and everyday life (see chapter 1). As bell hooks (2003) asserts, this rejection is central to the project of democratic education: "The democratic educator breaks through the false construction of the corporate university as set apart from real life and seeks to re-envision schooling as always a part of our real world experience, and our real life" (41). By recognizing and understanding the "multiple subjectivities, languages, identities" coconstituting the spaces and structure of a graduate program, we can reconstitute programs through our self-reflexive practice and social activity rather than reproduce disciplines and disciplinary members through "standard, product-oriented educational structures" and "single, consistent subjectivit[ies] that define academic experience" (Lerma et al., chapter 1). I agree with the authors that translingual praxis has the potential to reform graduate programs, not because the theory fills a gap in the scholarship or presents a fruitful subfield for our interconnected world system, but because it tunes us into the practices and social activities that coconstitute our programs and the places we make together. As Alastair Pennycook (2010) suggests, "Local practices construct locality" (7).

This potential for a more deliberate and responsive coconstruction of locality through practice points to a second way translingual and transnational orientations might help us respond effectively and ethically to our current moment. As Lerma et al. suggest, "Standard, one-size-fits all program structures and requirements seem particularly out of sync with the rapidly changing academic (and post COVID-19) job market" (see chapter 1). I'd add that they also seem irresponsibly out of sync with the global condition Guterres describes above. I suggest that attention to local language practice and coconstructions of localities, along with a commitment to the boundary-crossing work of democratic education, can broaden our understandings of graduate and postgraduate success and thus open up more possibilities for conceiving of and enacting graduate education as a public good.

Katina Rogers (2020) states that "an unstated purpose of graduate students' rigorous and creative work is to feed the knowledge they create back into the academy through both teaching and research. But why should scholarship be confined to such a narrow space?" She goes on to suggest that "it is easy to imagine a very different breadth and depth of engagement with communities of practice and with various publics, both in the way students learn and in how and where they apply their expertise" (9). If translingual and transnational orientations can help us focus on the language practices and mobilities that constitute our classrooms and programs, as Lerma et al. suggest, can't they also help shift our focus from discipline building and boundarying to intentional coconstructions of the places we share with each other and with neighbors across and beyond our universities—neighborhoods, cities, and regions?

The former chancellor of SU, Nancy Cantor (2006), described this shift as a focus on "local public scholarship," situated in reciprocal and sustained partnerships between scholars and community experts. In these collaborations, there "is an increasing awareness of the importance of the idea of *place* and the value of historical specificity and local knowledge and needs" (3; emphasis added). Of course, there is a long history of place-based community-engaged work in rhetoric and composition, most recognizable in groups like the Coalition of Community Writing and in journals like *Reflections* and the *Community Literacy Journal*. But while these forums represent a robust committment within the larger discipline, in my experience, Eli Goldblatt's (2007) observation in

Because We Live Here still holds true: professionalization in rhetoric and composition does not prepare us for the work of local public scholarship (5). How would valuing commitments to community building as much as discipline building reconfigure our admissions practices, curricular designs, dissertation projects, and the tenure and promotion guidelines that inform all of these? How would it reshape our hiring practices and the guidance and support we offer market-bound students?

Following Bou Ayash and Kilfoil's charge in the introduction to carefully listen to and consider the perspectives of graduate students in efforts to reform programs and practices in rhetoric and composition, I see Lerma et al.'s uptake of translingual praxis offering us a clear path: "A panoramic ethos is not about intrigue and achievement of previously established milestones, which give the illusion of something to grasp or obtain. It is about reframing our motivations for learning with and by each other" (see chapter 1). I can't imagine a more appropriate time to collectively reframe our motivations for teaching, learning, and disciplinary participation.

REFERENCES

AJMC. 2121. "A Timeline of COVID-19 Developments in 2020." https://www.ajmc.com /view/a-timeline-of-covid19-developments-in-2020.

Associated Press. 2019. "100-plus Rally in Protest of Fatal Shooting." ABC News, May 4. https://abcnews.go.com/US/wireStory/100-rally-protest-fatal-oklahoma-police-shoo ting-62823510.

Cantor, Nancy. 2006. "Scholarship in Action: The Case for Engagement." Syracuse University Chancellor's Collection, September 29. https://surface.syr.edu/chancellor/31.

Elks, Sonia. 2019. "Timeline: Greta Thunberg's Rise from Lone Protester to Nobel Favorite." Reuters, October 3. https://www.reuters.com/article/us-sweden-nobel-thun berg-timeline/timeline-greta-thunbergs-rise-from-lone-protester-to-nobel-favorite-idUS KBN1WI1RT.

Gilyard, Keith. 2016. "The Rhetoric of Translingualism." *College English* 73 (3): 284–89.

Goldblatt, Eli. 2007. *Because We Live Here: Sponsoring Literacy Beyond the Curriculum.* Cresskill, NJ: Hampton.

Guterres, António. 2021. "Secretary-General's Address to the 76th Session of the UN General Assembly." United Nations, September 21. https://www.un.org/sg/en/node /259283.

hooks, bell. 2003. *Teaching Community: A Pedagogy of Hope.* Routledge, New York.

Lu, Min-Zhan, and Bruce Horner. 2013. "Translingual Literacy, Language Difference, and Matters of Agency." *College English* 75 (6): 582–607.

Pennycook, Alastair. 2010. *Language as Local Practice.* New York: Routledge.

Rogers, Katina. 2020. *Putting the Humanities PhD to Work: Thriving in and Beyond the Classroom.* Durham, NC: Duke University Press.

Spring, Jake. 2019. "Brazil's Amazon Fires Worsen in September, Threaten Virgin Forests." Reuters, September 9. https://www.reuters.com/article/us-brazil-environment-fires /brazils-amazon-fires-worsen-in-september-threaten-virgin-forests-idUSKBN2601NP.

Tollefson, Jeff. 2019. "It's Official: Trump Begins Process to Exit Paris Climate Agreement." *Nature*, November 4. https://www.nature.com/articles/d41586-019-03230-y.

INDEX

ABOUT THE CONTRIBUTORS

Nancy Bou Ayash is associate professor of language and rhetoric at the University of Washington, in Seattle. Her work focuses on language ideologies, language politics in the study and teaching of writing, and translingual literacies in the transnational landscape of higher education. She has published in *College English, WPA: Writing Program Administration, Composition Forum,* the *Journal of Asian and African Studies,* and in several edited collections. She is the author of *Toward Translingual Realities in Composition: (Re)Working Local Language Representations and Practices* (Utah State University Press, 2019), winner of the 2021 Conference on College Composition and Communication's Research Impact Award and the 2022 MLA Mina P. Shaughnessy Prize.

Emily Yuko Cousins is currently an instructor in the English for Liberal Arts program at the International Christian University in Tokyo, Japan. She has an MA in English Studies from the University of Louisville, and previously taught first-year writing at universities in Bangladesh and Lebanon. Her interests include transnational writing program administration, translingualism, and writing center studies.

Lucía Durá is associate professor of rhetoric and writing studies in the English department and associate dean of the graduate school at the University of Texas at El Paso (UTEP). Her research focuses on understanding and leveraging community assets to solve complex problems. She uses participatory, constructivist methodologies to facilitate productive dialogues about risk and to design sustainable social and organizational change. She collaborates with local and global organizations, and she is increasingly working within the sphere of higher education. She cochairs the Hispanic Servingness Working Group at UTEP and contributes to leadership initiatives. She also represents UTEP on the Graduate Education Advisory Committee of the Texas Higher Education Coordinating Board and is an advisory board member of the Texas Center for Legal Ethics.

Patricia Flores is a doctoral candidate in rhetoric and composition studies at the University of Texas at El Paso (UTEP). She completed her BA and MA in communication studies at UTEP. Her research interest focuses on the rhetoric of health and medicine, border rhetoric, and first-year composition pedagogical practices. Paty is currently a doctoral fellow for the Humanities Collaborative at EPCC-UTEP.

Joseph Franklin is a newly appointed assistant Professor in the English Department at New York City College of Technology. Previously, he started up and directed a writing center at the University of Southampton in England. His primary research is in the global turn for writing studies, looking specifically at transnational writing program administration as a source for new knowledge.

Moisés García-Rentería, "Moy," is an assistant Professor of Rhetoric, Composition, and Literacy Studies at Wake Forest University. He researches and teaches Cultural Rhetorics, Latino Decolonial Thought, and Critical Pedagogy. His work on rhetorical criticism appears in the book Memoria de la identidad: una mirada panorámica a la diversidad cultural mexicana, published by Universidad de Guadalajara, and he has presented his research on Indigenous Latin American rhetorics and Latin American decolonial theories and methodologies at many domestic and international venues.

Bruce Horner teaches composition, composition theory and pedagogy, and literacy studies at the University of Louisville, where he's held the position of endowed chair in rhetoric and composition. His recent books include *Rewriting Composition: Terms of Exchange* and the coedited collections *Economies of Writing: Revaluations in Rhetoric and Composition* (with Brice Nordquist and Susan Ryan), *Teaching and Studying Transnational Composition* (with Christiane Donahue), *Mobility Work in Composition* (with Megan Favers Hartline, Ashanka Kumari, and Laura Sceniak Matravers), and *Crossing Divides: Exploring Translingual Writing Pedagogies and Programs* (with Laura Tetreault), winner of the 2018 MLA Mina P. Shaughnessy Prize.

Dr. Aimee Jones is an assistant Professor of English at Lynn University in Boca Raton, FL. She brings to her classrooms a background in composition pedagogy, professional writing, rhetorical history and theory, and multilingual and translingual literacies. Her research interests include multilingual and translingual literacy studies, writing center studies, and composition pedagogy. She has presented papers at numerous national and international conferences, including the Conference on College Composition and Communication Convention and the International Writing Centers Association Conference. Her scholarship has been published in *Sustainable Learning Spaces: Design, Infrastructure, and Technology*. She received the Marian C. Bashinski Award for Excellence in Teaching for her commitment to teaching first-year writing and the International Writing Centers Association President's Future Leaders Award for her research in writing center studies.

Carrie Byars Kilfoil is a lecturer in the analytical writing program at the University of California, San Diego. Her research focuses on translingual and transnational approaches to composition instruction, rhetoric and composition graduate education, and the material conditions of labor in writing programs. Her scholarship has appeared in *Composition Studies, Composition Forum, Rhetoric Review, JAC*, and the edited collection *Integrating Content and Language in Higher Education: From Theory to Practice.*

Corina Lerma is assistant instructor and doctoral student in the rhetoric and writing studies program at the University of Texas at El Paso (UTEP), and she is simultaneously pursuing an MA in philosophy at UTEP. She completed her BA in rhetoric and writing studies at the University of Texas at Austin and her MA in rhetoric from the University of Texas at El Paso. She has worked as a writing consultant for both EPCC and UTEP writing centers and is currently working as a teaching fellow for the Humanities Collaborative at EPCC-UTEP. Corina's research interests center on border rhetoric, immigration rhetoric, critical literacy, identity studies, and writing center/first-year composition pedagogical practices.

Kate Mangelsdorf is professor of rhetoric and writing studies at the University of Texas at El Paso, where she has directed first-year composition, the doctoral program in rhetoric and composition, and the university writing center. Her main research interests have been second-language writing and writing program administration, and she has focused in particular on the Mexico/US borderlands. With Char Ullman and Jair Muñoz, she has recently published *Graduate Students Becoming Qualitative Researchers: An Ethnographic Study* (Routledge, 2021). She is currently teaching grant writing to students from across the curriculum.

Brice Nordquist is associate professor of writing and rhetoric and dean's professor of community engagement at Syracuse University (SU). His book *Literacy and Mobility: Complexity, Uncertainty, and Agency at the Nexus of High School and College* received the 2019 Conference on College Composition and Communication's Advancement of Knowledge Award. He is the founder and director of SU's Engaged Humanities Network, which seeds, supports, and connects publicly engaged research, teaching, and creative work in Syracuse and Central New York. He is also the cofounder and codirector of the Narratio Fellowship, a storytelling and educational pipeline program for resettled refugee youth.

Madelyn Pawlowski is an independent scholar and UX researcher with a PhD in Rhetoric, Composition, and the Teaching of English from the University of Arizona. Her work on language awareness, writing teacher education, and teacher knowledge has appeared in Composition Forum, Writing Spaces, and The Journal of English for Academic Purposes.

Anselma Widha Prihandita is a doctoral candidate in language and rhetoric, writing instructor, and assistant director of the expository writing program at the University of Washington, in Seattle. Her research explores the intersections among writing pedagogy, decoloniality, and transnationalism. She is interested in questions such as: How can university, academic discourse, and global production of knowledge uphold epistemic racism? How can writing and language education be leveraged to undo this? and How can students and teachers who come from marginalized social and geopolitical locations navigate teaching and learning that are often not culturally sustaining for them?

Christine M. Tardy is professor of English applied linguistics at the University of Arizona. She teaches undergraduate and graduate courses in TESOL, applied linguistics, and writing. Her research explores the areas of second-language writing, genre and discourse studies, and policies and politics of English in higher education. Her work appears in journals such as *College Composition and Communication*, the *Journal of Second Language Writing*, *Research in the Teaching of English*, *TESOL Quarterly*, and *Written Communication*, as well as in numerous edited collections. Her monographs include *Genre-Based Writing: What Every ESL Teacher Needs to Know* (University of Michigan Press, 2019), *Beyond Convention: Genre Innovation in Academic Writing* (University of Michigan Press, 2016), and *Building Genre Knowledge* (Parlor Press, 2009).

Amy J. Wan (she/her/hers) is associate professor of English at Queens College and the Graduate Center, City University of New York. She is the author of *Producing Good Citizens: Literacy Training in Anxious Times* (University of Pittsburgh Press, 2014), an examination of citizenship, literacy, and the productive worker-citizen in the United States. Her writing has also appeared in *College English*, the *Journal of College Literacy and Learning*, *Literacy in Composition Studies*, *Rhetoric Review*, and *Radical Teacher*. Her article "In the Name of Citizenship," published in *College English* (74.1), was the recipient of the Richard Ohmann Outstanding Article Award in 2012. Her current project analyzes how to create spaces for change, resistance, and linguistic justice within the global US university through a historical and contemporary study of policies addressing access, diversity, race, and writing.

Alex Way is assistant professor in the Department of Rhetoric and Writing Studies at the University of Utah. He has taught English for Academic Purposes (EAP) at Kanazawa University in Japan, and English Composition at Washington State University and the University of Louisville. Alex's research interests include the sociolinguistics of writing, translingual and transmodal orientations to composition, and non-alphabetic literacies.

Joe Wilson is a doctoral candidate at the University of Washington, in Seattle. A former Fulbright student and graduate research fellow to Kazakhstan, his work considers questions of linguistic diversity as they are taken up by multiple trans approaches to rhetoric and composition, including translation studies, transnational approaches, and writing transfer.

Xiaoye You is liberal arts professor of English and Asian studies at Pennsylvania State University and founder of the Writing Education Across Borders (WEAB) Conference. His research focuses on comparative rhetoric, translingual writing, and cosmopolitan English. His first monograph, *Writing in the Devil's Tongue: A History of English Composition in China*, won the 2011 Conference on College Composition and Communication (CCCC) Outstanding Book Award. His recent book, *Cosmopolitan English and Transliteracy*, arguing for ethical use of English in everyday life and for cultivating global citizens in English literacy education, received the 2018 CCCC Research Impact Award.

Michelle Zaleski is assistant professor at Benedictine College, where she teaches composition and directs their writing center. Her research, which has appeared in *College English* and the *Routledge Handbook of Comparative World Rhetorics*, attempts to recover once-marginalized voices from the rhetorical past and present. Her current project traces the translingual practices of Jesuit rhetorical education in India during the early modern period.